GOODBYE TRUST

Incompetence and conceit – NOT woke – are destroying our institutions

DICK STROUD

CONTENTS

WHAT'S THE BOOK ABOUT?

" Advanced social science tells us trust was the secret to the rise of the West, the invisible forcefield that incubates a healthy, prosperous society. But now we in the UK are living through an age in which trust is slowly – almost imperceptibly – dissipating from public life.

Matthew Syed, *The Sunday Times*, June 2024

W hy spend a year of your life writing a book? Believe me, making money isn't the reason! You must have a tale to tell and the confidence it will resonate with others.

What drove me? A deep-seated distrust of the institutions – academia, the media, politics, business, the justice system and the financial regulators. They haven't merely lost my trust. That's putting it mildly. Frankly, I believe they're utterly busted.

That should be enough of a reason, but there is something else. I am sick of the world's ills being blamed on it 'going woke'. It's such a lazy phrase. When companies act like idiots, parading their virtue, the explanation is that it's 'woke capitalism'. Critics mock and chant, 'Go woke, go broke.' Calling something, anything, woke is supposed to explain everything.

When the English language is butchered to avoid using the word women, the reason is 'they have gone woke'. The same accusation is supposed to explain the upheavals in universities, the police's obsession with rooting out 'hate' and middle-aged politicians acting like children about the latest injustice. Woke is today's catch-all term to explain every behaviour and belief that annoys us.

Are these just the concerns of an old bloke longing for a time when all was well with the world? Being baffled by today's world doesn't necessarily mean anything is wrong. That what I read echoes my concerns is to be expected. We all live in an echo chamber that amplifies our prejudices and filters out challenging ideas.

To find out, I ventured outside my comfort zone, did some research... and that made me feel a whole lot worse. Everywhere I looked, trust in institutions is plummeting, especially among the young. This is compounded by a plague of unhappiness and mental health concerns that's gripping Western countries. Then there are the rumblings of nasty economic and social demons that threaten to break free.

What the hell is going on? Everybody has their pet explanation – it's the effect of the pandemic – social media is addling our minds – it's all Donald Trump's fault. Lots of Brits substitute Brexit for the Donald. And as Elon Musk believes, it's the woke mind virus.

You know what – I think it might be a bit more complicated.

Our institutions are in a mess and all we can do is blame it on them being woke! I think that's a dangerous oversimplification. If it isn't woke, what is it? This conundrum made naming the book easy: *Goodbye Trust*. Twelve months and 100,000 words later, I think I have worked out what's going on.

The book is a series of essays. One about each institution, with a couple of others investigating the manipulation of our language and the new moral and political beliefs that divide us. The concluding essay unravels the afflictions that are common to all institutions.

What I found scared me. A couple of the institutions are broken beyond repair. However, it's not all doom and gloom. Laughter is the only response to the behaviour of some of the actors, especially the politicians. Many business leaders have become so consumed with their self-importance that their antics read like a comedy. The determination of the elite to appear virtuous while amassing huge wealth is a feat to behold.

I have done my best to banish academic jargon while ensuring my conclusions are based on evidence, not conjecture. Much of the research is about the UK and US because their travails apply to the rest of the Western world.

Each essay is free-standing and follows a similar pattern: establish the facts, discard the prejudice and decide what it means. This gives you multiple ways of reading the book. If you are a traditionalist like me, start at page one and read to the end. Or you can pick and mix the essays that interest you. Maybe you find academia and the justice system bore you senseless – skip them.

If you want to start with the conclusions and then infill with the details, jump straight to 'So what's going on? Making sense of it all'. All the essays are summarised in 'Essays in brief – key points'; that might be your starting point.

Start with 'Politics – more showbiz than statesmanship' if you want a light-hearted introduction. 'Academia – the trashing of a priceless brand' is a microcosm of what's happening in the other institutions. If you are feeling gloomy, then leave that one for later.

Whichever way you read the book; I hope you enjoy it. Do tell me what you think using the website **www.goodbyetrust.com**.

ACADEMIA – THE TRASHING OF A PRICELESS BRAND

> In nearly 50 years of my affiliation with Harvard, I have never been as disillusioned and alienated as I am today.

Lawrence H. Summers, former president of Harvard and former US treasury secretary, following the university's response to Hamas's slaughter of Israelis

> The further a university drifts from its academic purpose, the less committed it will be to academic freedom.

Greg Lukianoff, president of the Foundation for Individual Rights and Expression

J ames Callaghan's 'great debate' speech at Ruskin College Oxford (1976) was about the failings of secondary education and was accompanied by the noise of students demonstrating with shouts of 'stop public sector spending cuts' and 'education not weapons'.

A few years before, my alma mater, Sussex University, was establishing a reputation for student militancy, with protests about the Vietnam War, Apartheid, nuclear disarmament, all things anti-American. Gripes about accommodation costs and the format of exams were tossed in for good measure.

I was a bystander to all this angst. Living in the seaside town of Brighton, studying the wonders of science and attempting to understand girls were my concerns – not edgy student politics.

Student demonstrations are nothing new. Mostly they are angry but peaceful. Occasionally they are violent, as events in Paris (1968), Tiananmen Square (1989) and Kent State University (1970) attest.

I recall these events to illustrate the timeless nature of university student activism. At Sussex, the demonstrators all seemed to come from the arts faculties. Those studying maths, science and engineering (me) were too busy with lectures and laboratory work. Scientists' preference for the student union bar, rather than screaming unachievable demands, was the argument we used to explain our political apathy.

I am sure the idealised world of academia still exists, where the brightest minds battle to extend the boundaries of knowledge. Alas, news coverage of universities and academics is, at best, mixed, often negative and sometimes insulting. Occasionally, we catch a glimpse of very bright people working together to do wonderful things, like the researchers at Oxford producing a Covid vaccine in an impossibly short time. Even the sheen from this achievement is wearing thin, with mounting concerns about its side effects and competitiveness; it was withdrawn in May 2024.

More often, the news is less flattering, with regular accounts of books and speakers being banned and students retreating to 'safe spaces', fearful of being harmed. Sometimes the stories are more alarming, with speakers and faculty being threatened and attacked.

When reading these stories, two thoughts come to mind. Parts of the media have long enjoyed ridiculing students, so isn't this business as usual? What enrages students today may be different from the past, but has anything materially changed? Academia has always been a mix of inspiring and infuriating.

From my early teens, it was clear that passing exams would expand my life chances. Let's be honest; it would also postpone the fateful day of getting a job. I knew nothing of universities, knew nobody who had ever been to one. My knowledge came from TV and radio, programmes like *University Challenge*, *The Brains Trust* and dramas set in Oxford and Cambridge with students in gowns hurrying from one inspiring tutorial to the next.

Studying at Sussex and Cranfield Business School and then spending time at London Business School and Southampton University as a lecturer exposed me to the reality of academia. Too many mediocre lecturers interspersed with the occasional inspiring teacher, lashings of petty politics and the antics of overly sensitive professors. And yet I have harboured an idealised vision of academia as a place free from day-to-day pressures where new ideas can flourish. Now I am not so sure.

Scepticism has become my immediate response when listening to academics speak. The titles of Dr, Professor, Reader and 'academic' have lost their cachet – at least to me. My instinct is that the brand of academia is becoming tarnished, if not worse.

As all good marketers know, a brand's most important asset is trust. We give great brands the benefit of the doubt once, maybe twice, but when they repeatedly disappoint, their aura vanishes fast. What has taken aeons to develop can be easily squandered.

My concern was this is happening to brand academia. I hoped this essay would dispel this fear – alas, I was horribly wrong.

WHAT HAS CHANGED

Much of what I am about to say is based on media reports and, yes, I know, I have also written about why we no longer trust the media ('Media – where did all the trust go?'). Unfortunately, my first-hand experience of academia is long ago and, in any case, it's unwise to base conclusions on personal experience. So, all the more reason to be ultra-careful and not to get swept along with the latest headlines and dominant narratives.

Let's start on safe ground by considering the quantifiable ways academia has changed.

I was among the 6% of my age group applying for university (1968). We were something of a rarity, especially among the working class. All my schoolmates were the first in their families to get a degree. I graduated in 1971 with 52,000 others, mostly men (70%).

My goddaughter was one of 600,000 when she began her degree (2021) and, as a woman, she was in the majority (57%). In some disciplines, this imbalance is much higher. An astonishing 68% of medical school applicants are women. Her mother was a graduate, as were most of her friends' parents. I had 50 universities to choose from; she had three times as many.

In the space of half a century, academia has expanded beyond recognition, as has the type of person it serves. Women are now in the majority (lucky guys) and attendance is no longer the preserve of the professional classes. However, the UK and US populations are still divided by levels of educational achievement. A third of people in the UK have a degree, yet 20% have no qualifications. Market researchers and political polling now segment the population into 'those with a degree' and the rest. I can't help thinking that is code for 'those who are intelligent' and 'the thickies'.

All these students need lots of lecturers. Like most employers, universities rely on a large pool of contract academic staff. In the US, only 30% are tenured or on a tenure stream; the others have little job security. The situation is the same in Australia, Canada and the UK.

This casualisation of the academic workforce – a more polite term than the 'gig economy' – does nothing to build loyalty to an institution.

Having been a contract lecturer at two UK universities, I have seen first-hand the different behaviour of those with and those without job security. When you are only as good as your last class appraisal, it changes your attitude. A highly acclaimed Oxbridge professor told me his advice to his untenured colleagues is to keep quiet – get tenure – then speak your mind. So much for dreaming spires and lively debate extending the boundaries of knowledge.

The final thing we know about academics is that they don't share the same political and social views as the larger population. Very roughly, there is a 50:50 divide between the right and the left in the UK and US, but academics are much more likely to be lefties. All the research I have studied concludes that fewer than 10% of academics admit to holding right-wing opinions, and it's even lower at Harvard (2%), where a resounding majority (82%) said they were liberal or very liberal. As for supporting Donald Trump or Brexit, the percentages are too small to measure.

There are signs that the upward trend in university attendance is slowing. In the US, student enrolment has fallen over 5% since 2019 and is forecast to keep falling. However, in the UK, the opposite is occurring, with a 5% increase since 2021. A word of warning, though: these numbers are distorted by changing demographics, the number of overseas students and the effects of the pandemic, so don't take them at face value.

What I am about to say is something younger readers might wish to skip, since it deals with the cost of getting a degree. Students starting at university in 2021 accumulated an average debt of £46,000. Tuition fees (£27,000) are the largest cost; the balance is for accommodation and the occasional meal and drink.

When I set off to Sussex in 1968, tuition fees didn't exist and, because of my dad's low income, the local authority paid most of my other living costs. This is not the place to get involved in fraught arguments about the 'fairness' of charging for higher education. However, I sympathise with young people's annoyance about paying for something their grandparents got for free. Arguing that 94% of my contemporaries left school at 15 to start work falls on deaf ears.

What's clear is that the size of academia has exploded. It's now big business, funded by £20 billion a year loaned to England's 1.5 million students. To put this into perspective, the amount of outstanding student debt is enough to fund the NHS for a year and then some (£205,000,000,000). Much of this will be paid by taxpayers, given that only a quarter of students are expected to repay their loans in full.

Despite so much state funding, the financial model of universities is under pressure from rising administrative costs and constraints on raising revenue (fees). As a result, the number and pay of academics have been tightly controlled. In the past, American universities spent a third of their budgets instructing students (2010) – today, it's closer to a quarter. UK universities are increasing the number of overseas students (who pay more fees). Over half the fee income of the top universities (the Russell Group) comes from non-UK students.

At face value, this explosion in academic capacity has been accompanied by an astonishing rise in the quality of the product, as measured by the level of degree awarded to students. When I graduated, only the very brightest got a 'First' – alas, I wasn't one of them. Hard work got you so far, but getting a First meant you were *extremely* bright, in the top 5% of the student population.

How the world has changed in the intervening years. In 2021, well over a third (37%) of graduating students could proudly display their First-class degree certificate. An astonishing 82% of students were awarded either an upper second or a First. Sussex University is doing even better, giving 90% of students these top degrees.

I look at these numbers in disbelief. How is it possible that

53% of mathematics graduates at University College London (UCL) get a 'First' but 'only' 33% at Cambridge (2016)? No disrespect to UCL but, in the university hierarchy, Cambridge is at the top for mathematicians.

The statistic that shocked me the most was the number of Firsts awarded to students entering university with A-level grades of 'DDD' and below. Between 2010 and 2020 this increased five-fold, from 5.3% to 28%. I appreciate that 'late achievers' can do far better than their top-of-the-class contemporaries, but are so many really doing this well? All my friends with Firsts had excelled at A-level, most taking them one to two years before us mere mortals.

The head of the Office for Students, an organisation tasked by the government with regulating England's higher education system and safeguarding the interest of students, said: 'Unmerited grade inflation is bad for students, graduates and employers, and damages the reputation of English higher education.' That's something of an understatement!

Things in the US are more complicated. The Grade Point Average (GPA) is used to measure students and is based on a rating (A, B, C, D, F) assigned for each course. There's little doubt that this is also inflating. At Harvard, the average GPA slowly rose from 2.5 in the 1950s to 2.8 in 1966, then shot up to 3.8 in 2022. It looks as if US students have been overdosing on the same intelligence-inducing drugs as their UK counterparts.

A landmark study concluded that: 'Without regulation, or at least strong guidelines, grades at American institutions of higher learning likely will continue to have less and less meaning.' This condemnation was published in 2009 and things have got a lot worse since then. Only half of US employers use the GPA score to screen college graduates from the class of 2021, down from three-quarters a few years before. Grade inflation has undoubtedly dented academia's credibility.

The reasons for this inexorable rise in grades aren't a mystery. All the performance measures of universities and their staff encourage it to happen. It's good for administrators to attract more students. Faculty are rarely criticised for the leniency of their marking, and happy students are more likely to give higher scores in teaching evaluations. Higher grades are likely to reduce the drop-out rates from courses. So where does the pushback come to maintain the grading integrity (replies to D. Stroud on a postcard!)?

Making degree education a mass-market product has changed the very foundations of academia, with grade inflation the easiest to quantify. How have its customers, the students, benefited or not from this upheaval? It's impossible to quantify the social and emotional gains but we do know how it affects graduate lifetime earning potential.

In England, the 'average' student is financially better off having a degree than those without. However, a quarter of male and 15% of female graduates earn less than their peers without a degree. According to Gallup, only 36% of Americans have a great deal or quite a lot of confidence in higher education institutions, down from 57% a decade before. It's not surprising that enrolment in US colleges has declined by 15% during this time.

The subjects studied greatly determine the future financial rewards. In England, graduates of economics, maths, medicine and computing are assured of a net positive return on their studies. For half of the women with degrees in the creative arts, English, agriculture and social care, it is financially worthwhile. Men fare far worse. Only 10% of those with degrees in the creative arts are financially better off than their school-leaving contemporaries.

For the past 30 years, education policy in the UK has targeted half of children going to university. No account was taken of demand for the credentials; it was all about achieving output targets. This has resulted in 'elite overproduction' – a mismatch between graduate supply and demand.

It's something of a misnomer, since there is nothing elite about a job that a few years ago would be done by A-level school leavers. 'Credential overproduction' is a more accurate term for a process that creates financial hardship for the individual and costs for the taxpayer. Having significant numbers of young people with 'elite' aspirations destined for run-of-the-mill employment can't be good. This situation will get worse with the number of 18-year-olds in the UK increasing 25% by 2030 and the threat of artificial intelligence (AI) decimating middle-ranking administrative jobs. There are also worrying signs that the booming demand for labour from not-for-profit employers and the public sector is ending.

While I was writing this essay the US released the 2022/2023 results for three standardised academic tests for pre-college students. The results were awful. The ACT (American College Testing) dropped to a new 30-year low, the SAT (Scholastic Assessment Test) recorded the fifth year of decline and the PISA maths test was the lowest since testing began in 2003. This can only have negative consequences for academia in years to come but is outside the scope of this essay.

Next, I wanted to see how academia fared during the Covid pandemic. It can be summarised as a mix of outstanding brilliance with catastrophically awful.

Scientists working at breakneck speed to create a vaccine displayed all the qualities you hoped academia possessed. Brilliant people cooperating globally, pushing the boundaries of science – all the dreams that originally made me want to study physics. Oxford University's partnership with AstraZeneca was a wonderful advert for academia and business working together. Unfortunately, the mounting criticism of the vaccine's safety and its withdrawal are sullying this memory.

Another less-known partnership was between technology

company Zoe and an academic at Kings College London (Prof Tim Spector). The university maintains the world's largest registry of twins to support research about how genetic variation relates to human health. A phone app was an ideal way of collecting data from this large group (14,000). Following the outbreak of Covid, the app was repurposed to measure the spread of the virus. Then came the 'lightbulb' moment. Why not make the app available to everybody in the UK so they could record their virus status and symptoms?

After 5 million people downloaded the app, Zoe had an unrivalled source of data about the pandemic in real time. A wonderful example of academia and business working for the collective good.

I am sure there were many other examples of academia enhancing its reputation during the pandemic. Unfortunately, there were also many instances where it displayed an unedifying face of intolerance and downright stupidity.

At no time during my life has academia been on such public display. Experts were listened to in hushed silence as they pronounced about the virus's spread and what we should be doing to stay safe.

In October 2020, three scientists from Oxford, Stanford and Harvard published an open letter expressing 'grave concerns about the damaging physical and mental health impacts of the prevailing Covid policies'. Instead of mass lockdowns, these scientists recommended focused protection for the most vulnerable. It was titled the Great Barrington Declaration, the name of the town where it was drafted.

Rather than debating the rights and wrongs of the proposal, academia's reaction was to criticise and silence them. One of the signatories, Prof Jay Bhattacharya, suffered a sustained attack from fellow academics. Later he recalled: 'When you take a position that is at odds with the scientific clerisy [consensus], your life becomes a living hell.' Later we discovered that he was blacklisted by social media companies at the request of agencies in the US government. The media echoed the voice of his critics.

It now appears that Anthony Fauci, a fellow scientist and chief medical adviser to the president, was central to the silencing operation. How ironic that when announcing his retirement, Fauci said: 'Stick with the science and never be afraid to tell somebody something that is the truth – but it's an inconvenient truth in which there might be the possibility of the messenger getting shot.'

Academics, and not just in the US, weren't prepared to consider alternative explanations about the pandemic's origins and the justification for the authorities' response. Worse still, they attacked those questioning the official narrative. They abandoned the central tenet of science: that it's continuously evolving and, in the case of Covid, evolving fast. We have now learnt that much of the 'settled science' they so determinedly protected was wrong. Worse still, they were fitting the science to support the narrative that the virus was naturally occurring, accompanied by a media campaign to lampoon those suggesting it was created in a Wuhan laboratory.

There's something worse than all of this, if that's possible. The authors of the academic paper *The proximal origin of SARS-CoV-2*, which was used to discredit those suggesting the virus came from a laboratory, questioned their own conclusions. Leaked emails and Slack conversations reveal their uncertainty but also their collective determination to quell any discussion about the virus being artificially created. Science was ditched to achieve the right message. The paper has never been retracted.

The reputational damage to academia was significant. Rather than being seen as a place where new theories have the freedom and resources to flourish, it ridiculed and dismissed new theories. As we will soon see, this might be the most enduring but it's not the only example of doctrinaire thinking.

Modelling and forecasting were other areas of academia thrust into the limelight and found wanting. Everybody was desperate to know how many cases, hospitalisations and deaths were expected and how they could be reduced. Academics were the people advising politicians and the health authorities, but increasingly they talked directly to the public and clearly enjoyed the experience.

We now know that the accuracy of the forecasts was dreadful. In the same way as other times when modelling had been used to determine policy for other disease outbreaks in the UK, they consistently grossly overestimated the severity of the situation.

In 2021, as the UK approached the Christmas holidays, forecasters claimed the UK would suffer fatalities between 600 and 6,000 each day and advised yet another lockdown. By now, a few politicians were questioning the usefulness of these numbers and had access to credible evidence from other parts of the world. Despite doom-laden warnings from the experts, no lockdown took place – and the daily death rate was less than half the forecast absolute minimum. The credibility of this branch of academia never recovered, especially with much of the media and the public.

In fairness, the consistently overly pessimistic forecasts, even if they were not encouraged by the politicians and the health authorities, were not sufficiently questioned. Both in the UK and the US the dramatic forecasts of deaths were used to justify the lockdown restrictions and vaccination policies. Politicians sheltered behind the credibility of the experts, who became part of the narrative. Some, including me, would call this 'propaganda'; others think it was people doing their best in difficult circumstances.

Society experienced an unprecedented period when personal freedoms were denied and astronomical social and economic costs incurred. The 'science' to justify these actions was in the hands of academic experts. Naturally, they were fallible and made mistakes. They aren't magicians. Observing these people, many seemed vain and unwilling to admit their faults. Another trait on display was intolerance to questioning opinions. This is a weakness we will continue to see exhibited throughout these essays.

Inevitably, the limitations (others would say failure) of the academics' ability to forecast the metrics of the pandemic have raised questions about the worth of their predictions about climate change. If they got things so wrong with events happening months in the future, what value should be placed on their views about half a century hence?

Nine months after all Covid restrictions were ended in the UK, over half of academic institutions had yet to return to pre-pandemic teaching methods. Some undergraduates will have completed their three-year degree in full- or semi-lockdown conditions. Long after supermarkets, restaurants, cinemas, theatres, pubs and public events had returned to normality, universities behaved as if the pandemic was still raging.

It seemed the more prestigious the university the more draconian the rules. At first, I thought Harvard's mask-wearing instructions were a joke, but they were for real. This is taken from a long spiel about using masks while eating. Remember, this is supposedly one of the world's leading universities with the brightest students. I am astonished that it didn't accompany the explanation with pictures – unlike the BBC, which provided pictorial guidance about 'five ways to make hugging safer'.

> *Practice 'Consume & Cover' – Consume your meal and immediately mask up when done. Use the 'Quick Sip Rule' – When drinking, lower your mask, take a sip, and then promptly cover your mouth and nose. If you're taking your time between bites and sips, put your mask back on. Conversation, checking email, and other activities should be masked, even when you're in a designated indoor dining area.*

The chances of 18–29-year-olds dying of or with Covid are 0.0098%. Death by a drug overdose or a car accident is much more likely. I was amazed at this minuscule risk and checked the mortality rates for the UK. These were even lower. Whichever way you view the numbers, students' risk of serious illness from Covid was minute.

Academics should have understood the statistics of risks far better than the general population. Their actions throughout the pandemic suggest they didn't. If they did, they allowed other factors to determine their response. I suspect parading their virtue was top of the list.

Other than disrupting student life you might dismiss the abandonment of face-to-face teaching and the elaborate rules about masks and social distancing as an excessive application of the precautionary principle. The words 'you can never be too careful' became educational institutions' favourite mantra.

There is a far darker side to this story concerning how some universities applied vaccine mandates. Columbia, Georgetown and the University of Pennsylvania were among those demanding all students had the original three vaccine doses and the bivalent booster. The argument about vaccine safety rages on, but one thing everybody agrees on is that myocarditis and pericarditis (chest pain caused by inflammation) are side effects and that young men are the most vulnerable – the same people who are at the lowest risk from the virus. No doubt, the justification would have been that vaccination prevented transmission of the virus, something that the vaccine producers never tested.

The Foundation for Individual Rights and Expression (FIRE) ranks US academic institutions by their attitude to ensuring free speech. They discovered the worst campuses for permitting free speech had the most draconian Covid rules. Those institutions that advised but didn't enforce vaccine use had the best ranking. Like many things to do with the pandemic, this relationship remains a mystery.

Our attitudes are only partially determined by facts. Reading about academia's rapid growth in student numbers and the grade of degrees, its mono-political culture and response to Covid, it's hard not to have an uneasy feeling that something is wrong, a feeling too easily confirmed by the constant stream of critical news stories.

MEDIA RIDICULE AND CRITICISM

Basing conclusions on the media's dominant narrative is a dangerous business. It's probably wrong and will almost certainly change over time. That said, it does more to determine public attitudes than any list of facts and figures.

Five storylines about academia's faults dominate the media; they criticise and ridicule in equal measure, perhaps with an element of fear mixed in. There's no doubt these are real problems; however, nobody knows if they are endemic or occasional events. Either way they damage trust since public opinion is formed by hunch, not logic. When you keep seeing the same storyline, it takes on the authority of a fact. That only 12% of the public associate the word 'trustworthy' with academics suggests all is not well (British Academy 2022).

Americans' opinion of higher education is on the same downward spiral, with 62% saying they have 'very little' or just 'some' confidence in colleges and universities. In 2015, that figure was 42%. This haemorrhaging has occurred in all parts of US society – Republicans and Democrats, those with college degrees, those without, men and women, young and old.

'Cancel culture' is the much-repeated term that describes academia's selective attachment to free speech. It is the most popular of the storylines and a good place to start.

Shouting down voices they don't want to hear

Students and academics have a long history of protesting at speakers they don't like. Whenever a disturbance occurs, the apologists claim 'the right' is weaponising free speech by provoking students and academics using controversial speakers with provocative views. Like all conspiracy theories, this contains some truth but doesn't explain or justify the events that are now unfolding.

What appears to have changed is the lengthening list of things deemed 'objectionable', 'provocative', 'problematic' and worst of all 'harmful'. In March 2023, the antics of the students and staff at Stanford Law School catapulted the issue of academic tolerance into the mainstream media (MSM) headlines. It ticked all the boxes – intolerance, partisan academics, warped notions about free speech and the dubious value of diversity, equity and inclusion (DEI) practitioners.

Kyle Duncan is a federal judge on the US Fifth Circuit and had been invited to speak to Stanford's Federalist Society. From the beginning, protesters led by a student coalition of 'Identity and Rights Affirmers for Trans Equality' booed and heckled his speech. After ten minutes, he gave up and asked Stanford's associate dean of DEI to restore order. Reading from a prepared speech she said:

> *For many people in this law school who work here, who study here and who live here, your advocacy, your opinions from the bench, land as absolute disenfranchisement of their rights. It impacts directly... they're people, humans, and their families. And I'm uncomfortable and it's uncomfortable to say this to you as a person. It's uncomfortable to say that for many people here, your work has caused harm.*

Several times during her address she said: 'Is the juice worth the squeeze?' I am sure Duncan guessed her meaning but he asked her to clarify: 'Is it worth the pain that this causes and the division that this causes? Do you have something so incredibly important to say that is worth this impact?'

What was Duncan's crime that was causing so much harm and distress? His most often quoted sins are being appointed by President Trump and refusing to call a transgender woman by the female pronouns. The protesters considered him harmful to the LGBTQ+ community.

From this bad start, events got worse. Duncan cut his speech short and left. Then the fun and games started. The associate dean for DEI disappeared 'on leave', Duncan was sent a letter of apology by the Law School's dean, whose office was then covered in signs criticising her apology.

Soon after the *Wall Street Journal*, *New York Times* and *Wash-*

ington Post published long opinion articles condemning the students and the DEI administrator. Normally, only national catastrophes result in these papers adopting the same stance. The UK *Daily Mail*'s headline about the event was to the point: 'Stanford law Dean of Equity is ON LEAVE after stoking woke students' protest against conservative judge'.

All the media made the same points. Those trying to stop free speech will likely be the US's future Supreme Court judges. If this were a one-off event, it might not have generated so much coverage, but protests have also occurred at Yale and the University of California.

Stanford's dean has now issued a 5,000-word document, *Academic Freedom, Free Speech, and Protests on University Campuses: Protest is Allowed but Disruption is Not Allowed.* My guess is the severity of her response resulted from the widespread condemnation but also the need to reassure the university's alumni, who are major donors, and the judges who will employ the students as interns. The DEI dean at the centre of the controversy left the university in July.

From the public's perspective, this was another event that confirmed their worries about academic intolerance, obsession with transgender issues and the disruptive role of the DEI function.

Another nasty tale of academic intolerance occurred at my old university. So much for its fine words about academic freedom:

> The University of Sussex values inclusivity, courage, kindness, integrity, and collaboration in all that we do. We are committed to promoting academic freedom and freedom of speech through providing an environment for the peaceful exchange of diverse viewpoints that can be scrutinised and explored with civility.

In October 2021 the notions of inclusivity and kindness were tested – and found wanting – when a group of students describing themselves as queer, trans and non-binary demonstrated to have

Prof Kathleen Stock fired. Her crime was 'espousing a bastardised version of radical feminism that excludes and endangers trans people'.

Matters got worse, and Stock quit her job (she had been there for 15 years) when protesters in balaclavas and masks started using flares; the police advised her to install CCTV at her home. When on campus, they suggested she be accompanied by security guards.

I have watched Stock lecture on many occasions. She is fair, sensitive and highly intelligent. The violent student protests that made her quit Sussex were dreadful but it was the lack of support from her colleagues, the university authorities and her trade union that hurt her the most.

How ironic that when she spoke at the Oxford Union, students were offered 'welfare resources' for those traumatised by her presence. The media's reporting of the event had great fun detailing how the famous Bodleian Library was providing bundles of coloured pencils to help students reduce stress by mindful colouring. Students were depicted as displaying a mix of petulance and infantile behaviour.

Before her departure from Sussex, Stock submitted grant proposals to Research England about gender identity that were subsequently successful and described as having 'created space in public and academic settings for more nuanced, evidence-informed debate'. There is no record of Sussex declining the grants.

My final example of student intolerance involves a sportswoman, not an academic. Riley Gaines was a 23-year-old US college swimming champion. She has been outspoken about male swimmers who have identified as being women and gone on to dominate the sport. After speaking at San Francisco State University, Gaines was surrounded by a hostile group calling her a 'f**king bitch' and telling her to 'go the f**k home'. Forced to take refuge, she was escorted by guards from the campus. Gaines accused the students of physical attacks, something they dispute. What happened next was truly astonishing. The university's vice-president for student affairs & enrolment management published a letter expressing commitment to the trans community. There wasn't a word of apology to Gaines but this statement of praise for the students:

> *Thank you to our students who participated peacefully in Thursday evening's event. It took tremendous bravery to stand in a challenging space. I am proud of the moments where we listened and asked insightful questions. I am also proud of the moments when our students demonstrated the value of free speech and the right to protest peacefully. These issues do not go away, and these values are very much at our core.*

Much of the media condemned the incident, especially when the president of the university commented that the event was 'deeply traumatic for the trans community'. Left-leaning papers (*The Guardian* and *The New York Times*) said nothing.

There are many more examples of students and faculty using physical intimidation against people they oppose for the temerity to question their views while simultaneously screaming about the psychological harm they are suffering. What's impossible to know is whether they represent the consensus view or are the extremist, activist fringe. It doesn't really matter, since the public just read about violent bullying students. Each incident chips away at the credibility and trust in the institution of academia.

You know a situation has got bad when the UK government appoints a 'tsar' to sort it out. In June 2023, a Cambridge professor of philosophy was appointed as the first 'free speech tsar' — his actual title is Director for Freedom of Speech and Academic Freedom, a role that's part of the administrative apparatus defined in the Higher Education (Freedom of Speech) Act 2023. That it has taken another government department (the Office for Students) over two years to fail to report about the horrendous treatment of Professor Stock at Sussex doesn't fill me with confidence that the machinery of government will do much good.

In the midst of so much intolerance, universities have a glaring blind spot over the behaviour of China – especially how it treats Uighur Muslims. Over 140,000 students from China are enrolled in UK undergraduate and postgraduate courses, up 50% from five years ago. Fee payments from China account for 6% of universities' total income and that doesn't include the funding China provides for research. With so much money comes the power to influence how academics and, it would seem, students behave.

It's a perverted logic that universities employ to justify banning goods from Israel while clamouring for Chinese money. I guess annoying Israel gets lots of virtue points. Doing the same to China would be a financial disaster.

In 2022, FIRE published a report titled *The Academic Mind in 2022 – What faculty think about free expression and academic freedom on campus*. I can't vouch for the thoroughness of the research; however, it gives the best available insights into the attitudes of academics and students. Faculty said shouting down a speaker is never acceptable (55%). Students were less sure (38%). Most faculty thought employing violence to block speakers was wrong (92%), as did students (80%).

Once the faculty's responses were segmented by age the younger ones were not that different from the students they teach. Should we be heartened or disturbed by these numbers? Knowing one in five students condone violent protest doesn't fill me with optimism.

Certain subjects, especially related to transgender and racial issues, are flashpoints resulting in aggressive actions against speakers and staff. As unfortunate as these are for those involved, they seem to be the exception, unlike another type of intolerance that is increasingly occurring.

You can't say and think that

We know academics are far more likely to ascribe to being left- rather than right-wing and there's little doubt that students are the same. Wasn't this ever so? Probably, but maybe not to the same extent – but that's a guess since there's no historical data.

As I discuss in another essay ('Beliefs – my moral compass is busted'), these descriptors of right and left are fast losing their relevance. Many of the most prominent people who are castigated, and worse, for saying the 'wrong thing' tick all the boxes for being old-style progressive lefties. For heaven's sake, I expect most of them still read *The Guardian* and *The New York Times*.

The dividing line between people is now determined by those upholding the canon of beliefs about the intersectionality of inequality, sexuality, ethnicity and disability and the supposed solutions to colonialism, racial injustice and climate change – and those that don't. Because of the religious ferocity with which these views are expressed, it's more appropriate to use theological language to describe this divide.

At one extreme are the 'believers' and the other the 'heretics'. Most people are somewhere in the middle – the 'agnostics', the 'don't care' and the 'prefer not to say'.

When the media reports on this subject, it's more in a tone of ridicule than disagreement. It's the equivalent of a naughty child being reprimanded by a parent, arms crossed, eyes rolled to the ceiling with a grimace of resignation and the hope the kid will soon grow out of this annoying phase.

These are some recent headlines:

- Censorship on campus: universities scrap 'challenging' books to protect students. *The Times*
- Universities accused of 'mollycoddling' students slapping content and trigger warnings on 1,000 books. *Daily Mail*
- Why is Durham University trying to 'decolonise' mathematics? *The Spectator*
- Oxford to 'decolonise' its computer degree. *The Daily Telegraph*

- Richard Dawkins plans to 'use every one' of the words woke scientists have banned. *Daily Express*

In case you were wondering what words Dawkins intends to use, they are 'invasive species' (considered xenophobic), 'double-blind' experiments (offensive to the disabled) and 'survival of the fittest' (an endorsement of eugenics).

It seems that each day universities ban more words. Today, it is the University of Washington alarmed that housekeeping 'feels gendered'. The University of Southern California's School of Social Work believes 'field work' might have unpleasant connotations of slavery and should be replaced with 'practicum'. Johns Hopkins University issued an online glossary of LGBTQ+ terms that defined a lesbian as a 'non-man attracted to non-men'. As you might expect – or maybe you don't – this attracted accusations of misogyny and a clumsy attempt to 'erase' women. It was defended as being inclusive of non-binary and transgender people; nevertheless, it disappeared from the university's website once it attracted the media's attention.

The 'believers' seem obsessed with policing what's said and written – something they continue after leaving university, as press reports about word-policing in the publishing industry, charities, non-governmental organisations and the NHS attest.

Much fun was made of the 92 pages required to explain Oxfam's *Inclusive Language Guide.* Hundreds of words and phrases were supposed to be avoided – 'standing with' (fear of alienating those who cannot stand), 'expectant mothers' (better to use 'people who can become pregnant') and 'empowerment' (people already have power; this is not something that can be bestowed by others). My heartfelt sympathy goes to authors (and editors) navigating this verbal minefield, who must live in fear of triggering impassioned accusations of 'hate speech' and a rush to the barricades to have them cancelled.

I expect for most people busy with their lives, these reports are no more than background noise, having the same importance as omens about AI causing mass unemployment and tales of a C-grade celebrity's peccadillos. The popular press uses them to generate copy to amuse their readers. For some, probably more among the oldies, these stories confirm their belief that the world is going to the dogs.

This obsession with language and beliefs becomes much more serious when it determines people's livelihood and reputation.

In 2022 the *Times Higher Education* published results of research intended to separate fact from fiction in the supposed academic gender culture wars. Fifty interviews were conducted with sociology, psychology and education academics. The researcher captured the full range of opinions and wrote what I thought was a balanced account of her findings.

She came to a disturbing conclusion:

> *Having approached the topic with an open mind, however, my discussions left me in no doubt that a culture of discrimination, silencing and fear has taken hold across universities in England, and many countries beyond.*

We have already seen how Prof Kathleen Stock was forced out of her position by student protest and the acquiescence of her fellow academics. The researcher discovered similar stories of 'intimidation, smears and losing career progression opportunities'.

Those holding opposing views were interviewed, detailing their many and extremely complicated opinions. Some believed 'sex' is a construct of oppressive systems, notably Western colonialism. 'Gender' was described using different constructs, performative, biopsychosocial and psychobiologist models. Though they didn't use the phrase 'the ends justify the means', they all believed in the rightness of their position; more than that, they believed their very existence was threatened by those holding opposing views.

Before beginning the project, she was warned, 'Are you not terrified – everybody is going to hate you.' And, that's what happened. She suffered online abuse, her research data was confiscated and she was 'let go' by her employer (City, University of London). Forced to use crowdfunding, she is challenging the punishments at an employment tribunal, claiming 'discrimination, harassment, victimisation and whistleblowing detriment'. Her research data has now been returned but her fight for justice continues.

When a journalist writes about intolerance in 'woke universities' – now a regular occurrence – there is no shortage of examples and titbits of mangled language to amuse the readers. The human rights professor at Bristol University was accused of Islamophobia, and the social anthropology lecturer at Edinburgh University alleged to be a racist. They were exonerated after lengthy investigations with little support from the university authorities.

As much as I avoid being carried along by the dominant narrative, it's hard to dismiss the view that academia is becoming increasingly doctrinaire and intolerant. Certainly, this applies to the toxic subjects of gender and racism, but I sense it spreads much further. How sad that a group of academics felt forced to create a Council for Academic Freedom, a basic right that most of us assume they already have.

It would be amusing, if it weren't so tragic, that academics have redefined the meaning of words to reconcile what's happening. Lewis Carroll would have had great fun with 21st-century academic speak. As we discovered, the universities' values statements are littered with sentiments about inclusivity, freedom of expression and valuing diversity – the antithesis of what is happening.

Redefining the language

When I was researching the history of secondary education, I read numerous academic and doctoral papers. Academic writing is the diametric opposite of plain English – the longer the sentence, the more multiple clauses and specialist vocabulary, the better. I was always left wondering if the difficulty in understanding the meaning was my fault or if the author was intentionally complicating the language to exaggerate their and the text's importance. For instance:

> *In the realm of pedagogical stratagems, the utilisation of experiential methodologies to facilitate the acquisition of knowledge necessitates the employment of a multifarious array of interactive, immersive, and student-centric practices, which endeavour to foster the enhancement of cognitive abilities, the inculcation of critical thinking, and the cultivation of a growth mindset amongst the pupils, thereby contributing to the overall scholastic outcomes and holistic development of the participants in the educational process.*

If anything, the situation has got worse. Good luck trying to decipher this statement:

> *The fluid and non-binary praxis of gender performativity predicates itself upon the recognition of the iterative reification of culturally constructed signifiers, which subsequently eschews the hegemonic and reductive binary schema typically employed to delineate the panoply of human gender identity and expression.*

I came to accept that this is how academics wrote. I hoped, for the sake of their friends and family, it wasn't how they spoke. Occasionally the effort of deciphering the complex verbiage was worth the effort and revealed some gems of wisdom.

'Academic speak' isn't new; it's part of the rites of passage when gaining the title of Dr or Professor. Using complicated grammar laden with technical language is all part and parcel of being an academic. Recently, however, the relationship with the English language has changed. In addition to complexity, academics are redefining the meanings of words and banning others they believe are so dangerous as to cause distress and harm.

The media has also played a significant role in tampering with the language, mainly to make stories more sensational and 'click-able'. Once upon a time, 'fury' described fierce passion, a disorder or tumult of mind. Now it means being very annoyed. A 'victim' was once somebody suffering extreme hardship and/or injury caused by an oppressive or destructive agency. Now it describes numerous racial or sexual groups. A 'revelation' was once a disclosure or communication by divine or supernatural means. Now it means the latest thing a journalist has discovered. Feeling 'exhausted' is to drain a person of strength or resources; now it means feeling a tad tired.

This inflation of the language makes the tone of news reporting more aggressive and louder. What academia is doing makes it downright confusing and dangerous.

Words are being banned for being harmful, and ideas are labelled as distressing. Students are portrayed as a collection of vulnerable minorities, each with their own sensitivities requiring protection. I expand on this subject in 'Language – from beautiful to brutal'.

The list of words and phrases that cause harm keeps growing. Students in the US are demanding that lecturers provide a 'trigger warning' anytime 'traumatic' content is about to be mentioned, especially about 'self-harm, domestic, racial or transphobic violence and homophobic harassment'. Books that might result in distress are being avoided. Universities are anxious to promote their havens of 'safe space' where students are protected from hurtful ideas. Some UK universities believe the word 'trigger' is itself provocative and offends some students and are using the term 'content notes' instead.

All of this is a far cry from the university culture of the 1970s. Yet again I wrestle with the thought that this description of fragile minds needing protection is a caricature. One that is easily substantiated by the actions of some universities but not representative of what it is like to be an undergraduate in 2024.

Maybe things have radically changed and universities have become dangerous places. Certainly, students at Leicester University think so, where its Centre for Hate Studies (note that word 'hate' again) found 40% of students claim to have been harassed. The charity for men's health Humen believes 57% of UK students have used counselling, helplines, self-help resources and wellbeing groups. The situation in the US is worse, with a quarter of university students taking some form of psychiatric medication. That's in addition to an unknown quantity of unregistered substances. For reasons I don't understand, women seem to be more prone to mental health conditions than men.

UK university students seem to want more control over what they read and discuss (HEPI, June 2022):

- 86% of students support trigger warnings (68% in 2016).
- 62% of students support safe-space policies (48% in 2016).
- 79% of students believe 'students that feel threatened should always have their demands for safety respected' (68% in 2016).
- 35% of students agree that 'if you debate an issue like sexism or racism, you make it acceptable' (17% in 2016).

When I read this research, a voice in the back of my mind is urging caution. Charities tend to, what shall we say, 'exaggerate' the magnitude of the problem they are established to address. That said, students' mental state seems to be fragile.

It's not surprising that the proportion of students believing 'universities are becoming less tolerant of a wide range of viewpoints' has risen to 38% (24% in 2016). Nearly half of US students feel uncomfortable speaking in class about controversial subjects, especially men. This fact, combined with the rising percentage of women students, now 57%, implies something – what, I am not sure.

Despite claims of valuing freedom of speech, it comes with conditions. There's no doubt that students want, and academics are providing, knowledge that is sanitised according to rules that it's hard to fathom. Well, certainly for an outsider trying to make sense of what's happening.

The rise and rise of diversity, equity and inclusion (DEI)

Until I wrote this essay, I had no idea that the scope of ambition of the DEI movement extends across all parts of academia. Starting with the assumption that academia is inherently unfair and biased, its mandate is to realign the entire academic system. Some of its initiatives get reported in the media:

- Ensuring 'fairness' in the recruitment and retention of staff.
- Training students and academics about unconscious bias, cultural competency and inclusive language and behaviour.
- Adapting all policies to ensure they meet DEI standards.
- Supporting minority groups, providing them with platforms to voice their concerns and contribute to the organisation's DEI goals.
- Incorporating accessible and inclusive design.
- Collecting data to measure the effectiveness of DEI initiatives.
- Implementing policies to eradicate microaggressions and discrimination.

These DEI mission statements from four world-class universities are brimming with warm and reassuring words. The devil is in the detail of how these aims are to be achieved.

> *Excellence is inclusive. We work across the university to create capacity, build community, and spark innovation in support of antiracist and inclusive initiatives to ensure that this is a place where everyone can thrive. (Harvard)*

We are committed to transparency, accountability, and promoting the integration of diversity, equity, and inclusion throughout the fabric of our educational mission. (Stanford)

DEI supports the university's commitment to fostering an inclusive culture which promotes equality, values diversity and maintains a working, learning and social environment in which the rights and dignity of all its staff and students are respected. (Oxford)

The university is committed in its pursuit of academic excellence to equality of opportunity and to a proactive and inclusive approach to equality, which supports and encourages all under-represented groups, promotes an inclusive culture, and values diversity. (Cambridge)

How strange that these same DEI departments attract so much opprobrium, like this statement from the *WSJ* (2023):

> *DEI attacks the integrity of the academic project. Instead of listening to divergent voices, ears are shut. Instead of the free expression of contrary opinions, chilling self-censorship takes place. Instead of a campus open to all, one finds a narrow doorway through which only an approved few may enter. If the right pieties and homilies aren't made, ostracisation and exclusion become the norm rather than the exception. Unanimity, inequality, and exclusion – Orwellian indeed.*

Let's consider a few facts before attempting to explain why the initials DEI cause so many people, mainly from the 'right' but increasingly from the legacy 'left', to get so angry.

In 2020, worldwide spending on DEI activities was reckoned to be $9.4 billion and set to reach $24.44 billion by 2040. That's a compound average growth rate of 12.6%. If only the UK and US economies were growing as fast! McKinsey believes the US alone spends about $8 billion a year on diversity training.

That's a lot of money and employment opportunities. A survey of 65 US universities (2021) found they employed an average of 45 people in their DEI administrations. Princeton had 70 staff, Ohio State 132, Stanford 177 and the University of Michigan, four times the average, with a budget of $85 million. The academics and students at Michigan must be very busy implementing the 2,800 action plans and 37 university-wide strategies their DEI group has generated. Alas, all this activity has done little to change the racial composition of its students.

If staff numbers are an indicator of priorities, then US universities are more concerned with DEI than providing services to students with disabilities. For every member of staff responsible for ensuring the universities provide the care specified by the Americans with Disabilities Act, four are involved in DEI. Of course, the demand for DEI resources might be that much more than for supporting disabled students – who knows?

The explosion of DEI employment opportunities has been fantastic business for universities that provide much of the training and accreditation. In the film *The Graduate*, Ben was advised there was a great future in 'plastics' – now he would be told it's 'DEI'. George Floyd's death and the rise and rise of BLM was the accelerant that fired the adoption of DEI throughout higher education.

My explanation about the workings of DEI is about to get more complicated. The words 'equality' and 'equity' are separated by two characters (al) that make a huge difference to the scope of DEI's remit. Harvard and Stanford, like most US universities, aim for 'equity'. Cambridge and Oxford strive for 'equality', along with other UK universities. By the time this book is published, I expect the UK institutions will also be dropping the 'al'.

Equality is all about treating everyone the same, regardless of their unique circumstances, while equity focuses on addressing the specific needs of individuals to achieve equal outcomes. Ensuring 'equity' requires being far more interventionist as well as having clarity and agreement about the 'specific needs of individuals' and the mechanisms of measuring equality of outcome.

The actions to achieve equity are at the heart of much of the controversy surrounding the role of DEI. For instance, abolishing bias, conscious or unconscious, sounds innocuous until you look at the way it's being achieved. Most US universities' DEI administrations operate bias reporting systems. If Cornell University's definition of bias is typical then they must be mighty busy.

> *A bias incident is action taken that one could reasonably and prudently conclude is motivated, in whole or in part, by the alleged offender's bias against an actual or perceived aspect of diversity, including, but not limited to, age, ancestry or ethnicity, color, creed, disability, gender, gender identity or expression, height, immigration or citizenship status, marital status, national origin, race, religion, religious practice, sexual orientation, socioeconomic status, or weight.*

Needless to say, this ultra-wide definition of bias (20 topics) and the equally wide scope of 'harm' is proving unpopular with many academics, who feel that they are constrained by the sensibilities of the most easily offended students. And we haven't even considered the contentious topic of 'microaggressions'.

The DEI industry is great news for kitemark-awarding organisations. Of the UK's top 100 most LGBTQ+ inclusive employers, according to Stonewall, 14 are universities. I don't know how many universities are part of their *Diversity Champions* programme, but I expect it's the majority, although a few universities are abandoning the scheme (UCL and LSE).

The Athena Swan Charter was originally established to increase the number of women studying the sciences. Recently it has expanded its horizons to include 'embedding intersectionality principles' throughout higher education. This means (I think) helping all minority groups by ensuring processes, like recruitment and promotion, are not only fair and seen to be fair but actively supporting nominated disadvantaged groups.

The B Corp Certification programme, discussed at length in 'Business – charting new paths or losing direction?', evaluates organisations on their performance in all things environmental and DEI.

Kitemark awards are emblems of DEI's success. Rather than evaluating their own performance, universities delegate these organisations to mark their homework.

What's happening in academia has parallels in healthcare. Once upon a time, medical staff exercised power, but in the quest for efficiency, the power has been captured by 'management'. Academic authority has been relinquished to the DEI administrators, not for reasons of efficiency but equity.

The DEI community has developed a language and framework for looking at the world that is alien to most people and attracts condemnation from politicians on the right. Not all academics are convinced by its value. This statement from the president of the University of Virginia crystallises the concern about the expanding influence of DEI administrators.

> *If faculty, staff, or students are required to assent to propositions that are debatable, as opposed to self-evident, such trainings would run the risk of crossing the line from education to enforced orthodoxy. If applicants have to describe how they are going to further DEI, it raises concerns that they will feel pressure to state particular beliefs in order to get hired. And if faculty are required to report on how their teaching or research efforts have promoted DEI, it risks infringing on academic freedom.*

The reference to 'how they are going to further DEI' is the practice, common in the US and now being adopted in the UK, of forcing job applicants and those seeking promotion to explain how they will uphold the tenets of the DEI mission statement. An astonishing three-quarters of job applicants at the University of California are rejected solely based on lack of commitment to the DEI agenda. The same percentage of faculty job opportunities at Arizona's university require applicants to declare their support for the DEI policies.

Those on the left either remain silent or attempt to dismiss this criticism as manufactured 'culture wars'. In some places, like Ohio, attempts are being made to limit the scope of diversity initiatives. If Ohio Senate Bill 83 becomes law it will ban mandatory DEI training and institutions taking positions on controversial issues. MIT has already decided to stop using diversity statements when recruiting. This didn't result from political pressure, but rather the absence of evidence they are effective. The university's president said: 'these statements impinge on freedom of expression, and they don't work'.

In June 2023, the US Supreme Court ruled that discrimination against Chinese Asian Americans was illegal and that race must not be used as a criterion for university admission. The judgement said: 'Eliminating racial discrimination means eliminating all of it.'

Academia spins the story as a judgement against black people at the hands of a Trump-appointed judge. President Biden said the judgement didn't come from 'a normal court' – the inference being it lacks legitimacy. Americans disagree, with only 20% thinking racial discrimination makes admission fairer. Approximately 70% of white, Hispanic and Asian adults believe the court's decision was a good thing. Only black adults retain support for affirmative action, probably because they are the greatest beneficiaries. Even so, their support has dropped to 50%.

It seems to me the diversity machine has worked well – in the class of 2024 at Stanford and Harvard, the percentage of whites (including Jews) is 21% and 34%, respectively – despite 75% of the country being white.

Colleges are already suggesting ways they can circumvent the law. The idea of 'adversity scores' is a favourite for giving colleges the mechanism to control the racial mix of students. Harvard now asks students to comment about: 'How will the life experiences that shape who you are today enable you to contribute to Harvard?' The University of Carolina asks applicants to 'Describe an aspect of your identity and how this has shaped your life experiences.' These could be innocuous questions or using 'life experiences' and 'identity' as proxies for race.

Those working in DEI feel under attack. From their perspective, all they are doing is trying to create a fairer society. The president of the National Association of Diversity Officers in Higher Education captures their frustration (2023):

 To now find ourselves in a situation where there's this very aggressive advocacy to turn the clock back is profoundly disappointing. It has had, I think, a chilling effect, not only in the context of faculty who teach curriculum that is being identified as a form of indoctrination, to the dismantling of what they refer to as 'diversity, equity, inclusion, bureaucracies,' to ways in which people feel threatened in terms of their work.

Academia is where the theory of DEI was born. Universities pioneered its implementation and exploited its business potential. Those involved must think the benefits of their work are self-evident. Clearly, not everybody outside the DEI bubble sees it that way.

Although variants of DEI ideology are now common in public and private sector organisations it is often ignored, rejected, ridiculed or condemned by large parts of the media and public. It shocked many people (including me) to learn that 10,000 UK public service jobs are focused exclusively on equality, diversity and inclusion at a cost of £557 million. The cash-strapped NHS spends £40 million a year on these staff, which is strange considering its high proportion of women and non-white workers.

According to LinkedIn, DEI jobs in Europe, the Middle East and Africa grew 1.6 times faster than HR jobs. People with the job title 'head of diversity' more than doubled in the five years to 2020. No wonder business schools are highlighting their DEI credentials – Wharton already allows MBA students to major in the subject.

Too often, the public debate (if there is a debate) is conducted by DEI's most vocal defenders and attackers. The results do nothing to improve DEI's or academia's reputation – quite the contrary. Those outside academia look on and wonder whatever happened to the idea that universities were about educating the best minds with the best teachers. What simplistic and reactionary thinking! It seems that the ideals of the University of California Berkeley are much more the order of the day:

 Excellence in advancing equity and inclusion must be considered on par with excellence in research and teaching.

Can we believe what academics say?

In the US, social science doctoral dissertations typically range from 75,000 to 100,000 words in length. Those in the natural sciences or engineering are shorter but have lots of graphs. Each year, over 50,000 of these additions to human knowledge are evaluated, published and archived, probably never to be read again.

The British Library created EThOS, a searchable database of over 600,000 UK doctoral theses. If each of these took on average three years to create, it's equivalent to 1.8 million years of human endeavour. A quick search revealed the strange things students had committed years to studying.

Practising the Urban Night in Newcastle-upon-Tyne: Rhythms, Frames, Affects, Assemblages and Subjectivities

Stratification and inclusivity in ethnically diverse adolescent athletes: an ethnography and theoretical evaluation of emerging masculinities in multi-cultural contexts

Cat-people: an ethnography of more-than-human interrelatedness in the 'cat fancy'

These examples are baffling and sound, what shall we say, slightly ridiculous. You can't help wondering about their usefulness, let alone why they require so much time to research. Of course, other research leads to wonderful outcomes that benefit us all.

Who knows what insights emerge from studying people with a 'cat fancy'?

This ultra-focused research on some obscure topic has long been criticised. I found articles dating from the 19th century, including *The Value of Useless Studies* (1892), lambasting universities for wasting public money. More recent examples – *We Must Stop the Avalanche of Low-Quality Research* (2010) – say much the same.

Doctoral theses are the tip of the iceberg of published research. Academics are judged and their promotion and funding depend on the number of peer-reviewed papers they produce and the quality of the journals that accept their work. The first rule of being a successful academic is 'publish or perish'.

Nobody knows the annual production – more than a million, less than two, would be a reasonable guess. In 2019, approximately half a million papers were published in US peer-reviewed journals, just within the fields of science and engineering. Meanwhile, UK journals published 130,000 papers in the same disciplines.

The need to 'publish or perish' isn't a new concept; the term was first used in 1928. The reputation and prestige of the journal is all-important, as is its 'impact', the number of citations per article published in the previous two years.

Theoretically, the journal publishing process should be an effective way of ensuring the best quality research gains the most exposure. Unfortunately, human frailty has meant this has never been true. There have always been accusations that 'fashionable' research is more likely to be published. That the 'old boys' network – yes, I know it should be 'old persons' – distorts the objectivity of the reviews. The opposite occurs when unpopular academics find it harder to be published for reasons other than quality. The same happens when attempting to publish papers that challenge the orthodoxy.

In 2018 three American academics highlighted the weakness of the peer-reviewed journal process when they submitted 20 concocted papers stuffed full of fashionable terms. This has become known as the 'grievance study hoax'. These examples must make academics wince:

An Ethnography of Breastaurant Masculinity: Themes of Objectification, Sexual Conquest, Male Control, and Masculine Toughness in a Sexually Objectifying Restaurant

Human Reactions to Rape Culture and Queer Performativity in Urban Dog Parks in Portland, Oregon

When the hoax was revealed, seven of the papers had been accepted for publication and seven were going through the review process; only six had been rejected. Stuffing academic papers with DEI terminology is not a guarantee for publication, but it doesn't do any harm.

This escapade has drawn attention to other ways that DEI thinking has become embedded in the publishing and referencing of journals. Academic research and books are littered with citations (references to the work of others). The number of times a work is referenced is important to the status of the authoring academic. The DEI movement has been promoting the notion of 'citation justice' whereby works are referenced not for their excellence/relevance but as a mechanism to raise the visibility of academics from marginalised groups. As the press reports, 'Ensuring straight white middle-aged men don't dominate the field'. I guess it's affirmative action applied to citations.

Critics of DEI ask, 'where is the knowledge, the research, that justifies its beliefs?' How do we know that 'critical race theory' isn't just that, a theory that has taken on the guise of a religious mantra? Where is the evidence that, at the last count, there are 69 different types of sexuality? How do we know that the notion of intersectionality is anything more than a collection of Venn diagrams? The response would be to quote a long list of papers by academics dripping with credentials. Is this justification valid, or does it demonstrate that credibility can be achieved by the volume of citations, not the thoroughness of the research? Perhaps the old saying 'never mind the quality, feel the width' extends to academia.

This concept is known as 'idea laundering', similar to money laundering. When enough academics publish papers using unsubstantiated concepts, those ideas eventually become the dominant narrative – at least in that area of academia. It's the magic of laundering a hypothesis so that it emerges as a fact.

I had first-hand experience of this phenomenon when researching the history of secondary education. Certain opinions evolved over time to become the accepted wisdom as alternative arguments and caveats evaporated. They were not supported by evidence but by their popularity.

Academic journals are adding additional rules enabling them to reject papers for reasons unconnected with the excellence of the research. For example, Springer publishes *The Nature Portfolio*, one of the most prestigious series of journals, and has recently issued a document entitled *Principles of scholarly freedom and scholarly responsibility*.

Academic freedom is defined as 'fundamental, but not unbounded'. Academic papers must meet all the usual standards (e.g. peer review) but will be refused if they might cause 'potential harms', a term so broad as to include just about anything:

 Researchers are asked to carefully consider the potential implications (including inadvertent consequences) of research on human groups defined by attributes of race, ethnicity, national or social origin, sex, gender identity, sexual orientation, religion, political or other beliefs, age,

disease, (dis)ability or other status, to be reflective of their authorial perspective if not part of the group under study, and contextualise their findings to minimize as much as possible potential misuse or risks of harm to the studied groups in the public sphere.

The other giant of the academic journal market (Elsevier) 'invites' editorial staff to self-report their gender identity, ethnic origins and race (diversity data) for the purpose of 'advancing DEI in research' so it can drive 'greater equity in publishing and research'. Thoughts about what that means on a postcard – please. What does it matter if the author of a paper about elementary particle physics is Chinese, Iranian, American or Nigerian?

That the editor of the *Journal of the American Medical Association* offered to resign because its website published a podcast questioning the existence of structural racism in American medicine shows the sensitivity of journals to saying the wrong thing.

The major academic publishers exercise huge control over the industry and academia; half of all revenues come from the five largest companies. Like the UK's royalty, academic journals should stay aloof from politics. As soon as they declare support for one faction of politicians, they are bound to annoy another. This seems obvious, yet *Nature* magazine appeared surprised that Republican academics (the few there are) lost trust in the journal after they published their support for President Biden. The *British Medical Journal* makes no apologies for being 'political'; rather, it keeps questioning if it is political enough.

Defenders of this policy would claim that politics is woven into all subjects. Maybe, maybe not, but the more journals take sides, the more enemies they make, and the easier it is to dismiss what they say.

The same arguments apply to scientists who brandish their political beliefs as much as their academic excellence. What possible good comes from Prof Michael Mann, the person the media love quoting about climate science, stating: 'Remember who the enemy is – Republicans'?

The bedrock of academia is the legitimacy of the peer-review process, yet nobody disputes its significant flaws. I was shocked to learn that over 10,000 research papers were retracted in 2023 (*Nature*), and that figure was thought to be 'only the tip of an iceberg'.

It is well known that 'predatory journals' don't have adequate (or any) quality control mechanisms. To the unwary, these journals appear as valid as those that have been peer-reviewed. Increasingly, journal papers that seemingly meet all the quality requirements are being questioned about their accuracy, especially in the replicability of the research data.

Nature magazine published research claiming that 70% of researchers have tried and failed to reproduce another scientist's experiments, and more than half have failed to reproduce their own experiments. The most damning testimony comes from the editor of the *British Medical Journal*: 'most of what is published in journals is just plain wrong or nonsense'.

Concern about academic research keeps emerging. Most recently, the US Department of the Treasury studied 67 papers, from 13 prestigious journals, and could only reproduce the findings in half of them. A study of papers in the field of psychology found a similar level of failure.

As already mentioned, publishing the *Proximal origin of SARS-CoV-2* paper sounds harmless enough, but it affected us all. It was written with the sole intent of closing debate about the origins of the Covid virus, yet correspondence released to a congressional subcommittee revealed the authors thought the Wuhan laboratory was a possible source, even 'friggin' likely', something now widely believed to be true. After the paper appeared in *Nature* debate about the virus's origins was treated as misinformation and banned by the social media companies.

At best, we can say that the academic publishing process has flaws. Like so much about academia, it's impossible to know if these imperfections are just that, things that can easily be remedied, or significant and growing problems. That the president of Stanford University resigned after papers he authored contained 'substandard practices' suggests even the mightiest of institutions are not immune.

CAUSE FOR CONCERN OR CRISIS?

There's much to criticise about the workings of academia, but then much about it doesn't attract attention and delivers huge benefits. Applying academic discipline to my own thinking, I should sit on the fence, claiming there's not enough evidence to draw firm conclusions.

Despite there being little I can say with certainty, I am concerned, very concerned. Parts of academia are on a path that is increasingly alienating the public. It's professing views that many (I think most) people dislike or don't understand. Its new priorities threaten the very thing that academia once cherished – excellence and impartiality. Its actions thrust it into a political arena that has never been more polarised. Already US states are attempting to pass legislation limiting universities' powers to implement DEI policies. The UK has passed the Higher Education (Freedom of Speech) Act 2023, enabling universities to be sued for failing to uphold the right to free speech.

It seems the concept of 'thinking the unthinkable' is being replaced by 'thinking within accepted boundaries'. The culture and bureaucracy of DEI are extending into the rules governing research funding, the guidelines for publishing academic papers, the recruitment of academics and the selection of students.

Academics seem to be suffering from an epidemic of cognitive dissonance. They are in an endless loop of striving to believe conflicting narratives simultaneously.

There's the traditional notion that universities are places

where new ideas flourish in a supportive environment valuing free speech. Yet they are also described as places strewn with danger, where vulnerable and fragile minds must be protected from harm. Not harm and distress resulting from physical abuse but from hearing words and beliefs they find abhorrent.

They are places where excellence can flourish, where the very brightest can achieve their full potential. At the same time, the academic process is manipulated to right the wrongs of past generations, valuing inclusion and equity as much as, if not more than, quality. Students study to expand their minds and explore new ideas – but only those echoing the canon of DEI beliefs. Universities labour to expand their diversity – all the time becoming more mono-cultured, with few espousing anything other than the progressive leftish agenda.

'Freedom of speech' is heralded as being fundamental to academia but is conditional upon the 'speech', the ideas being expressed, meeting criteria administered by the guardians of DEI and their supporters. Contrary thinking is readily extinguished at the first accusation of disinformation and 'hate speech'. I am sure many want to defend academic freedom but when you have a mortgage to pay and a career to build, it's safer to keep quiet.

Like so many human interactions, it's about gaining and exercising power. The disciples of DEI would agree, saying all they are doing is rebalancing the power struggle to the detriment of the old establishment to benefit the disadvantaged. To ensure the right decisions are made and to silence the distractions and lies of the reactionaries. A world facing multiple existential threats needs radical and immediate actions, not more debate.

This results in academics and students radiating a certainty and righteousness about their beliefs. Time is short – can't you see it's an emergency – we need action, not words. Those disagreeing are not only wrong, they are enemies of change, they are evil.

I find it hard to believe that all, even the majority, of students support these glaring contradictions between what universities espouse as their mission and what happens day to day. I comfort myself hoping they are too busy enjoying their social life to notice. However, I suspect it's easier to keep quiet, to self-censor, than confront the progressive disciples. Why rock the boat when they have paid their fees and stand a good chance of getting a First?

Academics have always had radical ideas, ones that conflict with the orthodoxy. But now it's not just academics, it's the whole process of academia that has coalesced around supporting a single agenda – diversity, equity and inclusion – that sees the world as a conflict between victims and oppressors. The right and the legacy left call this 'ideological capture'. The new progressives call it redressing past injustices.

Conflict happens when those outside academia are expected to believe and adhere to the new rules – when the rubber hits the road and DEI beliefs are translated into actions. Academia, the experts, are invariably involved in defending actions that the public, via the MSM, find objectionable, inexplicable and often comical. The word 'woke' is a scream that encapsulates their frustrations.

I sense there has never been more of a gap between the believers and the public. Media attention focuses on the antics of supposedly educated people saying ridiculous things. Academics and students have always held strong views, more so than Jo Public, but they were on the same spectrum of understanding about issues; they had a common language to discuss those topics. Today, academia obsesses about things that are a million miles from the concerns of the public. In the latest Pew Research about the US public's main concerns, not one related to DEI makes it into the top ten.

We are left with a question. Will the views of academia over time become accepted as the norm, and will we wonder what all the fuss was about? Will they retain the role of being experts, people we trust?

Alternatively, could it be they have eroded the trust of the general populace? Are universities constrained by a collective mentality restricting the freedom to consider radical ideas? Have funding authorities and peer-reviewed journals transformed from facilitators of academic progress into contributing to the problem?

Sadly, my money is on the latter.

I finished writing this essay in the middle of summer 2023. There were a few additions and corrections to incorporate in the final draft, but nothing of consequence. That all changed at 6.30a.m. on 7 October 2023, when Palestinians attacked Israeli civilians. I am sure you are aware of the gruesome details of the attack and the ensuing conflict, so I don't intend to repeat them here. However, it's important to realise the enormity of the event. It's been ranked as the third-worst terrorist attack in history, the equivalent of Israel suffering fifteen 9/11s simultaneously.

Like 9/11, civilians were the undisputed target of the attack. It was executed to maximise news coverage, being brutal and involving the worst excesses of violence. These were videoed and circulated using social media, often on the accounts of the victims.

When the news broke, I realised its significance as a major escalation of the conflict between the US and Iran. Stopping the diplomatic relationship between Israel and Saudi Arabia was another objective. I had no idea that it would also initiate events that 87 days later would result in the presidents of Harvard and Pennsylvania Universities resigning. All my concerns about universities' adherence to the nostrums of DEI would be graphically revealed as horrible problems. Long-time festering conflicts, largely ignored by the media, suddenly became headline news, all for the wrong reasons.

Within 24 hours of the attack, 30 student organisations at Harvard issued a statement that 'held the Israeli regime entirely responsible for all unfolding violence'. Protests targeted at Israel erupted at other US universities and soon spread to the UK. On US campuses, Jewish students were harassed, and cases of anti-semitism soared.

Harvard had been at the forefront of responding to the death of George Floyd:

> *We are outraged by the countless deaths of Black people at the hands of police officers and citizens caused by a system that treats Black people as expendable.*
>
> *Words alone cannot do justice to the centuries of trauma and violence that racism has inflicted, and continues to inflict, upon Black people and communities in the United States.*

It was among the first to express anger at Russia's invasion of Ukraine:

> *The deplorable actions of Vladimir Putin put at risk the lives of millions of people and undermine the concept of sovereignty. Institutions devoted to the perpetuation of democratic ideals and to the articulation of human rights have a responsibility to condemn such wanton aggression.*

This was the first statement issued by the president of Harvard after 7 October:

> *We write to you today heartbroken by the death and destruction unleashed by the attack by Hamas that targeted citizens in Israel this weekend and by the war in Israel and Gaza now underway.*

After criticism that maybe this didn't reflect the enormity of the event, another statement was issued:

> *As the events of recent days continue to reverberate, let there be no doubt that I condemn the terrorist atrocities perpetrated by Hamas. Such inhumanity is abhorrent, whatever one's individual views of the origins of longstanding conflicts in the region.*

Regarding the students' statement holding Israel responsible for the slaughter of its own people, Harvard's president said:

> *While our students have the right to speak for themselves, no student group – not even 30 student groups – speaks for Harvard University or its leadership.*

This unwillingness to condemn the latent antisemitism of so many Harvard students was too much for Larry Summers, a previous president of Harvard:

> *Harvard is being defined by the morally unconscionable statement apparently coming from two dozen student groups blaming all the violence on Israel. I am sickened. I cannot fathom the Administration's failure to disassociate the University and condemn this statement.*

As the conflict in Palestine increased, so did the hate (a word I use with caution) against Jewish students. All the much-trumpeted values about protecting vulnerable students from harm and hurt evaporated if they were Jewish.

To explain what their institutions were doing to combat antisemitism, the presidents of Harvard, MIT and the University of Pennsylvania were asked to give evidence to the House Education Committee (7 December 2023). This was never going to be a calm examination of the evidence. The Republicans were incensed at the universities' seeming acceptance of the hostile actions against Jews when they were so sensitive to all other types of hate.

Repeatedly asked what actions they were taking against

students who were flagrantly committing racist acts against Jews, the presidents responded with quasi-legal arguments. The final exchange between Republican Elise Stefanik and Claudine Gay (Harvard) immediately went viral:

 'So the answer is yes, that calling for the genocide of Jews violates Harvard code of conduct, correct?' Stefanik asked.

'Again, it depends on the context,' Gay said.

I am sure the words 'it depends on the context' will haunt Gay for the rest of her life. She was repeatedly asked why she was so emphatic about defending the rights of those calling for genocide against Jews when Harvard had an abysmal record of protecting free speech. In 2023 Harvard ranked the worst university in the US for allowing free speech according to the Foundation for Individual Rights and Expression (FIRE).

Four days later, the president of Pennsylvania resigned. Media attention turned on Harvard and to a lesser extent MIT; when would their presidents do the same?

Gay had only recently become Harvard's president (July 2023) and was faced with abiding by the decision of the US Supreme Court to prohibit positive discrimination (June 2023). This must have been difficult since her whole academic life had been about the economic and political effects of race. Among her special interests, she lists Black Politics in the Post-Civil Rights Era, Politics of Race, Ethnicity and Immigration. Being black and a woman, Gay was emblematic of everything DEI was about.

The attack on Gay became personal, questioning the paucity of her academic record, reports of plagiarism in her PhD dissertation and journal papers and her involvement in enquiries into fellow black academics who disagreed with her views about race.

At this point, two narratives developed. One believed Gay was being targeted by right-wing Republicans who saw an opportunity to bring down a person who represented everything they despised.

The BBC reporting was typical of this notion: 'Harvard's Claudine Gay [is] a casualty of campus culture wars' and Gay's departure was 'being celebrated as a high-profile victory by conservatives who have objected to her on ideological grounds'. And of course, it couldn't resist suggesting it was all about race: 'For her right-wing critics Dr Gay – who is black – represents much of what they loath about modern American higher education.'

Another narrative was based on a detailed analysis of her academic record, much of it focused on the instances of plagiarism in her writing, especially using the words and ideas of the black author Carol Miller Swain, a retired professor of political science and law at Vanderbilt University. To say Ms Swain was incensed by Gay's unattributed use of her work would be an understatement.

A 6,000-word detailed analysis of Gay's writing was anonymously sent to six journalists the day before her disastrous House appearance. It was titled: *Major Harvard tip: Claudine Gay plagiarism:*

 I'm sending this to several outlets because time is of the essence. Claudine Gay will testify before the House Committee on Education and Workforce on 12/5/2023 at 10:00 AM EST. If this information emerges before the hearing, she could be asked about it under oath.

Gay's publishing record, or the lack of it, was compared with other academics' and found to be wanting – one book and 11 journal papers in the past 26 years, with no ground-breaking research.

When she was dean of the College, Gay was involved in dismissing a member of the faculty for legally representing Harvey Weinstein. Another professor (Roland Fryer), a winner of a MacArthur Fellowship, researched the causes of racial disparities and concluded there were many factors involved, not only discrimination. He was not dismissed but had his research programme terminated. Gay was involved in his demise. Fryer, like Tony

Sewell in the UK, demonstrated the concept of systematic racism was deeply flawed, a concept at the heart of DEI theory and central to Gay's beliefs. More about this in the essay 'Justice – teetering on a slippery slope'.

There's no doubt there was a concerted campaign to remove Gay. The media positioned her as representing the worst aspects of DEI. By implication, her position as the head of, arguably, the world's leading university had nothing to do with academic distinction but with her race and sex.

When *The New York Times* agrees with the *Wall Street Journal* in their condemnation, you know the battle is lost. Gay resigned but retained her $900,000 annual salary.

To my mind, the hypocrisy of the response of academia to the 7 October massacre revealed that the ideals of DEI had a dark, dark side. All the warm words about inclusion and protecting the vulnerable come with a big condition – as long as they tick all the boxes. Gay, you might say, was unlucky, having her record dissected by the media. What it revealed was the consequences of DEI, and they were consequences it was impossible to defend.

I am not sure about the lasting effect this event will have on DEI's role in defining academia's future. What I do know is when the history of the period is written, it's for certain the name Claudine Gay, along with the phrase 'it depends on the context', will feature.

Alas, the 7 October attack continued reverberating throughout academia. In scenes reminiscent of the BLM demonstrations, students and faculty protested their support for Palestine and anger at Israel. Starting in the Ivy League universities, this soon spread to other institutions, with copycat protests throughout Europe. Most were peaceful, some less so, necessitating the police becoming involved.

Reactions to these events, like opinions about the Gaza conflict, were ultra-polarised. Supporters believed they were protesting about the evils committed by governments and displaying their compassion for the oppressed. Like the students of the 1960s, they held governments accountable for their actions. They were exercising their right to freedom of speech. Outside agitators, not students, were responsible for the violence.

Opponents ridiculed the protesters' simplistic, one-sided views that ignored the reality of the conflict, highlighting the blatant display of anti-Jewish placards and demands for Israel to be destroyed. As the students oscillated between being vulnerable, caring adolescents and mindless bullies, they reinforced the message that universities don't teach; they indoctrinate. Like the BLM protests, they all had lookalike placards, tents, uniforms, chants and demands. Blaming professional demonstrators for the violence was hard to accept when these students were supposedly the elite of the elite.

These opposing opinions were reflected in the partisan media reporting. Fox News and the *WSJ* highlighted the violence, destruction of property and ignorance of students about the Gaza conflict: 'The Ivy League's Anti-Israel Protest Meltdown' (*WSJ*). The *NYT* and CNN praised the students' bravery for their left-leaning activism: 'Student Protest Is an Essential Part of Education' (*NYT*).

What will be the lasting legacy of these events? I imagine the students' social media accounts will be littered with imagery of the events as proof they were there when 'history was being made'. Jews will feel even less safe in academia. The casual observer (most people) will remember images of face-masked, Keffiyeh-wearing students causing havoc. The informed observer will muse how these anxious young people, obsessed with 'hurtful language', microaggressions and all the other paraphernalia of identity politics, so quickly scream at anybody questioning their views. What became of 'cultural appropriation'? The cynics will think that these children of the elite are doing no more than reflect their parents' sense of entitlement.

Watching the demonstrations spread to the UK universities, I was taken back to my days at Sussex University in 1968, a supposed epicentre of student unrest. There were sporadic demonstrations with lots of shouting and banner-waving. Most students stood for a while to watch the commotion and then got on with their lectures and lounging in the student union. I guess that much the same happened with these protests. They ticked all the boxes for the left-wing radicals and the casual observers of being politically engaged students. No goals will be achieved, no opinions will be changed and nobody will benefit.

MEDIA – WHERE DID ALL THE TRUST GO?

> I think a lot of people in the world I once inhabited, in centre-left media and academia, don't realise they've slipped into a deeply unattractive habit of substituting checklists of unquestioned assumptions for thought.

Matt Taibbi, journalist

> When journalists arrogate to themselves the right to determine by their own consciences what shall be reported and for what purpose, democracy is unworkable.

Walter Lippmann in his 1920 book *Liberty and the News*

The Munk Debates are very 'Canadian'. They are civilised, well organised and without a hint of barracking and rowdy behaviour. Debaters keep to time; the audience asks sensible questions and applauds politely. They are a wonderful way of dissecting contentious subjects and measuring the effectiveness of the speaker's arguments. In November 2022 the debate's proposition was: 'be it resolved, don't trust mainstream media'.

Before proceedings began, the audience of 3,000 rejected the motion by a small majority (48%:52%). At the debate's conclusion, the vote was reversed (67%:33%), the largest audience opinion swing in the event's 15-year history.

What made the outcome even more surprising was that opposing the motion was Malcolm Gladwell, who is Canadian – and Canadians are usually supportive of their own. Alas, he was the weakest speaker and his debating style, with lots of personalised attacks, antagonised rather than convinced. His fellow speaker (Michelle Goldberg), a *New York Times* journalist, was adequate but uninspiring.

Their poor performance must have contributed to the 39% change in opinion, but it was the proposing speakers' (Matt Taibbi and Douglas Murray) systematic exposure of the media's lack of objectivity that made the audience re-evaluate. Memories of the media's lack of objectivity when reporting the Ottawa truckers' blockade were still fresh in their mind. The official investigation into the protest concluded that 'misinformation and disinformation about the protests was prone to amplification in the news media'. Murray's dissection of the media's failures was a tad more damning than 'prone to amplification'. Perhaps that swayed the audience? (Note: this was before the Federal Court found the government's invoking of the Emergencies Act wasn't justified.)

You can watch the event on YouTube. It's an education in debating skills and the perils of misjudging your audience. It also presents a microcosm of the media's frailty: rather than listening and engaging with those of differing opinions, it dismisses them.

I was surprised at the audience's initial high regard for the media. According to the Edelman Trust Barometer for Canada (2022) most people believed journalists were purposely trying to mislead them (61%). This is not dissimilar to Canada's next-door neighbour where, according to Gallup, 39% of Americans have no faith in the media. Way back in 1972 the figure was 6% and 68% had a great deal of faith – now that is 32%.

Levels of American and Canadian 'news aversion' are at an all-time high. Reasons given for avoiding watching, reading and listening to the news are lack of trust in its accuracy, feelings of powerlessness and the negative mood it generates.

The Brits are just as suspicious. Of the 27 countries surveyed by Edelman, only Japan and South Korea have a lower level. The BBC, once a 'national treasure', is trusted to be fair and accurate by under half of the people and is constantly accused of biased reporting. I expect trust levels will fall further after the errors and bias of its reporting of the 7 October massacre and ensuing conflict.

What's happening with the news media, and why are we so suspicious? Is it caught in the backwash of anger directed at other pillars of the state or is there something fundamentally wrong with how it operates?

STRUCTURAL CHANGES

Let's begin by drilling down into the facts before we start the conjecture. *The Economist* analysed 600,000 items from US news websites and the transcripts of prime-time TV channels. You will probably not be shocked by what they discovered:

 We find that there is indeed an affinity between the media and the left, because journalists tend to prefer the language used by Democratic lawmakers. Moreover, this disparity

has grown since the start of Donald Trump's presidency. As a result, the number of media sources covering politics in balanced language has dwindled.

How language has evolved – or should I say been manipulated? – is the subject of the essay 'Language – from beautiful to brutal'. The following are some of the reasons it has drifted from neutrality to a leftish partisan position.

Fewer journalists, more fact-checkers

Since 2008, newspapers in the US have lost 60% of their news reporting staff – probably more, since these figures don't reflect job losses during the pandemic. This has been partially offset by more people working in digital-only newsrooms, but total numbers are expected to decline for the foreseeable future.

Regional and local newspapers are closing at the rate of two a week. The same is happening in the UK as advertising revenues plummet, with 300 local and regional newspapers disappearing in the last decade. The UK's largest commercial news publisher (Reach) is reducing its national and regional workforce by 10%.

The career path of starting work in the regional press and graduating to national titles is fast disappearing. Once upon a time journalism was open to people from a wide range of backgrounds. It has now become an all-graduate industry based in major cities.

There's one recently evolved part of the news industry that's experiencing rapid growth – fact-checking businesses. Thanks to the supposed growth of misinformation and disinformation, there has been an explosion in organisations checking the media's reporting for the 'truth'. According to the Duke Reporters' Lab annual census, in 2021 there were 391 of these news-checking companies.

This growth was initially driven by fears that 'foreign disinformation' was behind the outcome of the Brexit vote and President Trump's election. Then came anxiety about climate change deniers and forces jeopardising governments' pandemic policies, especially mass vaccination. The customers of these organisations are large technology companies, government departments and wealthy individuals.

The Oxford Climate Journalism Network is a good example of how rich people influence the media. The organisation claims to 'support reporters and editors who want to make the climate crisis a central element of their journalism'. Sir Christopher Hohm helps fund this organisation along with Google and Meta. He is also a significant contributor to the activist group Extinction Rebellion. I suppose when you earn a million pounds a day it buys you a lot of influence.

These checkers and their sponsors are perfect examples of the 'third person effect'. Somehow, they think they are immune to the messaging they think determines others' behaviour. Often, they equate misinformation with views that conflict with their own. I would call it intellectual arrogance.

No doubt – well, a few doubts – their intentions are well-meaning. A concern shared by many, however, is they become a source of censorship of anything other than the accepted narrative. As soon as fact-checkers decide some facts are more valuable and important than others, they lose credibility.

It's ironic when the checkers are accused of spreading their own misinformation. Meta Australia was forced to sack its partner company (RMIT FactLab) for biased fact-checking during the 2023 referendum. Two months later they were reappointed.

Political outlook determines trust in the media

Having seen the inherent left-wing bias of reporting, these results come as no surprise. Gallup's research shows that political beliefs are a good predictor of a person's trust in the media. Back in the 1970s, Democrat and Republican voters were equally trusting. Today, just 14% of Republicans have a great/fair amount of trust compared with 70% of Democrats.

Reuters found that Brits exhibit the same political polarisation, with the 'left' being more likely to trust the BBC than those on the 'right'. The same applies to all the other news channels except Sky News. Irrespective of their readers' political views, trust in the accuracy of newspaper reporting has steadily declined for the past decade, too.

A person's choice of news channel is an excellent predictor of their political opinions. The divide in the US is most extreme with the audiences of TV news channels. Adults choosing MSNBC as their main source of news are overwhelmingly Democrats (95%); the same percentage of Republicans claim Fox News is their primary news channel. In the UK the press is similarly divided with the *Mail* reviled by the 'left' and *The Guardian* held in contempt by the 'right'.

This polarisation also extends to the fact-checking industry, with Republican voters believing these organisations are inherently biased and Democrats thinking they do a good job at suppressing misinformation.

Many young Brits and Americans (aged under 30), probably a majority, can't be bothered with any of the channels and have transferred their trust to social media as a source of news.

There might be disagreement about the importance of these structural changes, but few dispute that attitudes towards the news media are altering and not positively. Let's summarise the things we know for certain:

- Trust in all news sources is falling and this has accelerated during the Covid pandemic.
- News sources are becoming more partisan in their reporting.
- Social media is an important provider of news, especially among the young.
- Sources of online commentary have proliferated, increasing competition for subscription and advertising revenue.
- Digital technology has enabled 24/7 availability of news channels, replacing legacy media's fixed cycles of reporting.

Giving words meaning

Hopefully, the terms I have been using are well understood, but a few might benefit from further explanation. 'Legacy' media describes the old world when news and comment were associated with the channels of communication, such as TV, radio or newspaper. Of course, these discrete channels still exist, but they now broadcast their content to multiple devices – the phone being the most important.

The terms 'right' and 'left' have echoes from a bygone era. Research companies persist in using them to categorise people, so they still appear in this essay. Very roughly, the 'right' distrust the government's involvement in their life, believing it should be minimised and individuals allowed to determine their destiny. The 'left' hold opposite opinions. Other terms are 'progressive' and 'conservative', but they also sound dated. In the essay 'Beliefs – my moral compass is busted' I delve deeper into the murky waters of how we define our political beliefs.

It is easier to explain the term 'news and comment'. This is the material we use to form and sustain our opinions. It's much more than the news reports and includes comedy, discussions and in-depth commentary.

WHO IS TO BLAME?

There are two very different explanations for the erosion of trust and how it can be reversed. These quotes from the adversaries in the Munk Debate summarise these positions.

Michelle Goldberg, journalist with *The New York Times*:

> *Bias has become the key to an entire right-wing worldview...The conviction that conspiratorial forces are hiding the truth, and that only members of the movement are undeceived, justifies a refusal to acknowledge otherwise glaring realities.*

I have called this 'conspiratorial conservatism' with the 'right' and 'populists' (especially Trump) blamed for encouraging distrust, especially in the media.

The other perspective is described by Matt Taibbi, a one-time journalist with *Rolling Stone* magazine and now podcaster and Substack writer (Racket News):

> *Intellectual diversity that was normal in a newsroom once upon a time is vanishing. There's an expectation now among younger reporters to be a team player devoted to pursuing the same ideological framework.*

The term 'tribal groupthink' seems the best way to describe this explanation, whereby a vocal minority dictate the media's culture and what it reports.

Before attempting to judge who is right or wrong, let's expand on these two explanations. I have done my best to represent their positions, although I might have exaggerated a little to clarify their differences.

Conspiratorial conservatism

Wearing rose-tinted spectacles, proponents of this hark back to a golden age of news reporting that was unbiased and trusted by everybody. They are slow to adapt to new cultural norms. Rather than blaming themselves, they search for conspiracy theories to explain a world they don't understand or like.

Back in the day, their griping didn't matter. Now they have social media, podcasts and Substacks to air their grievances and large audiences sharing their views. It's left to the legacy media to counter their disinformation and hold them to account.

Their message about the 'deep state', the 'elite' or whatever it's called today, plays fast and loose with the truth. Trump and his acolytes constantly pumped out these lies, culminating in the insurrection at the Capital on 6 January. Destabilising a population by a constant stream of misinformation is a technique used by the enemies of democracy, foreign *and domestic*.

The mainstream media (MSM) is built upon self-correcting processes to ensure fair and honest reporting, whereas these dissent voices can say what they want – and they do. When they are criticised, they rationalise it as further proof of the conspiracy to extinguish free speech.

A free society must tolerate a wide spectrum of views, but there are limits, especially when opinions harm others. It should be no surprise that the media reflects society's values, those of tolerance and fighting injustices and inequality. This view can be opposed, but not at the expense of those least able to defend themselves. The media has no need to apologise for its role in helping the repressed and minorities.

These alternative voices like to call themselves 'contrarian' or 'heterodox' and peddle the view that they know the truth, which is different from what the media reports. Of course, journalists do make mistakes, but they do their best to report accurately. The MSM might be the worst system in the world, except for all the others.

Tribal groupthink

The commercial model of news companies has been rewritten by digital technologies. Reliance on advertising has been replaced with paid-for viewing, targeting specific demographic groups with content that maximises their screen time. Most often, these are younger people living in urban areas. Two-thirds of *The New York Times'* readers are under the age of 49 – and well over 90% vote Democrat.

To those who agree with the tribal groupthink position, the primary role of journalists and commentators should be to produce factually accurate and understandable accounts of events. This has been replaced by ideologically driven commentary that supports the values of its readers and the news channel. Neutrality has been replaced by institutional bias. Worse still, dissent is not tolerated.

The defining line between journalism and activism is disappearing. News channels are more about promoting their view of the world rather than educating and informing their readers. Lurking beneath their fine words about equality, diversity and sustainability is an ugly authoritarian culture. News output has become another form of political discourse, hell-bent on ridiculing the enemies and lauding the believers.

Journalists once came from a range of social backgrounds that mirrored the audience they were writing for. Many entered the profession by serving an apprenticeship on local newspapers and radio stations, a route that is no longer available. Today, journalists come from the professional classes; most have a university education (90%). Not surprisingly, their political views are very much left of centre.

Despite all the talk of ethnic diversity, journalism – like publishing and other creative industries – has become far more mono-cultured. Only those with family connections and wealth are likely to be able to make it in an industry that is based in major cities with sky-high property prices that aren't matched by salaries.

The notion of journalists being searchers for the truth is a quaint but dated idea. Success is measured by the reporter's ability to generate clicks and views. Judgement by online metrics results in simplified news reporting made 'accessible' to readers, who are made to feel comfortable. Fear of giving offence or causing 'harm' trumps all other considerations. Audiences want their views confirmed, not challenged.

Because negative and sensationalised news is 'clicky', especially if it supports the dominant ideology, the truth becomes distorted. When news stories contradict the narrative, they are mocked or ignored. The long-time *FT* journalist Lucy Kellaway recounts:

> *Thanks to a dastardly bit of software called Lantern, journalists have immediate, real-time feedback on how their pieces are doing online. For each article you can track the number of hits, shares, comments – as well as how long readers spent on the page. Worse, you can compare this data with any other article.*

Over time the groupthink becomes more pronounced as dissenting journalists leave or self-censor. The culture replicates and intensifies by recruiting only those sharing the same narrow set of values.

In the old days, 'the story was the boss' and the accuracy of reporting was paramount. Success in the MSM today is about promoting an ideology – despite the facts.

The symbiotic relationship between news channels and Donald Trump is the worst example of how the media have jettisoned objectivity for profit. Once Biden became president, *The Washington Post*'s digital audience shrank by a third. All the major TV cable networks lost significant numbers of subscribers. Who cares about objectivity when the louder you scream the demonic Trump, the more money you make? Perversely, it also makes it more likely he will be elected president again.

WAS IT EVER SO?

Let's start by questioning whether these conflicting views of the world are really new. Aren't they the same old divisions dressed up in new words? Every generation thinks the one before had deficiencies they don't. Perhaps today's 24/7 availability of news and social media means we are just more aware of these age-old differences.

For most of my life, newspapers and weekly publications have favoured one political opinion over another, based on the quaint English notions of class. Working-class supporters of the Labour Party read the *Daily Mirror*. Their Conservative-supporting contemporaries read the *Daily Express*. *The Times* was the voice of record read by the upper-class establishment. Everybody listened to the BBC, believing it was impartial and accurate. How simple life was.

The ownership of the MSM, on both sides of the Atlantic, has always been in the hands of a few wealthy and influential people. The 'left' in the UK believed there was an inbuilt bias against them, but in 1997 that all changed when Rupert Murdoch switched support and backed the election of the Labour Party's Tony Blair. How much this was influenced by ideology or commercial considerations (Blair was certain to win the election) is still being debated.

More important than the switch in allegiance to Labour, however, was that this blurred the division between politicians and the media. Andrew Neil, an editor of *The Sunday Times*, said: 'It was unprecedented almost Incestuous. The line between press and state became so blurred at one stage it was quite hard to tell which was which.'

The idea that news reporting was once free of partisan reporting is manifestly untrue. What is much harder to know is whether the degree of bias has increased and, if so, why. Some things are unique about today's world that might help explain what's happening.

The pandemic resulted in governments across the globe controlling their citizens' lives at levels only seen in wartime. For Europeans and the US, this unparalleled surrender of personal freedom hadn't occurred since WWII. The media's response (all the media) was overwhelmingly to support the government's decisions and to condemn dissenters. Questioning was replaced by simplistic propaganda.

Social media plays a major role in determining how and what the news channels report. Who is saying what on TikTok, Instagram and X (Twitter) is an inexpensive and immediate way of generating news content. It's becoming harder to know who is the chicken and who is the egg, the mainstream or social media.

Higher education is a rite of passage for most young Brits, Australians and Canadians. A slightly smaller percentage of Americans attend university, but the numbers are increasing. Great efforts have been made to recruit journalists from more diverse backgrounds. But few enter the profession who haven't attended university, probably sharing the same mindset that dominates academia.

Identity, not class is what now polarises opinions. As explained in the essay 'Beliefs – my moral compass is busted', divisions based on race, gender, sexuality and religion dominate much of the news reporting. In the old days, being a socialist or capitalist, a supporter of Keynes or Hayek, a believer in high tax and government spending or low tax and consumer choice, was what separated people and political parties. Divisions were about economic factors – tax rates, spending levels and interest rates. Today, it's about accepting or rejecting beliefs about inequality, sexuality and racial fairness.

Climate uncertainty is the first problem in our history that is truly global. Even during the world wars parts of the planet were insulated from the disputes. News and commentary about the climate is happening everywhere, consuming large amounts of news channels' bandwidth. Despite a tiny number of people understanding the science, everybody feels empowered to hold an opinion.

Experts' opinions are essential to explain scientifically complex subjects. Climate change and the pandemic are all about physics, biology and mathematics. Few of us understand these subjects, making us reliant on simplified accounts passed on by the news channels' experts. Science is 'messy': it's complex and full of uncertainties. Usually, there is a range of opinions. None of this is suited to being condensed into a two-minute news slot.

Economic constraints have led to media outlets lacking dedicated experts and the necessary time for in-depth research on intricate topics, increasing their dependence on think-tanks and activist groups for information.

These factors, in my opinion, have influenced the objectivity of news reporting, and not in a good way. For sure, there's never been a golden era of unbiased news reporting, but what we are experiencing today worries me more. It worries me a lot.

NEVER PERFECT BUT UNDERSTANDABLE

Believe me, I long ago discarded my rose-tinted spectacles about the MSM's behaviour. The 'popular press' has a long history of sensationalising the news and being overly aggressive to some personalities and deferential to others, switching allegiances overnight. Swarms of paparazzi, pursuing their target to get the photo that makes it onto next day's front page, epitomise this morally dubious sector of the news media.

As Michael Corleone says in *The Godfather*: 'It's not personal... It's strictly business.' This sums up my views about this tacky behaviour – I don't like it – I don't condone it – but I understand why it happens. It's all about journalists chasing personal fame and their employers chasing profits. Unedifying, certainly yes; malicious, maybe, but not something new. Likewise, I don't like the influence that money has on news reporting and the symbiotic relationship this causes between journalists and politicians, but I understand it.

Journalists work under intense time pressure and make mistakes. When I had first-hand knowledge of a news story, I invariably spotted errors in the reporting. That shouldn't happen, but it's understandable and forgivable by somebody who has made his fair share of writing blunders.

The forces that distorted news reporting used to be transparent. When Rupert Murdoch said, 'We are backing the Labour Party 200%', as he did in 1997, it was not whispered but shouted. This blatant and visible influence on news reporting has gone and been replaced with something much darker – a systemic manipulation of the media.

These worries started a decade ago, but in the past few years they have become a gnawing fear.

For most of my life, I was too busy to listen to the news. I might have heard the headlines while driving, and glanced at a newspaper, but that was it. The advent of online news probably increased my interest, but not by much. I guess most people, busy with careers and families, have this hands-off relationship with the media.

Things changed for me in 2000 when I started writing books and researching news stories. That's when I noticed that despite referencing multiple sources, the storyline, even the wording, was often very similar, which at the time I rationalised away as proof that it was correct. How naïve can you be?

Then in 2018, I began writing a history book about secondary education. I soon became irritated with the way authors relate historical events. Much of the complexity disappears, being replaced by a simplified version. The 'simplification problem' was succinctly expressed by the historian Mary Beard: 'We don't disseminate a complicated view of the past; we disseminate a simple view.' Worse still, over time, a single narrative of events emerges that is often proved wrong. It seemed that the most repeated account, let's call it the 'dominant narrative', was the one that triumphed, not the most accurate.

When asked what I had been doing for three years, other than writing 200,000 words, I would say 'reintroducing complexity' and 'questioning every dominant narrative'.

I am recounting this tale because the same mistakes, and they are mistakes, are now part of news and commentary reporting. Four events illustrate this issue: Brexit, the election of Donald Trump, the response to the Covid epidemic and climate change. The rights and wrongs of each of these are complex and far from straightforward but each has been reduced to a handful of simple arguments that their opponents and defenders deploy. Even news channels that pride themselves on their objectivity, like *The Economist*, repeatedly frame their arguments using a bundle of simplified narratives.

FROM WORRYING TO FRIGHTENING

News reporting is being stripped of all shades of grey; it is black or white. As many others have said, it's expressed more like the canons of a religion. The axioms are there and you either accept them, in their entirety, or you are an outcast. I know this sounds like an extreme statement so let me give you some examples.

Three experienced journalists have resigned from prestigious news organisations because of the intolerance they experienced when questioning the norms of the culture. These are extracts from the explanations of why they left.

Bari Wiess resigned from *The New York Times* in July 2020:

> *Stories are chosen and told in a way to satisfy the narrowest of audiences, rather than to allow a curious public to read about the world and then draw their own conclusions. I was always taught that journalists were charged with writing the first rough draft of history. Now, history itself is one more ephemeral thing molded to fit the needs of a predetermined narrative.*

Suzanne Moore resigned from *The Guardian* in November 2020:

> *My experience is that I have been censored more by the Left than the Right and it gives me no pleasure to say that. Laziness of thought is my big fear, this unthinking adherence to some simplistic orthodoxy. There are values and there is experience and there are people. Complicated fuckers, all of us.*

Tara Henley resigned from the Canada Broadcasting Corporation (CBC) in January 2022:

> *To work at CBC in the current climate is to embrace cognitive dissonance and to abandon journalistic integrity. It used to be that I was the one furthest to the left in any newsroom, occasionally causing strain in story meetings with my views on issues like the housing crisis. I am now easily the most*

*conservative, frequently sparking tension by questioning
identity politics. This happened in the span of about 18
months. My own politics did not change.*

Thankfully they have all found different channels to express
their views, none of them in the MSM. In the old language of politics, all of them would have been described as left-wing or progressive. I wonder what happened to the journalists with right-wing
views? I assume they left or were sacked long ago.

It's hard to condone organisations acting in this way, but at
least customers of the media can vote with their feet and use
other, less doctrinaire news channels, although that might be
easier said than done. What is far worse is when it seems that
most of the media is saying the same thing, as occurred during the
Covid pandemic and, to a lesser extent, about the Ukraine–Russia
war. A few lone voices held differing opinions, but they were the
rare exception.

During wartime, the state and the media work closely together
– it's called propaganda. What's happening in Ukraine is a real war.
The pandemic was not, yet that's how it was portrayed. Nurses
were 'on the frontline', ministers held 'war cabinets', the country
was 'beating the enemy', A&E departments were 'warzones' and,
lots and lots of the time, officials claimed to be 'winning the battle'
against the virus.

Perhaps the media felt compelled – or was compelled – to echo
and not question government statements? The same thing seemed
to happen throughout Europe and the US. Was I reading the news
or propaganda?

What's known for certain is that social media companies
applied a strict censorship policy against those daring to question the government's version of the 'truth'. Facebook and
Twitter (now X) accounts were suspended for suggesting the
virus originated in the Wuhan laboratory. Few people now
dispute this is how the pandemic started. Questioning the effectiveness of face masks was silenced despite the lack of definitive

proof. Suggesting natural immunity was as effective as vaccinations was silenced, now proven to be true. All discussion of vaccination side effects was silenced, despite undisputed evidence they occur.

Early on in the pandemic, the UK government changed its communications from informing and persuading to instructing and scaring. Tolerance of those questioning lockdown and vaccination policies evaporated, portraying them as 'enemies' – echoes again of wartime language – or fools (the 'tinfoil hat' brigade). Instead of questioning, the MSM reflected and amplified these sentiments in its reporting.

This essay isn't the place to discuss the rights and wrongs of the response to Covid. What can be said, without doubt, is the clampdown on dissenting voices, the language used to describe events and the MSM's role as an unquestioning communications channel of government resulted in a loss of trust. How much this is reflected in the previously discussed statistics is impossible to know.

Three events have occurred within the last six months (as I write this, in 2023) that graphically illustrate the deep divisions remaining in the MSM and how large parts of it are still manipulating the narrative.

In October 2022 Elon Musk concluded the deal to buy Twitter. Three months later the first of the 'Twitter files' was released by journalists given free access to the company's internal communications. At the date of writing, there have been 19 files revealing a frightening involvement (at least to me) by US government agencies in curtailing the freedom of speech. Twitter (now rebranded as X) users globally had their accounts closed or modified to limit their reach on the premise of distributing disinformation.

The second example began in 2016 when Russia's involvement with the presidential election and governing of Donald Trump dominated reporting in *The New York Times*, *The Washington Post*, MSNBC, CNN, ABC and all the other left-leaning media – that's most of the media except for Fox News and *The Wall Street Journal*.

For months on end, 'Russiagate', as it became known, was a favourite topic for this media and its UK counterparts.

There was one small problem. There was no proof it was true, as confirmed by the Mueller Report and the debunking of the Steele Dossier. The media's extreme bias in reporting about Trump is documented in astonishing detail in a series of four articles published by the prestigious *Columbia Journalism Review* (January 2023). The author (Jeff Gerth) explained why he wrote the articles:

> *I felt obligated to weigh in. Why? Because I am worried about journalism's declining credibility and society's increasing polarization... journalism's primary missions, informing the public and holding powerful interests accountable, have been undermined by the erosion of journalistic norms and the media's own lack of transparency about its work.*

The final event occurred in the UK when a journalist released the WhatsApp messages of the minister responsible for health during the lockdowns. These 100,000 messages revealed an unflattering account of how and why decisions were made. They exposed petty rivalries, game playing and all the behaviours that you hoped would have been suppressed during a national emergency.

To do justice to the Twitter and WhatsApp files would need a book, not an essay – a task others can, and I am sure will, undertake. What astonished me was the response of the MSM to these messages.

In the case of the Twitter files, Elon Musk was berated for his actions after purchasing the company. He had been outspoken about the previous management and staff and had sacked most of them. The journalists who accessed the files were also targeted. Their objectivity and intensions were questioned, as was the process of publishing their findings (using Twitter). What the messages revealed was dismissed as 'telling us nothing new'. And with that, the Twitter files were ignored, until the journalists appeared before the House Judiciary Select Subcommittee, where the Democrat representatives did exactly the same thing – ignored their content and attacked the messengers.

The response to the WhatsApp messages was almost identical, attacking the journalist who released the messages as being untrustworthy and dismissing the messages as 'not having any context' and 'telling us nothing new'. Six months later, the official Covid inquiry took more interest in their contents, mainly to illustrate the foul language of government ministers and their advisers.

As for the findings of the *Columbia Journalism Review*, they weren't countered but were ignored by the MSM. Other than a few wild comments about the author being part of the 'Trump–Russia revisionists' cabal, his findings have been largely ignored. Stories about Trump and Russia still circulate despite the lack of factual accuracy.

How opposing sides report the others' responses is just as divided. The 'it's telling us nothing new' group claim it's an attempt by the right wing to discredit lockdown policy – 'Anti-lockdowners are out in force filling a Covid Inquiry gap with their bogus ideology' says *The Observer*. Those incensed by the findings see the MSM's ridicule, followed by silence, as proving its collusion with the authorities – 'Other journalists don't like being confronted by their failure to hold the government to account' says *The Spectator*.

Whatever became of objective reporting?

SEARCHING FOR ANSWERS

The deeper I immersed myself in these stories the harder it was to find explanations for the extremes of reaction. Was the MSM living on a different planet, where the Covid pandemic played out very differently? Of course, some of the criticisms about the Twitter and WhatsApp messages have validity, but what they reveal is truly shocking. The Twitter files prove the US government's clandestine involvement in determining what people could read on social media. The WhatsApp messages expose the repeated failures of ministers and their officials. Historically, those on the left would be incensed by these revelations and attack the culprits with a vengeance, and rightly so. In both these instances, they were the loudest proponents of dismissing the files as an irrelevance.

I could go on with other examples of news channels stamping out diversity of opinion and, when faced with reality, manifestly lying. The sight of a CNN reporter explaining that the BLM protest he was covering was 'Fiery but mostly peaceful' despite the flames engulfing a building in the background would still be amusing to watch, if it were not so tragic. The editor of *The New York Times* (Joe Kahn) had to publicly intervene when a vocal group of his journalists attacked their colleagues for their views about transgender issues, saying they created a 'hostile working environment'.

By far the best explanation of what's happening was provided by an executive editor of *The Washington Post*. Writing in the newspaper, his article 'Newsrooms that move beyond "objectivity" can build trust' explains this counterintuitive belief:

> *Increasingly, reporters, editors and media critics argue that the concept of journalistic objectivity is a distortion of reality. They point out that the standard was dictated over decades by male editors in predominantly White newsrooms and reinforced their own view of the world.*
>
> *They believe that pursuing objectivity can lead to false balance in covering stories about race, the treatment of women, LGBTQ+ rights, income inequality, climate change and many other subjects. And, in today's diversifying newsrooms, they feel it negates many of their own identities, life experiences and cultural contexts, keeping them from pursuing truth in their work.*

Now it all makes sense. The CNN reporter didn't see a building on fire but a glowing emblem of racial freedom. *The New York Times* journalists weren't attacking their colleagues but mounting a heroic stand against the simplistic views of outdated feminism. Reporting the Twitter files would have emboldened Musk's right-wing beliefs. Publicising the WhatsApp messages would have weakened the collectivist strategy that defeated the virus. Saying one word in defence of President Trump would encourage his populist supporters, which is self-evidently wrong. And I thought objectivity was a virtue!

Journalists seem to be suffering from a bad dose of cognitive dissonance. Most reject the idea of 'bothsiderism', the notion that every side of an argument should be reported. At the same time, 'relativism' has never been more popular.

The idea that 'one man's terrorist is another man's freedom fighter' saw BBC presenters avoiding the word as if it was made of Uranimum-235 when reporting the 7 October slaughter. No wonder that when US journalists were asked which words best describe their industry, 'struggling' and 'chaos' were the most mentioned (Pew Research 2022).

As soon as the purpose of reporting events is not accuracy but adherence to ideology, you embark on a horribly slippery slope. It's treating readers like children with fingers stuffed in their ears screaming 'I can't hear you' whenever exposed to views they disagree with. Where do you stop when censoring content for being 'hurtful' or malinformation that will incense the vulnerable readership?

It's difficult not to conclude that the MSM is in a sorry state. How 'sorry' and who's to blame is where we started this essay. Is the MSM consumed by tribal groupthink or seeing the death throes of the old conspiratorial conservatism?

The simple and cowardly answer would be 'there are problems but not as bad as reported' and 'both groups are equally to blame'. But that's not what I believe.

My sympathies are far more with those believing the MSM is

in a very dark place where adherence to the narrative is valued more than objectivity. This puts me in the company of people with a worldview far to the left of my thinking. They feel betrayed that their ideals of fairness and balance have been trammelled by the new breed of activist journalists. My gripe, no, it's anger, is about the blatant partisan way events are reported. Too often, the journalist's simplistic agenda takes precedence over accurate reporting. More often than not they don't attempt to disguise their prejudices.

It's beyond my comprehension how the MSM can ignore the dialogue between those in power, showing many of the UK's lockdown rules were decided by politics not science. These weren't trivial rules; they affected children's education and access to old people isolated in care homes. These journalists were forever trumpeting the message about 'following the science', which didn't occur, and they don't seem to care.

The final, most contentious and hardest question to answer is the extent the public influences the MSM's reporting. It's easy to think of consumers of news as a passive group having their views determined by what they see and hear. But that's not true. They have opinions they prefer to have confirmed rather than challenged (confirmation bias), are attracted to negative news more than good (negativity bias) and overly value the last thing they read (availability bias). Most people committed a huge amount of emotional capital to following the rules throughout the pandemic. I expect the MSM knows there is no commercial advantage in making readers question that decision.

A similar explanation applies to the lack of reporting of the Twitter files, with those suffering the most from state censorship being those despised by many readers. It's as if Trump's election caused politicians, journalists and readers to jettison their belief in democratic justice. Ensuring this man and his supporters never control the political process again made it easier for them to adopt the adage 'the ends justify the means'. Needless to say, their actions have incensed a lot of people.

Regretfully, the exposé of the media's bias in its reporting of Trump and Russian influence hasn't changed many minds. Those detesting Trump will still detest him. Those convinced of the media's corruption see it as confirming their beliefs.

I wish I could foresee reasons why the chasm between these opposing views of the news media will shrink or at least stabilise. Alas, all I see is it getting wider as levels of trust plummet. The more the media polarises, the more incentives it has to curate the news to please its readership, fuelling a destructive feedback loop with commercially disastrous consequences.

Adding to the divisions is the 'Fox News fallacy'. Anybody the news channel criticises gets knee-jerk support from the Democrats, irrespective of whether the accusation is right or wrong. Republicans are no better, believing anything on MSNBC, a channel known for its left-wing views, is automatically wrong.

Surely, there must be some reasons for hope. Although this might be grasping at straws, there are a few things that might at least slow the decline and, who knows, nudge the MSM to a safer place.

There is only so long you can be angry, and that is what much of today's reporting is, 'red in the face' anger directed at 'them' who stop the world from being the safe, equitable, diverse, sustainable, caring, protective and carbon-neutral place it should be. High ideals are great, but we inhabit Planet Reality. Eventually, exhaustion and the infighting that results from failure intervene. Already, we're seeing pushback from journalists rejecting their workplace's ideological constraints.

Many of the beliefs of activist journalists are either irrelevant or incomprehensible to many, I would guess most, of their audience. The shrill language about ethnicity, diversity, sexuality and the environment is sounding dated and contrived. When these beliefs are tested with real-life situations, the public invariably win. Defending transgender rights suddenly becomes a very different story when a male rapist is sent to a female prison. Ask the ex-premier of Scotland how that worked out.

A sizeable group of people, I would guess the majority, live busy lives and just want the MSM to keep them informed of what's happening, not to lecture them on what to believe. There is only so much hectoring, negative, angry news people can take.

Something is very wrong when the top five topics reported by the media don't make it into the top ten issues of concern to the public. Worries about crime, gas prices and inflation topped the list – climate change, the war in Ukraine, Covid and LGBTQ issues didn't feature (Rasmussen Report 2022).

Finally, you can get your daily dose of bias-confirming stories from the zillions of online sources so why bother with the MSM? If you tire of the media's bullying style there's the fast-growing world of alternative journalism. That's been my solution. And let's remember we are only just beginning to see the power of AI to curate and deliver content.

How confident am I of things improving? With looming American presidential elections, I would make a sizeable bet that when Reuters and Gallup next report their index of the public's trust in the media, it will have declined.

The 7 October massacre of Israelis occurred after I wrote this essay. Alas, the media's reporting of the event and the subsequent conflict has reinforced many of the failures I described.

These are two of the worst errors that have been made.

On 17 October, *The New York Times*, *The Washington Post*, *The Wall Street Journal*, ABC, NBC, CBS, FOX, CNN, the Associated Press, *The Guardian* and the BBC reported that an explosion at a hospital in Gaza had killed 500 people. Most of these organisations went on to blame Israel for the explosion. In case their readers weren't shocked enough by the headlines, *The New York Times* attached a photo of a bombed building in another part of Gaza. The BBC blamed Israel for the attack.

We now know that the explosion occurred in a car park and was caused by a missile launched by Hamas. Blaming Israel was a total failure of the news media, which made a huge leap of logic and arrived at a totally wrong conclusion.

On 15 November Reuters reported:

> *In a statement, the military said: 'Based on intelligence information and an operational necessity, IDF forces are carrying out a precise and targeted operation against Hamas in a specified area in the Shifa Hospital... The IDF forces include medical teams and Arabic speakers, who have undergone specified training to prepare for this complex and sensitive environment, with the intent that no harm is caused to the civilians.'*

Somehow the BBC managed to report this news as:

> *We are hearing from Reuters, that is reporting that Israel – it says its forces are carrying out an operation against Hamas in Gaza's Al Shifa Hospital and they are targeting people, including medical teams as well as Arab speakers.*

Later corrected, it should have read, 'IDF forces included medical teams and *Arabic* speakers for this operation.' By then the damage was done.

Time after time, the BBC and other parts of the news media either got the story totally wrong or reported it without due care and attention. I think we can add political bias to that list of mistakes. Lack of resources is definitely not an excuse when it can employ a thousand people to broadcast the Glastonbury Festival.

So much for the arguments that the legacy media has the processes and 'guardrails' to ensure the accuracy of its reporting. Good grief, the BBC has 60 journalists working in its disinformation unit (Verify).

You know things are bad when the BBC's former head of television calls for an independent review into the organisation's reporting of the war, accusing its diplomatic correspondent of pro-Palestine bias.

Reporting about wars is extremely difficult and made harder by social media. The mistakes that have already emerged suggest there's a chasm between the reporting and reality. When the conflict has ended in Gaza and Ukraine, I fear we are in for many more shocks.

At 21.00 EDT the first of the US presidential debates started. One and a half hours later it ended and much of the world's media suddenly discovered that Joseph Robinette Biden Jr is a frail old man who struggles to end sentences and is frequently incoherent.

So ended a period of gaslighting by much of the media that had instructed its readers, despite all the evidence to the contrary, that Biden possessed the physical and mental ability to govern the world's premier power – not just now but for a further four years.

When his stumbles, wandering and other lapses of memory were questioned it was attributed to fake news and misinformation of the hard right, the MAGA Republicans and all the other hate figures of the caring, progressive left.

These excruciating 90 minutes were so bad that the charade couldn't be maintained any longer.

If you needed more evidence that large swathes of the media have abandoned objective (and truthful) reporting, it was there to be seen as this poor old man left the stage and even *The New York Times* admitted it was time he retired.

POLITICS – MORE SHOWBIZ THAN STATESMANSHIP

Giving money and power to government is like giving whiskey and car keys to teenage boys. Our government: what the f*** do they do all day and why does it cost so goddamned much money.

P.J. O'Rourke, *Parliament of Whores*

All political lives, unless they are cut off in midstream at a happy juncture, end in failure, because that is the nature of politics and of human affairs.

Enoch Powell, *Life of Joseph Chamberlain*, 1977

Why have I lost interest in UK politics? No, it's more than that; it's a crushing boredom about the UK's system of government. When friends ask what do I think about XYZ politician or the fuss about implementing ABC legislation, my eyes glaze over. There was a time I read about the machinations of the Conservative and Labour parties and the town council's latest intrigues. Today, I might spend five minutes muttering about the local parish councillor's unsuccessful attempts to fix the potholes in the road, but that's it.

Ask me about the shenanigans in the US presidential election and I am brimming with opinions. Thoughts about the prime minister's latest scrap with the leader of the opposition – not a clue. I can bore you for hours about China's expansionist policies, use of AI technology and ageing populations. What's the government's latest pledge to restrict economic migration? All you would get is a blank face and a shrug of the shoulders. Claims by the Labour Party they are going to build zillions of houses by ignoring their much hated NIMBYs and spend tens of zillions on green technology – another shrug of disinterest and disbelief. If the words ever had any substance they will have dissolved by tomorrow.

It worries me (a little) that I don't care what's happening in my own country, at Westminster, Whitehall and my local town hall. For heaven's sake, I pay huge amounts of tax and my day-to-day existence is governed by their rules.

When I pay attention it's for the entertainment value, to revel in their outlandish behaviour and daft comments. Is this disinterest 'an age thing', the result of watching politician after politician, bubbling with enthusiasm, promising the earth and delivering little? Have I replaced the inevitable disappointment about their performance with the humorous value of their antics? It's impossible to know, but I suspect something more fundamental has occurred. We blame the pandemic and social media for most things, so perhaps they shoulder some of the blame.

If the title of this essay is correct and politics is more showbiz than statesmanship, does it matter? That's a big question, with few facts to support or contradict the premise. So beware, this essay is low on substantiated arguments and high on my opinions.

Another admission is my examples are mostly from the UK – apologies to readers from the US and elsewhere. However, as I start writing, a man who will be 86 if he wins the next US presidential election is likely to contest it with somebody who sends half his country into a state of apoplexy and faces 91 (and counting) legal charges. Even the revered *The Economist* magazine is in meltdown, concerned about a new breed of European politicians called 'populists' that propose the outrageous idea of listening to voters and doing what they want.

Surely laughter is the only way to reconcile these absurdities. Maybe it's not just a 'UK thing', and my thoughts will resonate in other parts of the Anglosphere.

WE LOVE THE THEATRE OF POLITICS

There are lots of people who are intrigued by politics and the minutiae of the battles between the good and the bad guys. I just read a Substack written by a bright young chap who has spent ages analysing the outcomes of the UK's local elections. His enthusiasm about the subject was matched by the hundreds of people commenting, all brimming with interest and excitement.

UK newspapers all contain political commentary, and there is an endless supply of podcasts and YouTube channels dedicated to politics. Undoubtedly, many people are still interested in this stuff – or are they?

The facts, as sparse as they are, suggest many share my views, probably the majority, and have given up caring. Parliament is clearly worried and commissioned research to answer the question: 'Political disengagement in the UK: Who is disengaged?' (2022).

Unfortunately, the study went wrong from the start with its

definition of 'politically disengaged', putting me firmly in the engaged camp, somewhere I am most definitely not:

> *People are politically disengaged if they do not know, value*
> *or participate in the democratic process.*

I do know about the democratic process and vote at general elections – not for a party I like but for the best of the hopeless alternatives. It's the 'value' part of the definition that gives me problems. I don't think politicians, national or local, have the power and machinery to do what they say – even if they understand what they mean.

I am sure the 650 MPs, two-thirds men and 85% graduates, a few of whom have science degrees (17%), are (mostly) sincere in wanting to do good. What 'good' is differs between political parties, but making that 'good' happen, delivering the 'value', is where – in my opinion – they fail, big time.

What interests the young man with his Substack, political commentators and 'politically engaged' members of the public is the theatre of it all, the preening actors strutting around the stage, desperate to convince us of their sincerity. Mostly they are performing a lengthy, complicated tragedy with oodles of opportunities for the audience to top up on their confirmation bias. I watch and think, 'what's the point?' I know how the drama ends; it's an adaptation of a script that has been performed countless times.

It's the theatre of the absurd, and I am tired of watching. But when the plot flips, and it morphs into a comedy, as it invariably does, then it becomes interesting. At least it will make me laugh.

What do we know about the Great British Public's attitude to politics? The simple answer is lots of speculation among academics about their foibles but little hard data. When the Hansard Society last published its annual audit of political engagement (2019), it found two-thirds of people said they discussed politics a few times a month or less. I dare not think how little interest would be recorded if the research was done today.

Parliamentary research from 1991 recorded about 50% of people claiming to 'trust government to put the needs of the nation first'. By 2017, that had plummeted to 15%, although it recovered to 20% in 2021. It is anybody's guess how low it has fallen now.

For the past 25 years only 10% of people agreed with the statement: 'They trust politicians to tell the truth when they are in a tight corner.'

None of these are resounding endorsements of faith in the political class. Ironically, my responses would have been more flattering as I think politicians are mostly motivated to do good and mostly tell the truth – well, their version of the truth.

Political engagement is often equated with the turnout at general elections, figures that must give politicians more hope. Peaking in the 1950s (84%) it fell to a low in 2001 (60%), crawling back to 67% (2019). Only a third of the electorate can be bothered to vote in local elections, the same percentage as in the European Parliamentary elections (pre-Brexit).

Better educated, richer people vote more than the poor. Older people vote more than their grandchildren. At the last general election, three-quarters of the over-65s staggered to the polling booth. Just over half the 18–24 age group couldn't be bothered.

Voting occurs every four to five years, takes a few minutes and requires little thought. It is not an arduous task and is a mighty low threshold for measuring political engagement. It is less than driving to the local supermarket for the weekly shop.

The best academic research I encountered (probably because it resonated with my prejudices) found the electorate united in believing politicians pursue short-term headlines and are self-serving, protecting the interests of the rich and powerful. It was a bit more nuanced than that, but those were the main messages.

Opinions are divided about their ability to make decent policy decisions, again reflecting my feelings – sometimes they do, mostly they don't. Where I depart from the research findings is about politicians' ability to 'make a difference'. A resounding 87% of respondents thought they could. I am resoundingly sure they can't and don't.

The electorate believes in the *potential value* of politicians and government to make the world a better place. Most people believe the UK's democracy is good but doubt the current crop of representatives can be trusted and are up to the job.

Things are no better in the US, where only 4% think it is working extremely well and two-thirds say they feel exhausted thinking about the subject (Pew Research, 2023).

My interpretation of these findings is probably too cynical, but it appears my fellow voters want (need) to believe the fairytale of politics; that somewhere, there are nice competent people who will do the right thing to make their lives better. Yet, the longer voters are around, the more disappointed they become, repeatedly seeing the fantasy turn into a comedy, a horror story or both.

But hold on a minute, if this is true you would think older people wouldn't bother voting and the young, yet to be disillusioned by disappointment, would be flocking to the ballot box.

This brings us to the crux of my argument. What motivates older people to vote is a mixture of past horrors and rose-tinted memories. If you suffered badly under a past Labour or Conservative government, you will be adamant that they shouldn't be re-elected. You are voting for a negative outcome. Alternatively, you might believe a golden age of politics was when Mrs Thatcher or Mr Blair were prime minister and harbour the vague hope that today's politicians will replicate their success. This is the 'long memories, perpetual optimist theory' rationale.

Younger people aren't constrained or informed by what's happened before. Their interest, if they have it, is the drama playing out now, something like a TikTok video. Are politicians people they 'identify' with – are they good TV performers? What goodies are they promising to give away? Today's young will also want to hear a stream of platitudes about diversity, inclusion and how they will be protected from harm.

As with all generations, their views are left of their parents'. Voting for the Conservatives is an anathema. Their politics are determined by youthful naïvety and believing 'nothing could be worse than the current bunch'. Hmmm, disappointment is just around the corner.

Whereas my disillusionment with politics results in feelings of despair and detachment, the young appear to conclude a better alternative is to dump assemblies and elections and rely on a strong leader to take control. These were the findings of the Open Society Foundations study (2023). I have some sympathy with this notion. Unfortunately, when the 'strong leader' approach has been tried, it hasn't ended too well. So yes, I would prefer a faulty, spluttering system of democratic government to that alternative, just.

This is going to sound awful, but I don't think most people, young or old, have a clue what is really happening in the world around them. They skim a few news channels – well, those that confirm the views they already hold – but don't dig any deeper. They don't have the time, inclination or ability to go far below the superficiality of the political theatre. The same applies to most politicians. This is not a criticism; it's an observation. The business of government is mighty complicated. Expecting MPs, let alone the electorate, to grasp more than the soundbites of everything from fiscal to environmental policy is naïve and wishful thinking.

We all collude with the farce that becoming an MP conveys mystical powers. One day you are part of the audience. Maybe a junior administrator at the town hall, school teacher or trainee lawyer, the next, after winning on election night, you become an MP and acquire the mantle of wisdom to decide our futures.

They will not have come from the lumpenproletariat but the

professional classes, much more at home with a laptop than a power drill, great with PowerPoint slides, hopeless with anything remotely practical. Having clambered to the top of the greasy pole they cling on for dear life as their deficiencies are exposed and then slide down and away into obscurity.

And there we have it. Like actors, politicians must learn their lines and try and appear authentic and knowledgeable, all the while keeping the audience engaged and enthralled. Some politicians are natural performers worthy of Oscar awards. Most aren't and are soon forgotten.

THE ACTOR-POLITICIAN

In the past half century, 2,500 people have taken the role of MP in the UK and strutted the political stage. All are hopeful of landing a starring role; a few get bit-parts; most must be satisfied with walk-on roles. It has been a predominantly male profession (75%), but in recent performances many more women have joined the show. For some strange reason, the average age of the troupe remains constant at 50 years old.

How many of these thespians can you remember? I would wager more for their dud performances than their virtuosity.

Those that stick in the memory were great character actors – like them or loathe them. Immediately they divided the audience into staunch supporters and outraged opponents and had lines that stick in the memory long after their retirement.

A recording of Margaret Thatcher generates sighs and mutterings of 'evil woman' or 'best ever', pretty much in equal quantities. Her saying – 'You turn if you want; the lady's not for turning' – is regularly trotted out to illustrate her obstinacy or steadfastness, depending on your views.

Jeremy Corbyn spent most of his life playing small parts with few lines that nobody could understand and few recall. After 40 years, he got a lucky break and shot to star billing. More out of sympathy than expectation of success, he was nominated to contest the leadership of the Labour Party. Much to everybody's amazement, he won.

His role was a mix of two characters. Chance the Gardener, in the film *Being There,* played by Peter Sellers. A simple, naïve soul who radiated being ponderous, calculating and complex. His most insightful line was:

> *In the garden, growth has its seasons. First comes spring and summer, but then we have fall and winter. And then we get spring and summer again.*

These soft attributes were supplemented with an edgier character, The High Sparrow from *Game of Thrones.* He was an aesthetic, religious man, surrounded by ultra-loyal supporters who radiated purity of mind and hatred of the ruling elite. One of his best lines was:

> *We have no names, no family. Every one of us is poor and powerless. And yet together, we can overthrow an empire.*

Corbyn was a natural for the part and packed theatres with a new audience of young idealists and disgruntled oldies. Readership of *The Guardian* newspaper went through the roof. It's rumoured that his interest in drains and manhole covers ignited a national craze that is only now subsiding.

Unfortunately for him, this character was an anathema to most other people, especially those living outside the urban areas of the south. They 'didn't take to the man' is the politest way of putting it. It is rumoured he was the original target for the saying 'the worst prime minister we never had'.

Without a doubt, the greatest character actor in post-war times was Boris Johnson. He was renowned for forgetting his lines and making them up as he went along. Full of bluster and energy, he was an Oxford Classics graduate. Despite his qualifications and reputation for a 'fine mind' you always wondered if he would complete a sentence and if it would make any sense.

His TV and journalism experience was perfect preparation for being mayor of London and his parliamentary career. He was a great exponent of the simple short message (Get Brexit Done) that became firmly embedded in the audience's memory. His dishevelled appearance, blond hair pointing in all directions, and stooped body, in need of losing weight, made him instantly recognisable.

Boris's knock-about musical hall style was a million miles away from David 'call me Dave' Cameron's ever-reasonable, ever-obliging persona. Both were graduates of Eton and Oxford and nearly the same age, yet their acting styles couldn't have been more different. Dave had a mission to make people like him and his party. If this required photoshoots of hugging a hoodie and huskie – not simultaneously – so be it. His downfall was believing foreign actors shared his wishy-washy compromising style. Much to everybody's surprise he dashed for the exit after losing the Brexit vote and was thought lost to the stage.

For a short time, he was in a duo with a nice chap called Clegg, who brimmed with bonhomie. Alas, the crowd turned against him. After a brief time in obscurity, Clegg burst onto the international stage alongside Mark Zuckerberg. OK, the job has its downsides, defending Facebook's misdemeanours, but the rewards are considerable, last estimated at £15 million a year.

Much to everybody's surprise, Dave has made something of a comeback. After an unfortunate period in the lobbying industry, he found solace on his pig farm. Then came the call all actors dream about – 'Are you interested in a leading part?' The downside is the show isn't likely to run for long but, what the hell.

As for Boris, he has returned to his journalistic roots and is financing his growing family by amusing corporate leaders with gossip and tales of his acting days. I expect he is also waiting for 'the call' but that might not come for a year or two.

Occasionally there are double acts that rise to prominence.

Tony Blair and Gordon Brown were two characters who dominated the political scene for well over a decade. They based their roles on Roger Hargreaves' Mr Men children's books. Tony was a mixture of Mr Happy and Mr Good. Always with a smile on his face, forever reasonable, prepared to see all sides of the argument and determined to do good. His excellent stagecraft may have been inherited from his stage performer grandmother.

Gordon was Mr Grumpy – or was Mr Grumpy Gordon Brown? The son of a minister in the Church of Scotland, he was a menacing figure who struck fear into the rest of the cast. His best-known quote is 'that bigoted woman' barked at one of his supporters. He loved confusing the audience with facts and figures like his 'five economic tests' for joining the euro and his musings about post neoclassical endogenous growth theory. Like so many double acts it all went wrong when the partnership split. Tony moved on to make a fortune and Gordon assumed the starring role, but his popularity dived as audiences realised he didn't believe in anything and tired of his relentless pessimism.

Until recently all performances took place in London but regional theatres now operate in Scotland, Wales and Northern Ireland. I think the politest thing to say is that these have had their teething problems and have resembled a bizarre form of experimental theatre. Their most memorable stars, Martin McGuinness and Nicola Sturgeon, have left the cast under a cloud. Sturgeon's successor performed for just 400 days before disappearing into oblivion. Mark Drakeford retired, leaving Wales with a 20mph speed limit that's only slightly slower than its economic decline. Despite this, the electorate believe him to be a good guy, probably due to his relentless anti-English dialogue. Little can be said about the Northern Ireland Assembly, which has been suspended more than it has been opened.

A few words should be said about the theatre for exhausted politicians and other ageing odd-balls with a penchant for dressing up in gowns and wearing wigs. Known as the House of Lords, it provides a daily fare of boring speeches renowned for their pomposity rather than insight.

Returning to tales about the main theatre. The longest-running and most popular play is Prime Minister's Questions (PMQ). A half-hour knock-about comedy that takes place at 12.00 every Wednesday. This spectacle involves the two leading actors, supported by their acolytes, doing their darnedest to embarrass each other. Questions are asked and answers given. Rarely are the two connected. It is a marvellous example of theatrical sparring with points awarded for manufactured indignation, voice projection and put-down lines. Thirty minutes of nonsense that's great fun to watch.

John Major, a prime minister renowned for his monotonous dialogue and lack of audience engagement, should have performed wonderfully at PMQ. His father was a comedian who plied his trade in the UK's musical halls. After he retired, Major wrote a history of these entertainment venues in which he said: 'PMQ often resembled my father's description of a raucous night at the Glasgow Empire' – somewhere famed for the projectiles thrown by the audience.

Actors are naturals in the theatre of politics. The accomplished actress Glenda Jackson, winner of two Academy Awards, extended her theatrical career by becoming a member of parliament for the Labour Party. Italians found Beppe Grillo's jokes more appealing than those spouted by their head of state, Silvio Berlusconi, the man famed for his Bunga Bunga stories. And of course, there is Volodymyr Oleksandrovych Zelensky, the Ukrainian comedian turned head of state and worldwide personality who is leading his country against the dastardly Vladimir Putin.

Let's not forget those American actors who seamlessly made the transition to become politicians – Ronald Reagan (53 films, non-memorable), Arnie 'The Terminator' Schwarzenegger, Clint 'Dirty Harry' Eastwood and of course Donald Trump, who hosted the first 14 series of *The Apprentice USA*.

The migration from actor to politician goes in both directions.

A career on TV can turn around a mediocre or disastrous period in politics. Sometimes it works well – Michael Portillo single-handedly increased train travel in the UK with his series about *Bradshaw's Guide,* a sentimental meander around the railways and culture of yesteryear.

Sometimes things go very wrong. The chap who was minister for health during the pandemic went from political outcast, via *I'm A Celebrity... Get Me Out Of Here* and *Celebrity SAS: Who Dares Wins* to theatrical outcast. Who knows, third time lucky? Nigel Farage is a 'populist' actor who skirmishes on the outskirts of politics. Between parts he dashed to Australia and did surprisingly well on the 'get me out of here' show. That his fellow contestants were unknown and objectionable helped his cause. The UK's general election in July 2024 was too much of a temptation for the man. Declaring himself leader of the Reform Party he has set his sights on destroying the bad old Tories.

American audiences of *Traitors* must have wondered about the strange little Brit, John Bercow (the ex-speaker of the House of Commons). But not for long, as he soon disappeared from the show.

Strictly Come Dancing (UK) and *Dancing with the Stars* (US) have long been a way of re-launching the careers of tarnished politicians as their ritual humiliation revealed their softer, caring sides, if not their sense of timing and flexibility. The memorable performances of Ann Widdecombe, Vince Cable and Ed Balls can still be watched on YouTube.

What separates the star performers from the rest is their ability to act as anti-politicians while obviously being one. Getting audiences to suspend reality, to identify with their character is a rare gift. Stage props help – Nigel Farage is forever grasping a pint of beer; Boris loved wearing funny hats – but their genius is making the masses believe the unbelievable – time and time again.

When the inevitable fall from grace happens their performance skills are not wasted. Most move to the conference speaking circuit, where for vast sums of money they entertain corporate audiences about their past achievements and the indiscretions of their opponents. Most write books that few people buy.

MEANINGLESS AND UNBELIEVABLE RHETORIC

Believing what politicians say is meaningful and truthful requires a huge dose of make-believe. Mostly, the audience is far too busy talking, eating popcorn and ignoring the drama, allowing nonsense to masquerade as wisdom.

Until recent times political dialogue had to have some morsel of substance, some anchor to the real world. The advent of 'word salad' has changed this, permitting politicians to say the first words that come into their heads. It's all about talking with conviction and using as many fashionable terms as possible. The leading exponent of nonsense speech is the American vice-president Kamala Harris, who will govern the US the instant the ageing incumbent's senility can no longer be ignored.

Here are some of Kamala's memorable performances.

Reflections on – I am not sure:

> *It's very important. As you have heard from so many incredible leaders for us at every moment in time, and certainly this one, to seize the moment in time in which we exist in our present and to be able to contextualise it, understand where we exist, in the history, in the moment, not only as it relates to the past but to the future.*

Her reflections on climate change are almost understandable:

> *One of the young leaders was talking to me about climate mental health, I said tell me what but unpack it for me and she talked about how her peers are thinking about it, one example is, whether when they are ready, could they start a family* [very long pause and much shaking of the

head] *worried about what that would mean and the stress of it, they were talking about it in terms of their peers trying to figure out what they are going to have to get a job and make a living, can they do it and adapt the education they have to their activism.*

Harris is permitted to talk utter gibberish because for most of the time the audience pays her little attention. Those who do, can't believe the VP of the US can be so inarticulate. They rationalise that it must be their fault for not understanding her stream of random words. Her acting skills are poor, as is the synchronisation of her speech and body and facial movement. Despite these faults, she maintains her star billing but not her popularity, which remains at rock bottom.

Audiences are astonishingly forgiving, perhaps I mean naïve, about what politicians say. This example is from the UK and involves Theresa May, a prime minister who struggled with her lines and failed to establish a memorable character. She was taking her final curtain call and suddenly declared the UK would reach 'net zero' by 2050. This got the audience to its feet, many shouting, 'We haven't got that long – make it by 2030.'

Nobody had a clue what this meant or how it could be achieved, but it sounded like a great idea – a wonderful new storyline – one you couldn't oppose – only five people did. Such a momentous decision took less than an hour and was based on the flimsiest of arguments. At the end of her career, she skilfully used the wheeze that the further into the future the commitment, the easier it is to support. All the credit accrues to the originator of the idea and all the acrimony to those making it happen. It's an old acting trick, but it keeps on working.

Politicians are endlessly telling the audience why their policies will improve people's life by curbing economic migration, saving the NHS, getting the workshy working, reducing inflation and solving other intractable problems. The lines are said with conviction but soon forgotten, until the next policy announcement about solving the same problem, which has invariably worsened. Thankfully the audience has a short memory and is easily distracted by the latest Netflix drama series.

Obsession with trivialities and a reticence to confront big issues are other traits of the political class. A packed House of Commons debated the intrigue of the birthday drinks parties held during lockdown. A little later, only three MPs bothered to discuss why an unexpected number of UK citizens keep dying each week for reasons nobody can (or wants to) explain. A few members of the audience try to make sense of these warped priorities; most are much more excited by who was at the drinks party.

Endless hours of parliamentary time were taken up with legislation to stamp out the barbaric practice of eating our own dogs. There was no evidence this was happening, but 'better safe than sorry'. This came to a screeching halt, however, when concerns were raised about offending cultural sensitivities in the Far East. Some bright spark thought that banning power showers would help conserve water (yet more legislation). Maybe tackling the three billion litres of water a day lost through leaky pipes might be a better use of time? If ever there was a displacement activity, it's passing worthless legislation.

Lack of consistency is another political trait the audience tolerates. During the pandemic, everything was an emergency. Vaccines that should take decades to test were approved in months, closing the country down was agreed on the nod, suspending civil rights, the work of a moment, yet the public inquiry into the pandemic is moving at a snail's pace.

Hundreds of lawyers have been employed, millions of pounds spent, and nobody has a clue when it will conclude. Worse still, nobody seems to care since the audience finds the play monumentally boring. It's a drama they hope will never be resurrected. If past inquiries are a guide, then we are in for a long wait. The review into a two-hour period on a Sunday afternoon in Belfast 50 years ago cost £200 million and ran for 12 years. In the past 30 years governments have spent £640 million on these naval-gazing exercises, resulting in 2,265 recommendations. That's a little shy of £300,000 per recommendation, most of which were never implemented. The portents that the Covid inquiry will be any different aren't good. Worse still, it seems that it has already decided its conclusions and is extending the show for as long as possible to top up the pensions of the support staff (lawyers).

Politicians act the role of people who are in charge, knowledgeable people who can make things happen, an illusion the best of them can maintain for years. Despite repeated failures, they keep coming back with more convincing speeches, and the audience keeps applauding. We want to believe their stories; we want them to deliver a happy ending. Eventually, even the most forgiving has to admit it's all nonsense. But never despair, there is always another star waiting to take their place with even more convincing lines.

WHAT'S GOING ON?

It's good fun portraying politicians as hopeless characters, strutting about acting out a drama about governing the country. Depicting voters as a witless audience, easily distracted and prepared to tolerate abysmal performances might make some readers wince. Perhaps our expectations are so low that when the inevitable failure occurs, we really don't care.

Some might believe the wealthier members of the audience have too much influence over the actors' lines and dictate the script. Having made their fortune, the fat-cat philanthropists are compelled to help the poorer, ill-educated members of the audience. Most of the time, it's impossible to understand what they are achieving other than bolstering their self-importance. Paying people to block the roads to the theatre for the good of the environment and increasing travel costs seems a strange way to help.

I will leave it to you to decide how much of my analogy is appropriate. However you view the political theatre – a hopeless shambles or good people doing their best – it isn't working very well. We all have our own rationale why; this is mine.

Forgive me, but I am going to use another analogy. Think of politicians as car drivers following a map – their election manifesto. Navigation instructions are displayed on the GPS screen showing the fastest route and details about obstacles, speed limits and road works. The civil service is the machine powering the car, purring away with a reassuring hum, the Rolls-Royce of ultra-efficient electric, carbon-neutral engines.

Reality is very different. The GPS doesn't work and the route is devilishly difficult to follow, with numerous road works, accidents and other assorted obstacles. The steering wheel no longer controls the wheels and the brakes keep engaging for no apparent reason. Worst of all, the engine is spluttering, losing power and acting as if it has a mind of its own. Finding a charging point (that's working) is devilishly difficult, causing extreme 'range anxiety'.

What's going on? Boris Johnson discovered the failings of the 'machine' that was supposedly running the state at the worst of times, during the pandemic. Dastardly Dom (Dominic Cummings) recalled Boris kept saying:

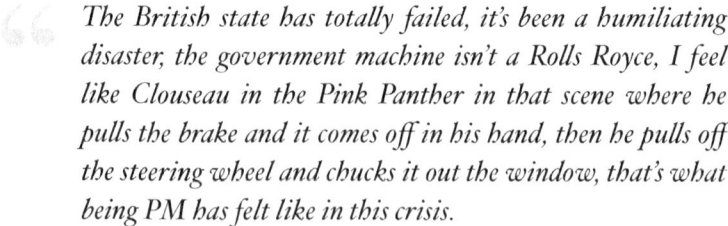

> *The British state has totally failed, it's been a humiliating disaster, the government machine isn't a Rolls Royce, I feel like Clouseau in the Pink Panther in that scene where he pulls the brake and it comes off in his hand, then he pulls off the steering wheel and chucks it out the window, that's what being PM has felt like in this crisis.*

Had Johnson been more diligent in his studies, he would have realised the 'machine' has been busted for ages. Way back in 1981, a fellow Conservative (Sir Keith Joseph) was discovered wandering around his ministry screaming 'where are the levers?' He had just become responsible for the country's education and discovered his powerlessness to make things happen.

Powerless to act

Politicians, be they lowly MPs, ministers or even the prime minister, have far fewer degrees of freedom to govern than they or the electorate believe. The political theatre depends on the assumption that citizens elect politicians to do what they promise. In the US, that might be true, but not in the UK. Their levers of control are surprisingly few and getting fewer.

The EU, UN, WHO, World Bank and IMF all want to dictate the plot. Many people believe their actors are superior to our homegrown bunch. For sure, they are better paid and have longer titles, but that doesn't correlate with competence.

Monetary policy affects much of our lives and is outside politicians' control:

- Interest rates are set by the Bank of England (BoE), which follows the US Federal Reserve.
- The BoE theoretically controls inflation. In reality, it is determined by global events and often made worse by the bank's ponderous reactions.

The little influence politicians have on fiscal policy is fast disappearing:

- The Office for Budget Responsibility is the arbiter of the public finances and decides if policies are sustainable.
- 'The markets', especially those trading currencies and government bonds, have far more power than the prime minister. If in doubt, ask former PM Liz Truss.

Just when they think they have discovered the levers of power, a marauding QUANGO appears and grasps control. These quasi-autonomous non-governmental organisations are funded by the state and theoretically controlled by politicians. In reality, most of them have gone feral and do their own bidding. At last count, there were 1,000 of them ready to pounce and devour the unsuspecting politician.

Inertia and the urgency of the 'ticking clock' pervade every aspect of political life. Everything takes longer than expected, even when everybody agrees – a rarity among the political class. Time is short. There are five years to convince the electorate that your policies work and get elected again. First, you must grapple with your new role. Maybe you were a lawyer and must become an instant expert in transport or fisheries, empty the 'in tray' from your predecessor and only then fathom out your own agenda.

Ministers come and go at a frightening speed. For example, the Department for Education has had 42 bosses since the end of WWII. Their average time in charge is just two years. That's not long to understand the job, formulate policy and get it implemented. It's ridiculously short and explains why so many mistakes are made.

And then there are the institutional, constitutional, legal and procedural barriers. Those wanting to derail government policy no longer have to prove it is wrong or provide a better solution. Enmeshing policies in legal challenges works just as well. When all else fails, there's always some aspect of human rights legislation that can be applied and droves of virtuous lawyers anxious to claim their 15 minutes of fame.

The judiciary, on both sides of the Atlantic, seems only too willing to intervene and overrule politicians. More on this and the growth of 'lawfare' in the essay 'Justice – teetering on a slippery slope'.

Finally, there are 'events', those unknown, unknowns that suddenly become horribly real. War in Ukraine, Covid and carnage in the Middle East. One day, all is well, the next, a new event that demands immediate attention.

And you thought politicians had the power to do stuff. What little influence they have is asymmetric. They can easily make our lives harder by raising taxes and restricting our freedoms but are woefully slow at making things better.

Policies must impress

Political policies are invariably determined by the 'ticking clock' of the electoral cycle. In a perfect world, government decisions provide the optimum benefits to their citizens. Of course, it's never that simple, with numerous other factors involved. One that shouldn't matter, but does, is the media's reaction. Will the press coverage impress the audience and provide memorable emblems of political achievement? Whatever politicians do, there's always an eye on the next election and how to beat the opposition.

For example, if you are going to spend £20 billion improving the UK's railway infrastructure with the option of spreading it over numerous projects, none of which will make headlines, or splashing it all on one that generates masses of media coverage, which do you choose?

Building a super-high-speed railway line from London to 'the north' was portrayed as Britain at its cutting-edge best (2009). London, Heathrow Airport and the cities of the north, connected by super-fast trains with the memorable name HS2. That was headline-grabbing, with numerous photo opportunities. Far more to brag about than improving the track and signalling between Skegness and Sleaford or improving the toilets at Barnstaple station.

This approach is extremely risky. When the policies don't work – which is more likely than not – they attract negative media coverage. Lots of it. This was the fate of HS2. Fifteen years later and much reduced in scale, not reaching central London until after 2040 (maybe), the bill has topped £100 billion and is still going up. Of course, the politicians picking up the tab for the failure weren't those who benefited from the accolades. When they then cancel large parts of the project they are covered in political excrement. However, all is not lost – HS2's annual diversity, equality and inclusion statement must be one of the longest and most expensively produced in the UK (52 pages).

The year the UK's NHS was created, its costs were double

those predicted – horrible portents of its ability to consume vast sums of money. It was a wonderful project for the Labour Party that grabbed the audience's attention and gratitude. It's the mega-project of all mega-projects. Originally costing way less than 1% of GDP, it's now the largest single item of public spending (12%) and always needing more money. By 2036 it will employ half the public sector workforce; that's one in 11 of all workers in England.

Three-quarters of a century after its inception, the NHS is a nightmare, a problem all governments have to endure. Satisfaction with the NHS is the lowest since records began, 40 years ago. Less than a quarter of Brits are satisfied with the service, a 5% drop on the previous year.

Tony Blair was no exception. On taking office he had a couple of headline policies that would boost its performance. The Private Finance Initiative was a clever way to build hospitals while deferring and hiding the costs. It provided numerous photos of Labour politicians opening brand spanking new hospitals, with future governments left paying the bills. The total lifetime cost for this venture is enormous, probably five times more than it would have been had the hospitals been funded normally.

Blair's other big policy was the National Patient System. This was a huge computer project involving multiple vendors and untried technology. Words like 'state of the art', 'cutting edge' and 'fit for the 21st century' filled the news. A beaming Tony Blair and Bill Gates (Microsoft) were photographed on the steps of Downing Street. This was a brave prime minister willing to use innovative technology leading the UK towards a bright future.

He must have known the public sector's aversion to all things digital, especially when used by the NHS. Surely his civil servants warned him? Of course it failed, costing taxpayers over £10 billion, and has become a case study for abysmal IT projects. More recently, another politician (Matt Hancock) fell into the same trap. Along comes an entrepreneur with some fancy IT that will, in a single leap, improve the NHS's productivity (Babylon). What could go wrong? After the flurry of supportive press headlines, things turned sour. Yet another bright idea ending in disaster when the company collapsed into liquidation.

Building new motorways is a lengthy process, expensive and bad for the environment. Why not use technology to make better use of the existing tarmac? Give it a catchy name – 'a smart motorway' – and let media acclaim begin. Like me, millions of motorists must have sat in the long delays during their construction, wondering how they would work without increasing the risk of accidents. The answer is that they didn't and were soon abandoned.

The audience, the ones that politicians are desperate to please, aren't without blame. We like politicians who do things, and do big things, not lots of boring little things. Aren't we looking for politicians with 'vision' who 'think big'? And that's what we get. Policies explained with impressive soundbites and images, policies with the promise of quickly fixing problems that have been decades in the making. And so the show goes on. Politicians give the audience what they want, and nobody is happy.

All is not well with the government machine

The prime minister, ably assisted by their cabinet, decides policy, and an army of 500,000 civil servants makes it happen. Often called the 'governing marriage' this has a simple elegance and efficiency (in theory). Politicians come and go but the engine of government, the administrative state, with its long institutional memory, its procedures and safeguards, remains a reassuring constant. Politically neutral and faithful to the residents of Downing Street, it's the Rolls-Royce of administration. And now the story about cows jumping over the moon.

An article in *The Economist*, 'From Rolls Royce to old banger', beautifully described the fractious relationship that so often exists. Politicians blame the civil service for incompetence in implementing their policies. Civil servants respond that failure results because politicians fail to listen and take their advice. At the time of *The Economist*'s article, the prime minister (Blair) had just received a report from a Labour-supporting think tank (Institute for Public Policy Research) saying:

> *Whitehall is poor at reflecting on its purpose, strategic thinking, dealing with inadequate performance, managing change effectively, learning from mistakes or working across departments.*
>
> *The anachronistic and severely inadequate constitutional conventions governing relations between the civil service, ministers, Parliament and the public have become a recipe for ambiguity, confusion, weak leadership and buck passing.*

This was written 15 years ago, and things have gone downhill since then.

Those politicians and the officials I have encountered were (with a few exceptions) well-meaning and motivated people. Unfortunately, their cultures, priorities, timescales and expectations are hopelessly misaligned. I am reminded of the book *Men are from Mars, Women are from Venus,* which relates the very different mindsets of men and women.

Politicians want the seamless conversion of their ideas into actions; civil servants want to maintain order and retain the status quo. Politicians exist in electoral time, civil servants in career time – politicians are rewarded by 'quick wins', civil servants by not being associated with mistakes and playing by the rules. Yes, yes, I know these are crude generalisations, but they illustrate the massive difference between the two.

Having started to make generalisations, I am going to make one that I think goes to the heart of the problem. The civil service culture values its ability to advise far more than its ability to implement. Politicians and their political advisers increasingly know (or think they know) what they want to happen. They expect the civil service to make it a reality. And there you have one mega-mismatch of expectations.

Some might call this 'creative tension', others 'conflict' – disaster is the word I would use. Whatever the name, it has got a lot worse since 2020. This date has a lovely mathematical symmetry but will be remembered for two monumental events. In January, the UK left the EU; in March, the country's business and social life was suspended during the first Covid lockdown.

Since 2016 the number of civil servants has jumped by a quarter, supposedly because of the Brexit vote. The theory was that the government administration would need to expand to deliver services provided by the EU. Nobody knows how civil servants voted in the referendum, but there's little doubt the majority wanted to remain, and here they are, expanding their numbers and learning new skills for something they didn't want to happen. Then Covid struck and they were sent home with their laptops to work from their dining room table, and that's where most of them remain.

As I am writing this essay there are two competing narratives. Many politicians believe the highly unionised civil service is actively sabotaging the implementation of policies they don't like. By refusing to return to their offices, they are compromising the efficiency of all parts of the government machine. All this has been compounded by lengthy periods of strike action for inflation-busting pay increases. Civil servants' salaries match those in the private sector, yet their pension benefits are infinitely better.

The other narrative is that civil servants are being failed by politicians who expect them to implement unworkable policies and are being intentionally aggressive to them individually and as a group. The head of the civil service trade union criticises ministers for calling officials 'lazy, woke, inefficient, Remainer snowflakes' or branding them 'Machiavellian geniuses' trying to unseat the government. Worst of all, they detest being called 'The Blob'.

What's beyond doubt is the public sector's productivity is nosediving. More is being spent on education, the health service, the police and all the other services the state provides, and it's delivering less (ONS, 2024).

Personally, I think the idea of a neutral, efficient civil service is wishful thinking; however, as a comedy, it could be the basis for a TV series. Whoops, somebody has already had that idea (*Yes Minister*, first shown in 1980).

One moment, the Home Office's director general for asylum was supposedly implementing government policy. The next, she is the head of Amnesty International UK, screaming about the government's asylum policies. The senior civil servant pivotal in the demise of Boris Johnson, the Conservative prime minister, soon after resigns and becomes the Labour Party's chief of staff. These examples make a mockery of the notion of civil service neutrality.

On a gloomy day, it's easy to despair that there has been a total breakdown in trust and that the workings of the public administration are permanently damaged. What's for certain is confidence in the current crop of politicians and the idea of an efficient, neutral civil service eager to implement their policies are in tatters.

For now, the audience is on the side of civil servants, expressing four times more confidence in them than politicians. My bet is this will not continue.

This is a very gloomy point on which to conclude this essay. A young reader will say it's typical of a miserable old sod. They might be right. But then they might be wrong. I will keep attending the political theatre but only for comedies. There's a new one in rehearsal called 'The Labour takes power.' The first act is bound to be solemn and serious but it will soon morph into a farce. That's when I will get my popcorn and start watching.

BUSINESS – CHARTING NEW PATHS OR LOSING DIRECTION?

It is an immutable law in business that words are words, explanations are explanations, promises are promises – but only performance is reality.

Harold S. Geneen, president of ITT Corp

To act on the belief that we possess the knowledge and the power which enable us to shape the processes of society entirely to our liking, knowledge which in fact we do not possess, is likely to make us do much harm.

Friedrich August von Hayek, *Nobel Prize Lecture*, 1974

Back in ancient history (1977), I attended business school and left brandishing a master's in business administration (MBA). For 12 months I was immersed in the intricacies of finance, tax, law, marketing, logistics and business strategy. I was being groomed to become a smart-arsed manager, a large cog in the corporate world with the promise of a big pay cheque.

I learnt how to minimise the corporate tax bill by financial engineering and transfer pricing; ways to escape watertight contracts by manipulating the law; techniques for tempting consumers to buy products; and most importantly how to get to the top of the greasy pole, ASAP. It was like going to West Point or Sandhurst except we learnt about business not war.

Half a century later, business seems much the same. Ego and ambition still trump dedication and loyalty. Of course it has moved from analogue to digital and adapted to changing cultural values. However, I sense there is something more going on than natural evolution.

It's as if the purpose of the corporate world has expanded way beyond satisfying customer needs to tackling the ills of society. Companies seem anxious to have a moral purpose that's beyond making money, paying tax (as little as possible) and employing people (the fewer the better).

Maybe this is a story being peddled by the media, lacking in substance? But, perhaps companies are responding to their customers' demand for altruism as well as decent products and services. Are, as the media suggests, young employees expecting employers to give purpose to their lives as well as pay a fat salary? Hopefully, by the end of this essay, I will know if these are myths or reality.

What better place to start than to look at what Harvard Business School, the granddaddy (whoops, grandperson) of business schools, is teaching its students? Much to my surprise the syllabus is little changed from what I studied. I recognise most of the module titles but, like my physics degree, the detail has long since flown my memory. Some new subjects are covered but they seem tacked on as an afterthought.

A module titled 'Inclusion' promises to 'take students and faculty through the journey of inclusive change'. 'Leadership and Corporate Accountability' examines the legal, ethical and economic responsibilities of corporate leaders. 'Social Purpose of the Firm' studies how companies can address society's greatest challenges (e.g. climate change, poverty and economic development). All this sounds very worthy, but I doubt if it comprises more than 10% of the total.

I decided to investigate further. Little has changed from my time lecturing at London Business School. The syllabus there still contains lots and lots about finance with a dash of 'social responsibility and ethics'. The MBA syllabus at my alma mater has a few words like 'stakeholder' and 'inclusion' tossed in; otherwise, it's all familiar. Part of me was disappointed that the body of knowledge of business had evolved so little.

These superficial changes are nowhere near enough to explain my concerns. Before going further, perhaps it would be wise to understand what it is about contemporary business that makes me uneasy.

BUSINESS TAKES SIDES

Business has never existed in a vacuum and has always tried influencing the political agenda to further its interests. For most of my early life the Labour Party in the UK and Democrats in the US were the parties of the workers. Conservatives and Republicans supported business. Of course, it wasn't as simple as this, with lots of exceptions.

I have no idea about the political affiliation of senior managers in the UK but research from Harvard sheds light on the US situation. It seems Republicans outnumber Democrats, among S&P 500 senior executives, by a margin of 69% to 31%.

Ten years ago, the Confederation of British Industry (CBI) was the main lobbying group for business, along with the Institute of Directors (IoD). Much of their work took place at the EU in Brussels, not Whitehall in London. Trade unions promoted workers' rights and wages using the Trades Union Congress (TUC) as their channel to government.

I am not that knowledgeable about the US equivalent, but it appears companies used industry lobbying groups and the chambers of commerce to influence government, whereas trade unions bought influence with politicians.

Much has changed in the UK. The CBI is now moribund after a series of allegations of sexual impropriety. Since the early 2000s, membership of the IoD has collapsed by two-thirds and, of course, the UK is no longer in the EU, leaving lots of empty offices in Brussels.

Trade union membership has been shrinking since the 1980s and now is mostly public sector employees. Much the same has happened in the US, where only 6% of private sector workers are union members.

The days when these monolithic organisations represented the unified voice of their business and worker constituencies are long since gone, as are the days when business and party politics were aligned. Today's companies seem intent on demonstrating their allegiance, not to politicians or economic systems but to causes.

This next sentence is the most shocking of this essay – are you ready?

According to the most authoritative global research about trust (Edleman Trust Barometer), '*business is the only trusted institution* with government and the media fuelling a cycle of distrust' (emphasis added). Business was not seen as being all virtue – 63% thought business leaders purposely mislead people by saying things they know are false or gross exaggerations. You can imagine how little trust people had in journalists and politicians.

So it seems companies are taking a rational decision, distancing themselves from government. As trust in other institutions plummets, they are filling the vacuum and providing moral direction along with products and services. If this is their intention, then 'God help us'. That's a comment from somebody who has spent his life in business.

Let's get down to the specifics of how this moral leadership is manifesting itself. These examples are in no order of importance. All of them make me distinctly uneasy.

Financial institutions display their progressive credentials

Perhaps it's because the financial institutions' misdemeanours caused such economic chaos that they feel compelled to be visibly progressive in their behaviour. The HR director of Lloyds Banking Group was so incensed by debates at the Conservative Party conference that she emailed employees offering them counselling if they were 'triggered by the rhetoric heard'. This bank's language guide advises using 'separated' rather than 'widow' because the latter is 'unnecessarily vivid' and, worse still, may 'trigger unwarranted personal memories of trauma and upsetting situations'. This seems odd since the bank owns an insurance company called Scottish Widows. We wait to see if it will be rebranded as Scottish Separated.

So concerned is the CEO of Aviva that her company is not achieving its diversity targets that she insists on personally approving all senior white male appointments.

These gestures generate the usual derision in the mainstream media (MSM) but nothing to match the next example. If a bank suspects a customer of illegal activities, it can close their accounts and tag them with a marker that makes it near to impossible for them to find alternative banking facilities. According to the consumer champion Which?, 30% of these account closures are mistakes.

Of course, institutions need to protect themselves and their customers from fraudulent activity but, recently, accounts have been closed for reasons that have nothing to do with the customer's finances. Toby Young is a UK journalist who could best be described as a contrarian and somebody who fights for the freedom to express views that grate with the establishment. Without warning, his personal and business PayPal accounts were closed for breaching their 'hate, violence or racial intolerance' policy and spreading 'Covid misinformation'. He appealed and asked for details of his supposed breach of their rules – none were ever provided.

He is a journalist with connections throughout the UK media. Soon it was in the MSM and on TV and being discussed in the UK Parliament. PayPal suddenly found he hadn't broken any rules and his accounts were reinstated, accompanied by one of those excruciating boilerplate apologies: 'We hope this didn't cause you any inconvenience.'

A similar situation occurred with a prominent UK politician, Nigel Farage. One day, he had a bank account with Coutts Bank; the next, he didn't. Reluctantly the bank was forced to release the documents justifying its decision. He was 'exited' because his views 'do not align with our values'. To add further clarification, 'this was not a political decision but one centred around inclusivity and Purpose'. Heavens knows what this means and why the capital P?

Not satisfied with this gobbledygook, Farage pursued the case and discovered a rationale that was comical, frightening and beyond naïve. Within a day, it was the main story in the UK media. Like PayPal, the bank backed down, issued an apology and hoped the story would die. If the CEO of NatWest (owner of Coutts) hadn't leaked the story to the BBC, that might have happened. Worse still, she suggested Farage's account was closed for financial reasons.

The scandal escalated and after a week of excuses and bravado, she resigned, receiving a £2.4 million payoff, her legal fees paid and £60,000 to help find another job. Surely, somebody being paid £5 million a year shouldn't make such an awful mistake? What would have happened to a junior banker – paid 0.6% of that salary – if they had stood on the high street and denigrated a customer's financial affairs? Instant dismissal (likely) – a leaving bonus (unlikely) – money to find a new job (never).

How could the management of these organisations have been so naïve and failed to predict the resulting backlash? A few months after this kerfuffle, Mr Farage appeared on *I'm A Celebrity... Get Me Out Of Here* for a reported fee of £1.5 million. Where he banked the money remains unknown.

The driving force for removing Farage appears to have been the bank's membership of the B Corp network, an organisation like Stonewall that awards kitemarks to organisations obeying its rules. I guess it also defines the moral code of acceptable customers. More on B Corp a little later.

For every one of these high-profile 'mistakes' there are hundreds (probably thousands) of people who find themselves without banking facilities, not for illegal activity but because of something they said or did that was contrary to the institution's professed values. This happened to a feminist group that questioned the claim that 'trans women are women'. The same bank continued providing services to another customer convicted of murder and hideous acts of torture.

I am sure these organisations believe they are parading their moral authority by hurting the baddies. In their world, such actions are not only acceptable but the right thing to do. I guess you can't blame them for this attitude when senior members of the Labour Party aligned themselves with Farage's bank, accusing the government of 'bullying' the disgraced CEO. Howls of anguish came from the left-wing media, accusing Farage of manipulating events for his own purpose and 'whipping up a populist storm'.

That the bank behaved this way and that there were those attempting to defend its actions make me uneasy. No, it's more than that – it annoys the hell out of me.

Trashing a brand for the best of reasons

Forbes magazine announced: 'The Super Bowl will kick off a new marketing era for Bud Light, and a woman is at the helm for this new direction' (February 2023). This is a marketer's dream of being entrusted with an iconic brand.

Three months later, marketer Alissa Heinerscheid's world

caved in following the release of a 20-second Instagram video that she commissioned. What could go wrong with using the transgender influencer Dylan Mulvaney to promote a beer?

Social media is a brilliant way of targeting your brand to niche audiences. It is inexpensive and quick to implement, but when it goes wrong, it goes horribly wrong. Portents of the reaction were exposed 48 hours earlier in an interview where Heinerscheid described her strategy:

> *Bud Light is a brand in decline. It's been in decline for a really long time. And if we do not attract young drinkers to come and drink this brand, there will be no future for Bud Light. So I had this super clear mandate. It's like we need to evolve and elevate this incredibly iconic brand.*

When asked to explain what 'elevate' meant she replied:

> *It means inclusivity. It means shifting the tone. It means having a campaign that's truly inclusive and feels lighter and brighter and different. And appeals to women and to men.*

I am sure all of this is correct. When I was a marketing consultant, it's the sort of stuff I would advise clients to do; however, a cardinal rule is that these words stay inside the company. Even supportive media will interpret them as something very different. The story reported by the MSM was that Bud Lite was insulting its older male customers.

A marketing professor (Mark Ritson) expressed the same disquiet that I felt:

> *There is a significant absence of respect for the current Bud Light consumer. She was too quick to talk about who the brand needs to recruit and silent about the loyal consumers that made the brand what it is today.*

Adopting a purpose and being driven by a social agenda are wonderful things, but they do not necessarily go hand-in-hand with short- or long-term profitability.

Since the event, the beer's rating among twentysomething women has increased from -6 to +0.5. Among Republicans, it has gone in the opposite direction (+13 to -8). I guess you could say that Heinerscheid's objective of improving the beer's reputation with young women has been achieved – but at a cost. Brand tracking surveys show that among the general population, the beer lost 75% of its popularity. In April the beer's sales fell 21% compared with March.

Photographs of the Bud Light team of marketers were very telling. All were young (under 30), and most were women. Among this group, the idea of a transgender influencer promoting the beer must have seemed pioneering and exciting. I fear they exist in a cultural bubble that is very different from the world inhabited by their customers. Not only did they not understand the resulting reaction, I doubt if they cared, until reality intervened and the beer sales plummeted.

That intelligent, well-meaning people can be so naïve and careless with a brand's value is unforgiveable. Equally surprising was when so-called experts at the *Financial Times* were dismissive of the beer's boycott:

> *AB InBev (owner of Bud Light) should stick with its marketing approach, rather than wringing its hands weakly. These efforts to broaden the beer's reach made perfect sense and it has since gained free publicity.*

Alas, there are no signs the free publicity is turning into sales. After researching 170,000 of the beer's customers, the brewer discovered: 'They want Bud Light to engage with topics relevant to all consumers like music and sport.' What a surprise.

The 'Mulvaney effect' has been longer lasting than even I

would have guessed. Despite the parent company AB InBev making lots of conciliatory, or was it grovelling, noises to Bud's older customers, sales in the US continued to fall, down 17.4% in the final quarter of 2023.

Nike 'Just do it' wrong

This tale is almost identical to the Bud Lite saga. In my view, it was much worse and should have received even more ridicule. Nike has consistently created some of the industry's best advertising. Never using the word 'inclusive' to describe its advertising; it just did it. The wonderful campaigns 'This is us', 'Dream Crazier' and 'Find your Greatness' were innovative and had the highest production values.

Then in 2023 Nike announced that it:

> *Exists to champion athletes and sport. We believe women and girls aren't just the future of sport – they're on the leading edge of change. They are redefining what sport is and the opportunity it represents to serve a new generation.*

As part of this campaign the same Dylan Mulvaney was hired to promote Nike's women's sports bras and leggings. A TikTok video was released showing Mulvaney 'exercising'. I have no idea what Nike was trying to achieve, but it certainly generated a torrent of criticism.

Former Olympians commented, including: 'Have some decency while being inclusive. This is an outrage' – Caitlin Jenner (herself transgender).

'The ad feels like a parody of what women are. In the past it's always been seen as an insult to say "run like a girl," and here we've got someone behaving in a way that's very un-sporty and very unathletic' – Sharon Davies, Olympic swimming medal winner.

Davies is right, it's a caricature of Nike's own advertisement 'Run like a girl' that did so much to dispel the stereotypes about how boys and girls compete in sports.

All mention of the video has disappeared from Nike's website in the hope that the event is soon forgotten. All companies, even Nike, make the occasional mistake. But for a short time, it revealed the company's management thinking and it was an ugly sight. Being inclusive means, as Nike has always shown, embracing all types of people rather than ridiculing one group at the expense of another.

How not to support 'Pride Month' – ask Target

As part of celebrating Pride Month, the US retailer Target launched over 2,000 new themed products, including 'gender fluid' mugs, 'queer all year' calendars and books for children aged two to eight titled *Bye Bye, Binary*, *Pride 1, 2, 3* and *I'm Not a Girl*.

The company has been supporting Pride events for over a decade, but this year's campaign extended to transgender merchandise for children. I suspect that was where it all went wrong.

Like the Bud Lite advert, it triggered a torrent of adverse publicity and customer reaction. The company quickly removed the offending products but not fast enough to halt the backlash, which affected its financial results, forcing the company to lower its year-end profit forecast.

Talking with reporters, the CEO said: 'As we navigate an ever-changing operating and social environment, we are applying what we learned.' That's another version of the familiar 'lessons have been learnt' comment. The chief financial officer was a little more forthcoming: 'It is a signal for us to pause, adapt and learn so that our future approach to these moments balances celebration, inclusivity and broad-based appeal.' That's code for next year we will try not to offend large swathes of our customers.

Promising to continue supporting Pride Month, Target said it will have a more 'focused assortment of merchandise'. This strategy has worked, with the company surviving the 2024 Pride Month, receiving equal criticism from LGBT+ activists and their detractors.

Advertising for business or virtue

Back in the day, companies advertised to improve their business performance. It might be as simple as encouraging people to buy a product or with the vague objective of improving their corporate or brand awareness. Usually, it was easy to understand an advertisement's marketing objectives.

I must admit that much of today's advertising baffles me. It seems a mishmash of brand awareness and promoting the company's diversity. The representation of black and Asian minorities has surged, alongside championing environmental sustainability and sexual diversity.

Campaign magazine highlighted three ads, primarily featuring black actors, and evaluated their emotional impact. On average, the ads received a score of 2.4 when assessed by a diverse sample of viewers.

Ads with notable score disparities between black viewers and the broader audience were from Asda supermarket (5.4 versus 2.1), Virgin Media (5.0 versus 1.9) and Nationwide (4.8 versus 2.1). Personally, I'd have rated all three as zero, but I understand I'm not the primary demographic, the under-35s.

Given that 82% of the UK's population is white, these companies seem to be intentionally targeting a minority audience. Whatever the reasons, it doesn't appear to be related to business performance.

In the name of promoting their inclusivity, two companies, Costa Coffee and Dr Martens, thought it was sensible to use imagery of a young transgender person with breast removal scars on their chest. Perhaps it is because of my age and sympathy for women forced to have mastectomies, but I find this disturbing, especially with the high degree of mental illness among the young, the target for this imagery. Surely, the companies realised the negative reaction these pictures would cause. Maybe they didn't, maybe they didn't care, maybe it was intentional, whatever explanation, I can't believe it was good for their business.

Reading the content on the World Federation of Advertisers (WFA) website and the manifestos of the Conscious Advertising Network (CAN) helps explain what's happening and provides insights into why Nike and Bud Lite behaved as they did. Most advertising agencies are members of one or both of these organisations.

WFA thought that: 'Issues around Bud Light in the US and the attack on its choice of influencer partners, may have put greater emphasis on the real DEI agenda and taking real action' (DEI: diversity, equity and inclusion). It was a strange choice of priorities, the 'attack on the influencer partner', not the huge loss in business.

CAN believes that:

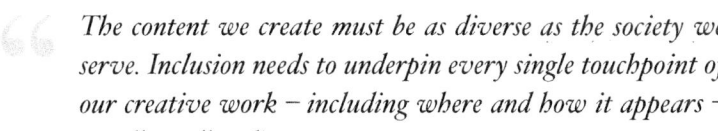

> *The content we create must be as diverse as the society we serve. Inclusion needs to underpin every single touchpoint of our creative work – including where and how it appears – to talk to all audiences.*

CAN's objectives are laudable, but have companies gone too far in trying to achieve these goals at the expense of alienating their mainstream customers?

Let's not forget that advertising agencies do the bidding of their clients. That doesn't stop them from protecting against naïve marketers who are willing to risk their brand's equity. That's a part of their job they seem to have jettisoned.

Way back when I worked for a living, I coined the term age-neutral marketing. It meant that marketing should work for all age groups. The exceptions are very young and old people who have specific product requirements. Markets should never be treated as a zero-sum-game. The same applies to the customer's sex and race. Excluding one group to benefit another is crazy, something you learn in marketing 101.

Achieving a neutral approach is not easy. That's why advertising agencies charge such high fees. When it fails, which is most of the time, it makes advertisements look like simple attempts to promote the company's diversity beliefs – maybe that is what this is?

Clumsy advertising isn't just a waste of money. It risks trust in a brand, and that's an expensive mistake.

Making entertainment inclusive

I used the word 'clumsy' in the context of advertising. The same word applies to meddling with the rules for films to win the Best Picture Oscar. The Academy Award-winning actor Richard Dreyfuss expressed a more extreme sentiment – 'they make me vomit'.

The new 'standards' are a crude way of forcing film companies to increase the number of actors and supporting staff employed from underrepresented groups and to dictate the storyline. If there ever was a recipe for blatant tokenism dictating the process of creating entertainment, this is it. Reaction from actors and directors suggests this might be a step too far, even for the progressively minded Hollywood.

Once you start applying racial conditions to the awarding of prizes, where do you stop? In the post-October 7 surge in anti-semitism, 250 Jewish entertainers signed a letter requesting their race be included in the list of protected racial groups.

 There is a duty for the entertainment world to do its part in disseminating whole and human depictions of Jews, to increase understanding and empathy in viewers in these dangerous times. We ask the Motion Picture Academy leadership to do its part in advancing a just cause that has been ignored for too long.

Outside the world of 'luvvies' (I wonder if that word is banned yet), the intrigue and machinations of awarding the Oscars are of little interest until they involve actors behaving as prima donnas, not uncommon, then it creates excellent clickbait. These mechanistic, tick-box rules reveal the film industry's obsession with inclusivity.

I guess there's a risk that scriptwriters become too obsessed with race and identity at the expense of the environment. This is hard to believe since most new films include a storyline about the heartless capitalist trashing the planet and the heroine fighting back against all the odds. Bloomberg's Philanthropies believes more can be done and has launched goodenergystories.com, which *The New York Times* calls 'Hollywood's Climate Adviser'. Hopefully, somewhere in Tinseltown there is somebody promoting the idea of making films that people want to watch.

Google 'missed the mark'

There is only one story in the digital town and that's artificial intelligence (AI). Since the beginning of 2024 the share price of Nvidia, the specialist AI chip producer, has increased by 64%, giving it a market value larger than Alphabet and Amazon. By the time you read this, of course, its shares might have plummeted but there's no doubt that AI is the hot topic of 2024.

Microsoft's ChatGPT is my trusty sidekick, but Google is desperate for my attention. I had such high hopes when Google's boss launched Gemini in December 2023, describing it as:

> *The next step on our journey with Gemini, our most capable and general model yet, with state-of-the-art performance across many leading benchmarks. I'm genuinely excited for what's ahead, and for the opportunities Gemini will unlock for people everywhere.*

During February 2024, Google's AI product grabbed the headlines for all the wrong reasons. What the product 'unlocked' were gasps of horror and ridicule when its image generator behaved as if it was obsessed with inclusivity. Whatever you asked, its response was images of women and black people. OK, I am exaggerating a tad.

The image of *Girl with a Pearl Earring* by Johannes Vermeer was a black lady. Medieval knights and Vikings were all black people. Pictures of a mayo sandwich were black people eating white bread. George Washington was a black man, as was the Pope (both male and female options). As some wag commented 'It looks like

Google put its DEI supremo in charge of the product.' In the weeks following the incident ex-Google employees commented that they weren't in the least surprised. They portray a company obsessed with inclusivity targets that has abandoned excellence for DEI box ticking.

Google issued a rather lame statement saying that Gemini had 'missed the mark' and immediately took it offline. The incident might have ended there – but journalists unearthed the social media posts of the product's boss. He was a right-on Democrat and a vocal supporter of critical race theory:

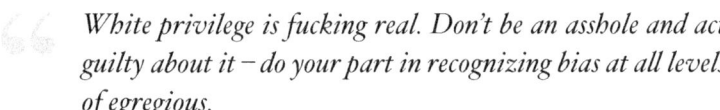

> *White privilege is fucking real. Don't be an asshole and act guilty about it – do your part in recognizing bias at all levels of egregious.*

> *... I've been crying in intermittent bursts for the past 24 hours since casting my ballot. Filling that Biden/Harris line felt cathartic.*

> *... Today's inauguration speech will go down as one of the greatest ever – acknowledging systemic racism.*

It's difficult not to laugh about this incident but then you are overtaken by a wave of horror. AI technology is only as good as those controlling how it learns, processes and responds.

It would be better if Google was less obsessed with disinformation and fake news and more concerned that its AI products weren't reflecting the sensibilities of its latest recruit from Harvard on a mission to save the world.

No wonder Google's CEO's next response stressed the seriousness of the mistake:

> *We know that some of its responses have offended our users and shown bias – to be clear, that's completely unacceptable and we got it wrong.*

As the story went viral, the pundits wondered if this incident had revealed an ugly side of Google's culture that was supporting censorship and acting as a dogmatic parent telling users what we can and cannot do.

Failing while parading its virtue

The Bank of England has made an abysmal mess of controlling the UK's rate of inflation as the country exited the pandemic. Economists might debate the extent of its responsibility, but nobody defends its actions. It should have raised interest rates earlier. Public confidence in its performance is the worst since it began collecting data in 1999.

There are many explanations for what went wrong. What is known is that during the period when the Bank should have been acting, it was mounting a PR campaign explaining how it was decolonising its art collection, actively pursuing its 'climate transition plan', making itself more diverse, creating gender-neutral toilets and helping staff pay for gender reassignment treatment. These well-meaning ventures generated as much media commentary as its efforts to control inflation.

I doubt there is a correlation between the Bank's failure and its activities to tick all the boxes in the DEI checklist. But like the NatWest saga, it raises legitimate questions about the competence of the organisation's management to do their primary job. This was the main conclusion of a damning report from the Lords Economic Affairs Committee. At least one of the goals that it failed to achieve – reducing climate change – has been removed from its objectives.

Another blunder by the bank is the cost of its quantitative easing programme. What seemed like a free way of funding government expenditure by printing money now looks like it will have a very high price tag. The latest estimate puts the cost at £85 billion.

The former Federal Reserve chair Ben Bernanke was asked to review the BoE's forecasting and related processes and concluded there were 'significant shortcomings', including using outdated software that was unable to function when there were large changes in the economy.

There are no reports of Bernanke's opinion about the bank's DEI strategy but I expect it was exemplary.

Vogue's blatant posturing of its DEI credentials

The England women's football team came within a whisker of winning the football World Cup. Katarina Johnson-Thompson became heptathlon world champion (again) after recovering from a horrific injury, a couple of years before. The nation's women's cycling team is packed with world record holders. The women's Hundred cricket competition has been a huge success, attracting a new audience of girls. Britain's women's sport has never been more successful, packed with charismatic winners.

'The Vogue 25' is the list of women *Vogue* magazine honours for 'Defining – and redefining – Britain in 2023'. Among its number were a couple I know personally and was astonished to see listed – the less said, the better.

Women's sport has been so successful, yet only one sportswoman was named, and they attracted all the media attention. With so many stars to choose from, *Vogue* selected somebody who, three years ago, was a junior male cyclist. Why, asked the media, did *Vogue* select somebody who never has or will reach the elite level?

Did *Vogue* genuinely think they deserved the honour more than all the world-class stars? What rationale did the prestigious magazine use to come to this decision?

The cynical me thinks it was to cause controversy and generate press coverage that would parade its LGBTQQIP2SAA credentials. I doubt this will have any effect on the subscriber numbers of the magazine, who might well agree with the choice. But I'd like to know if anybody at the publication gave an instant's thought to what this conveys to the thousands of young women striving to be world champions. I guess *Vogue* doesn't see them as potential customers!

Each of these stories can be dismissed as aberrations of normal business operations that have been dramatised and exaggerated by the media. It's all too easy to highlight events that support a popular narrative, and soon you discover a conspiracy – that businesses and businesspeople are becoming more interested in promoting virtue than doing the day job of running successful enterprises. This is undoubtedly happening, but I doubt it's the norm (I hope not).

However, I do think businesses, especially large multinationals, do believe it's their role and within their power to help solve society's ills. These examples show how inept some are at the task. Eventually, even the largest companies are forced to bow to market forces. After a year when seven of the eight major theatrical releases significantly underperformed in the US and overseas (2023) the head of Disney said:

> *Creators lost sight of what their No. 1 objective needed to be. We have to entertain first. It's not about messages.*

WHAT'S GOING ON?

Indulge me for a moment while I recount a couple of personal anecdotes from the past. What's the difference between 'gay' and 'grey'? Back in 2009 the answer was 'not much'.

In a previous business incarnation, I owned a marketing consultancy focusing on older consumers – back then called the grey market. I was speaking at a conference about 'niche markets', following somebody explaining the importance of marketing to gay people – back then known as the pink market (can you believe it).

If you replaced the word 'gay' with 'grey' our presentations were almost the same. Both of us were trying to convince the audience about the business potential of markets that most companies ignored. We weren't suggesting they do this for altruistic reasons; rather, they were missing out on an untapped source of profits.

Afterwards, we got together and produced some marketing

papers explaining the similarities between these consumers and the techniques companies could employ to capture their business. It was great fun, and I learnt a lot about what was then called the LGBT community, a term that most of its members detested.

At the same time, I got to know some people active within Greenpeace, the environmental pressure group. Our paths crossed when learning Tai Chi. I remember hearing about their campaigns and the indifference of companies to the environment. Back then, LGBT and environmental causes were worthy but not important. Racial equality was assumed, and the concept of racial equity was a gleam in an academic's eye. These issues were not on companies' agendas; they were avoided for fear of creating adverse publicity.

Corporate life was not devoid of all concerns for society. Most large companies had some sort of corporate social responsibility (CSR) plan that described how they wanted the world to be a better place. This concept had been around in business literature since the 1950s but only took shape in the late 1990s. My old employer (IBM) enabled employees to spend time using their business skills to help charities. The cost to the company was small, as was its impact on the community; however, it resulted in good photos for IBM's annual report.

How different the world is today. A passion for saving the environment, fighting racism and celebrating all variants of sexuality are taken for granted. Alas, a lack of interest in older consumers is still the norm.

What was it that caused companies to embrace these goals of inclusivity and sustainability? Did they have a collective 'road to Damascus' moment? If so, where and when did it happen?

I believe there are two possible explanations. Let's start with the one assuming it was a logical evolution.

Natural evolution

I rely on the 'Law of Economy' when seeking an explanation for events. Better known as Occam's Razor, it proposes that when deciding between competing theories, the simplest is most likely to be correct. This implies businesses changed because the world around them changed, not because of some conspiracy – it is as simple as that.

This is a brief summary of the major events that have pressurised companies to adapt...

As the mass of scientific evidence mounted, so did dire predictions about the environment. This became headline news in 2006 with the dramatic claims of Al Gore's film *An Inconvenient Truth* and the following year when he and the UN's panel on climate change received the Nobel Peace Prize for raising awareness about man-made climate change.

Concern for the environment soon became a global issue that companies couldn't ignore. Indeed, by embracing it they could exploit its profit potential.

The United Nations Climate Change Conferences (COPs) have become larger and more regular as countries attempt to reach agreements about controlling carbon emissions. COP3 in Kyoto had 10,000 delegates, tiny compared to COP28 in UAE, with 97,000 attendees. Cynics claim the fine weather and opulence of Dubai explain the doubling of the audience from when it was held in rainy Glasgow two years earlier.

I am never sure of what these events achieve other than providing a wonderful stage for politicians and corporate leaders to parade their environmental virtues. The achievement of the latest event was an agreement to 'transition away from fossil fuels', something I thought had long ago been agreed.

National and supranational governments have enacted masses of environmental policies requiring businesses to adapt. Suddenly, an issue that had been the responsibility of the lowly CSR department shot to the top of the corporate agenda.

Attitudes to the social factors of race and sexuality have also evolved, providing challenges and opportunities for business.

Sixty years ago (1963) Martin Luther King gave his famous 'I have a dream' speech describing his vision of racial equality. Barak Obama's election as president and the activism of the Black Lives Matter movement (2013) increased pressure for businesses to take notice. And then, the graphic murder of George Floyd (2020) ignited outrage that went viral. Many believed the legal framework enforcing racial equality wasn't working and that the problems were deep-seated within society. Parts of government and business embraced the ideas of race theory that had previously been confined to academia. Race joined the environment on board agendas.

In most parts of the West, same-sex marriage is now legal. The barriers preventing gays and lesbians from achieving positions of power in government and business have disappeared. Despite achieving the original objectives of the LGBT community, other, more vocal groups wanted a radically different attitude to sex, gender and equality.

Sexuality has become extremely contentious and complicated. The new LGBTQQIP2SAA activist lobby is driving the agenda to recognise the multitude of gender variations. Charities, NGOs and government agencies readily accepted their ideas, which are now determining the behaviour of many companies.

It has been a long battle for women to achieve equality with men and to overcome the predatory nature that some males display. Now more girls than boys go to university and in most subjects they achieve better grades. Yet, old prejudices and behaviours persist that were graphically highlighted in 2017 when the actress Alyssa Milano tweeted a request to her followers: 'If you've been sexually harassed or assaulted, write "me too" as a reply to this tweet.' The rest is history as the campaign snowballed. According to *The New York Times* #MeToo brought down over 200 powerful men, with Harvey Weinstein being the most prominent. This event was a game changer and caused institutions to question their role in ensuring women's safety and equality.

A timeless rule of business is that unless issues get the sustained attention of senior management, they're not addressed. Concerns for the environment, racial and sexual diversity and equality most certainly got that attention. Like in academia, the mechanism to create and manage the tactical policies was the diversity, equity and inclusion (DEI) department.

Another driver of change started back in the 1960s when activist investors pressured companies to stop trading with South Africa and producing tobacco products, forcing businesses to be socially responsible as well as increasing shareholder value. This idea evolved into the environmental, social and governance (ESG) movement, allowing investors to evaluate companies by their ESG rating, creating further incentives to embrace a socially responsible approach.

I am part of the Boomer generation that controlled much of business for the past few decades. Many of us are now retired or close to retirement. Another generation of managers is taking control – the Millennials – who are being influenced by Gen Z, not long out of university. The younger generations' attitudes to the relationship between employer and employee are very different from mine and my parents'. They have entered the workforce when labour supply is limited and are exerting their negotiating position by increasing their salaries. At this stage in their career they are the highest-paid generation ever (*The Economist*).

Much is made about the different technological literacy of the generations. That's an issue but not as significant as the different attitudes to the role of business and its social values. For example, half of those working in marketing are aged between 26 and 35 and were at university when DEI culture was rapidly evolving.

Customers are also undergoing a generational change as the spending power of older consumers declines. How this will be replaced by the young is unclear. Unlike their parents, they have educational debt and sky-high housing costs that consume much of their income. The dynamics of intergenerational finance are fascinating but must remain a story for another day.

The young and old have always had different product requirements, but now the generational differences extend to attitudes about how companies behave. Managing the generational transition without alienating large swathes of existing customers is difficult, as the management of Bud Lite and Target have discovered.

The role of business and how it relates to society has evolved, hurried along by the accelerant of social media. And then there are the effects of the pandemic, like the widespread adoption of working from home. No single event caused this change. Rather, issues that had been smouldering for decades suddenly ignited, all in the space of a few years.

There's a variant of this evolutionary explanation that includes the self-centred, manipulating side of human nature.

It's a cunning plan

There's no disputing the chronology and importance of the events just discussed. However, there are some additional factors involved in explaining management's change of attitude. Let's start by describing how the business world nearly ended in 2008 and how it fell in love with globalisation and cheap overseas labour.

Trigger warning – this is a cynical interpretation of events.

Do you remember the Millennium Bug? Despite all the preparation, the worry persisted that when the second millennium ended, computers would go berserk as their clocks reset to the 1900s. The fears turned out to be misplaced. All was well; no planes crashed, computers kept working and the IT industry made a fortune. Full disclosure – I was a beneficiary.

Celebrations were short-lived. The new era in which companies fell in love with internet technology, driving the price of technology stocks to eye-watering levels, ended abruptly. The NASDAQ stock market index increased by 800% between 1995 and March 2000, then went into a nosedive, losing most of this gain and sending shock waves throughout the financial industry. Much introspection followed, along with reassurances that 'lessons had been learnt' from the dot.com bubble.

Much, much worse was to come in 2008, when the housing and stock markets collapsed, bringing the global financial system near to breaking point. A staggering $5,000,000,000,000 of US pension savings, real estate and bonds disappeared, causing 8 million people to lose their jobs and 6 million their houses.

It could have been far worse if governments hadn't intervened. Within days, cash dispensers would have stopped dispensing, supermarket shelves emptied and anarchy reigned. For financiers, politicians and CEOs, it was like facing a terminal cancer diagnosis. There was a potential cure, but it was dangerous; it was a life-changing treatment.

Trillions of dollars, pounds and euros were poured into the economy; interest rates soon plummeted to near zero, where they stayed for over a decade. Magically, the world returned to normal. But for most people, it didn't, only they didn't realise it. We will come back to the reasons.

For much of the past two decades, companies (and consumers) benefited from reduced costs. Globalisation helped companies increase their margins and consumers experienced lower prices. As China became the 'world's factory' it flooded Western markets with products. Some boldly bore the 'made in China' label, while others, like the Apple iPhone, had the country of manufacture hidden away in the small print. I bet you didn't know there are over a million China-based merchants on Amazon, contributing much of its revenue. China's low prices kept inflation in check and exploded product choice. Everybody seemed to be a winner.

Another huge benefit for business was the use of well-qualified foreign workers to fuel growth and maintain wage stability (a nice term for keeping wages stagnant). Even the UK's exit from the EU and the pandemic didn't stem the flow. In 2022, net migration increased by 600,000.

I am not a religious person, but I think this quote from the bible explains the results of these events.

 For whosoever hath, to him shall be given, and he shall have more abundance: but whosoever hath not, from him shall be taken away even that he hath.

Thomas Piketty, the French economist, used a formula to express a similar sentiment in his book *Capital in the Twenty-first Century* (2013):

> *r > g, where r = interest in the form of the average return on capital and g = growth rate of the economy.*

I am taking huge logical liberties equating these quotes, but what the hell, they convey what happened. Those with assets prospered. Those who benefited from globalisation and immigration prospered. Those working in industries based on digital technology prospered. Those who didn't have assets or benefit from globalisation or working in digital technologies, didn't prosper – in fact, for large sections of the population, life didn't improve. It got a lot harder.

Between 1998 and 2021, more than 5 million manufacturing jobs disappeared – not all to China; many went to India. Western Europe was similarly affected. Those employed in the industries where China and India excelled lost their jobs.

The massive increase in the money supply pushed down interest rates, doing the reverse to asset prices. Those with wealth had a wonderful time. Those without were left scrabbling to catch up. The stock market surged, as did property prices. London properties have increased by 350% since 2000. After losing 36% of its value in 2008, the S&P 500 index averaged 21% annual return for the next 13 years.

This is how Piketty described wealth and its distribution.

> *For millions of people, 'wealth' amounts to little more than a few weeks' wages in a checking account or low-interest savings account, a car, and a few pieces of furniture. The inescapable reality is this: wealth is so concentrated that a large segment of society is virtually unaware of its existence.*

Accounting for inflation, wages in the US have approximately the same purchasing power as 40 years ago. Most of the real income growth has been experienced by the highest-paid workers. Much the same has happened in Europe. In Italy, wage growth has been stagnant for 30 years. The economic pain has spread into the middle classes, where social mobility has gone into reverse, with the young doubting they will achieve their parents' standard of living. Only 36% of those born in the 1980s own property, unlike the 60% of their parents' generation (born in the 50s and 60s).

And then came the pandemic, which disproportionately affected poorer people. Digital technologies enabled the credentialled 'laptop class' to work from home. Everybody else had to muddle through the best they could. Half of high-income workers watched their savings increase from the safety of their home.

Add to this the effects of rising inflation and interest rates, and you have all the ingredients for an angry electorate. Most people realise that something is awfully wrong but don't know why.

Now here is the amazing thing. As trust in politicians has plummeted, the opposite has occurred for businesses. Blame for all these wrongs is focused on the political class and their supporters. As I mentioned at the beginning of this essay: 'Business is the only institution seen as competent and ethical' (2023 Edleman Trust Barometer).

With so much attention focused on fairness and inclusion, the management class has worked a wonderful trick of engendering trust while accumulating astronomical levels of wealth.

FTSE 100 CEOs earn £119 every time the average UK full-time worker earns £1. S&P 500 CEOs are paid even more, with a whopping average annual salary of $16.7 million (2022). Hard to believe, but that's 272 times the pay of their median workers.

Increasing inflation, rising interest rates and surging energy prices pushed many households into serious debt. Life was much better for the bosses of BP and Shell, each making over £10 million a year. Those running the supermarket giants Sainsbury's and Tesco earned well over £4 million. On average, heads of FTSE 100 companies had an extra £500,000 in salary, an increase of 16%, way above inflation.

The average pay for Google UK's staff is over £256,000 a year. Have some sympathy for Meta (Facebook) UK employees, scratching out an existence on a miserly £134,000 a year. I could go on to quote the record speed at which millionaires and billionaires are being created and the eye-watering salaries and bonuses paid to those in the finance sector. The senior echelons of big business and those employed in the digital industries have prospered while Jo and Jemima Average watched their living standards fall.

Harry Potter, eat your heart out – this is magic indeed.

But that's not all. Business leaders have forged their personal reputations as social reformers as the size of their bank balances exploded. Even Voldemort would be impressed by this trick.

Am I saying that businesses have used their passion for social issues and climate change as a smokescreen to divert the public's gaze away from their personal behaviour and financial rewards? No, not really, because I don't think they are that smart. However, the fact that 20% of the companies listed as the top employers of LGBTQ+ employees are in the finance industry makes me wonder. That 13% of them are legal firms makes me even more suspicious.

I do think corporates have been extremely lucky that the anger of the perpetually angry has been diverted away from class and inequality to the muddy waters of identity politics, climate change and achieving equity.

Those who would have joined the Occupy Wall Street protesters turned their anger on oil companies sponsoring the arts. It's easier getting activists angry about authors accused of transphobia than their publishers' enormous salaries. When the CEO of a bank who's paid millions a year breaches customer confidentiality to the BBC, the progressive left is more concerned with the victim's politics.

Businesses adopted the guise of good global citizens in reaction to external events; it cost them very little (until now) and allowed things to continue pretty much as before. That's about to end as companies are forced to make good on their promises. It's easy to commission a PR campaign promoting your green credentials and pepper your website with reassuring words, but sooner or later, these must be converted into actions.

We have reached that time when good intentions need to become actions.

It's delivery time

Much to my embarrassment, I often slipped the phrase 'pick the low-hanging fruit' into my client consultancy reports. I was a great one for advising management to concentrate on 'going for quick wins', taking the 'no-brainer' decisions (a phrase on many banned lists) and focusing on 'high-return, low-risk decisions'.

Companies wanting to adapt to the changing culture and priorities have been spoilt by a bountiful supply of over-ripe fruit scattered at their feet that also provided some great marketing opportunities.

Continuing with the business metaphors, I think we are entering the next phase, where 'the rubber hits the road'. A few more phrases I have used: 'things just got real', 'when theory is put into practice' and 'where the fun starts'. Let's look at some examples that illustrate this painful evolution from intentions to actions.

The rise and fall of ESG

It all began in 2004 with a report, *Who Cares Wins* – what an imaginative name, a rip-off from the motto of the SAS, Britain's elite special forces (Who Dares Wins).

Funded by the Swiss, this joint initiative of financial institutions, mandated by the UN's Secretary General, developed guidelines and recommendations for integrating environmental, social and corporate governance (ESG) issues in analysis, asset management and securities brokerage.

According to one of the lead authors, there was much debate about what to call the overall topic, with the favourite proposed name being GES, because governance was seen as being the most important issue. The downside was that 'social', being at the end, was likely to be ignored because of its vagueness. 'Environmental' was the 'sexiest' term, so that was put first. Hey presto, environmental, social and governance (ESG) was born with the concept of 'sustainable finance and responsible investment', which was warmly embraced by NGOs but largely ignored by corporates and the capital markets.

Like so much in the world, all this changed following the financial crash of 2008.

In the aftermath, the finance industry was blamed for the resulting horrors. Politicians screamed that bankers were only concerned with profitability and personal earnings and oblivious to the chaos they caused in the real economy. It was time for a very public display of contrition. Lessons had to be visibly learnt. Finance companies had to demonstrate they were doing more than making profits and paying huge salaries. ESG was an off-the-shelf 'feel-good' model just waiting to be adopted. Well, that was the theory.

The young loved the idea of ESG. They now had a way of distinguishing between the bad old profit-obsessed companies and those embracing the rights of all stakeholders, especially those actively reducing their impact on the environment.

Stanford Business School researched the attitudes of investors (2022) and found that Millennials and Generation Z were twice as worried about environmental issues as Baby Boomers. The same age variation occurred for concern about workplace diversity, income inequality and workplace conditions. Young people wanted to know their hard-earned money was invested in the right sort of companies and the Finance Industry was anxious to help.

To further justify the value of ESG funds, studies from 2013 onwards indicated that these ideals not only benefited the environment but also resulted in more profitable companies. Recently, research has shown the exact opposite, but mysteriously that hasn't received much publicity. The most recent study concluded:

'We find no relation between ESG ratings and worldwide stock returns across the period 2001–2020' (2022).

From 2014 to 2018, the value of ESG-rated assets grew at a compounded rate of 16%, and by 2022 they represented a quarter of all market assets – about $3 trillion.

Given this trend, many believed we were observing a transformative shift in business towards universally embracing ESG principles. The finance industry flourishes by offering intricate products that are hard to comprehend and ESG added to this complexity.

And then reality raised its ugly head, asked some difficult questions and the tyres came off.

The fundamental challenge with ESG is determining how to measure consistently and accurately each of its elements and how to weigh one against the other. How do you know if a fund's ESG claims aren't superficial ('greenwashing')? Can a strong 'G' rating compensate for weak 'E' and 'S' scores? The following anomalies would be amusing if they didn't have such major financial consequences for the companies and investors.

Before its directors were arrested, the American crypto exchange superstar FTX had a better 'leadership and governance' ESG score than ExxonMobil, though it only had three directors and ran its accounts using QuickBooks – the same software I use for my tiny business.

In 2022, Tesla, then the world's largest producer of electric cars and the company that has done more than any other to popularise electric vehicle (EV) technology, was removed from the S&P ESG index because of claims of racial discrimination and faults with its governance. It was readmitted in 2023 but not before Elon Musk had belittled the ESG rating, calling it a scam. Maybe the final straw for him was when the world's largest tobacco companies were awarded higher ESG scores than Tesla.

Those defending such nonsense plead the need for flexibility when ranking multiple industries. Critics say it is fatally flawed by the ambiguity of the concept. The war in Ukraine and the resulting disruption of energy supplies have greatly strengthened the latter's case.

ESG investment funds that treated defence companies like the Black Death suddenly changed their opinion when those companies' weapons were being used to fight the evil Vladimir Putin. As is often the case, war changes everything – that's what happened to these companies' ESG rankings. The same happened to oil and gas companies that needed extra funding to increase their output because of Russia's pipeline closures.

BlackRock and Vanguard are the world's largest asset managers and have been vocal supporters of ESG. Both have been forced to change their policies. Vanguard is no longer refusing investments in fossil fuel projects and only approved 2% of the environmental and social resolutions brought by shareholders. BlackRock announced it will vote against climate lobbyists pursuing a ban on new oil and gas production.

You would think that the scientific properties of lithium were well understood and not a political issue. Alas, no, since the metal can be dangerous to humans and is labelled 'toxic' within the EU but not in China, the US and the UK. This difference in definition affects the standards (and costs) of mining and using the substance. It is a perfect example of the messiness of business, which is always about trade-offs. Fossil fuels are bad, but so are the constituents of electric batteries. War is awful; so is the tyranny of unopposed megalomaniacs. ESG frameworks tie themselves in knots trying to rationalise why mining coal is bad, but exposing humans to lithium is OK.

In the middle of this mess are the rating agencies that award the companies' ESG scores. In August 2023, S&P announced that 'effective immediately' it will no longer provide a numerical score and will now rely on text to describe a company's ESG compliance.

Where all of this leaves the EU's proposal that European firms with more than 250 employees must collect and report ESG data on every single company in their supply chain is anybody's guess. Mine is that it will result in a mountain of bureaucracy that favours large companies and creates terabytes of reports that deliver very little. Yet again the EU demonstrates its mastery of regulating. If only it was a fraction as good at innovating.

The ideals of ESG are great and have made lots of financiers lots of money. As to saving the planet? The jury is out and not expected back anytime soon. On a personal note, if four years ago I had sold my 'clean' energy shares and invested in the 'dirty' variety (oil and gas), I would be a lot wealthier now.

DEI – from words to actions

What are we going to do about #MeToo, #BlackLivesMatter and #Trans, a chum of mine was asked by his employees. His is a small company, so if anybody was going to do something, it was him. But what? He threw the question back to his employees and said, 'you come up with a proposal'. Everybody was enthusiastic but very busy. He is still waiting for their ideas. Had this been a larger company, the task would have been handed to human resources (HR).

Sorry if this will annoy those readers who work(ed) in HR but during my time in business, it was seen more as an obstacle than as an enabler. It set the rules for recruiting and firing people and ensured the company complied with employment legislation. I always thought it could do a lot more – especially about skills planning – but mostly, it arranged the mechanics of training courses and recruitment.

As the volume and complexity of employment legislation grew, so did the importance of HR. Between 2011 and 2021 their numbers in the UK grew by 42%, four times as fast as the overall workforce. And then came the interest in diversity, inequality (equity) and inclusion and the birth of DEI that is explained in my essay 'Academia – the trashing of a priceless brand'.

Soon this culture and its associated bureaucracy was embraced by companies, either by expanding the HR function or by creating free-standing DEI departments. The adoption of DEI was boosted when McKinsey started publishing reports claiming there was a link between a company's diversity and profitability – *Diver-*

sity Matters (2015), *Delivering through Diversity* (2018) and *Diversity Wins: How Inclusion Matters* (2020). Not only did diversity demonstrate companies' caring side, it increased their bottom line.

These claims have been repeatedly questioned. Most recently, a paper in *Econ Journal Watch* (2024) concluded:

> *We conducted a quasi-replication of McKinsey's tests using data for US S&P 500 firms and found no statistically significant relations between McKinsey's measures of executive racial/ethnic diversity and not only industry-adjusted EBIT margin, but also industry-adjusted sales growth, gross margin, return on assets, return on equity, and total shareholder return.*

Despite this research questioning the business benefits of diversity, more than 80% of Fortune 500 companies use the 'diversity equals improved business performance' justification on their website.

Note: Many things have changed about business. A constant is senior managers' desire to expand their fiefdom and visibility. This was a once-in-a-lifetime opportunity for HR to extend its influence.

At this point, we enter the world of conjecture. When consultants advise companies about making significant changes, the caveat is always the CEO must be involved and seen to be involved. It seems this advice was readily accepted, with 96% of them agreeing that DEI is a 'personal strategic priority' (*Fortune* magazine and Deloitte, 2020).

What happened next is a Dick Stroud guess. Perhaps senior management perceived DEI as a contributor to better performance but for sure it could enhance their personal reputation. An added bonus was it echoed the views of the progressive elite and their young employees.

So, the cynical view is that it's an inexpensive way of being on the side of the good guys and polishing the shine on the CEO's virtue. Those more trusting of human nature would say it was done with the best of intentions since it was inherently the right thing to do.

The best analogy I can think of is when, back in the late 1990s, companies discovered the importance of 'quality'. Much more than a basic requirement of business, it became a strategic mission the CEO was committed to achieving. Suddenly, companies were undertaking numerous quality audits and achieving 'best practice'. Once the initial enthusiasm waned and it was discovered that these disconnected activities were not working, a more measured approach was adopted. I sense we are approaching the same point with DEI.

DEI is beginning to have a hard time, especially in the US, where it has become a totem political issue. Democrats believe it is a good thing, Republicans aren't convinced. Its problems have been exacerbated by the economic downturn that has reduced staff numbers in the early adopters of the DEI culture.

Although the Supreme Court's decision to end 45 years of affirmative action applies only to academia, it has also made companies more conscious about its use in their recruiting practices. For example, PwC has revisited its diversity targets and decided scholarships can no longer exclude white applicants. It said it was applying 'rigour' to its DEI policies. Well, that's good to know.

Whenever companies attempt to 'change their culture', they invariably make the same mistakes. Adopting DEI is no different, as related in the *FT* article 'Why diversity strategies fail' (2023):

> *There's a rush to implement 'solutions' without thoroughly analysing the problem they are trying to fix. Expectations are set unrealistically high, believing a few one-off – high visibility – events will change embedded attitudes (i.e. running training courses, altering the website text and publishing a new mission statement and staff guides).*

What this article did not mention was the danger when the

cultural change antagonises significant numbers of employees, let alone customers, as illustrated by the previous examples. As long as DEI stayed within the domain of HR it attracted little attention. When it became involved in marketing, new product development and dictating how workers and consumers behave, it was exposed to social media attention – much of it negative.

It's relatively easy to recruit staff and give them a budget and a mission. The box has been ticked, allowing management to bask in the glory of promoting their social credentials. We are now at the point of what comes next. Middle management and their support staff have taken the delegated authority, created the DEI policies and managed their implementation. Now, companies are facing the consequences. As we have seen, these risk angering customers and the media and, worse still, attracting ridicule.

A panel of experts advising the UK government (2024) found employers are anxious 'to do the right thing' yet implement DEI in a haphazard way, without measuring its effectiveness, the harm that can result and whether it contravenes employment law.

Research undertaken by the *Harvard Business Review* attempted to answer 'Why DEI leaders are burning out' and concluded: 'The job demands constant emotional labour and surface acting, particularly for professionals of colour.' This translates to: 'The job demands being nice to people you don't like.' From memory, this is a basic prerequisite of being in business.

I am unsure if we are witnessing the teething problems of corporate DEI or its demise. No doubt it will become embedded in some industries, such as publishing and not-for-profits. My guess is that its influence will wane, becoming another layer of HR administrative bureaucracy.

The trust mark industry

The Kitemark symbol is one of the first trust marks received widespread recognition from both companies and consumers. Established by the British Standards Institute, it verifies a product's quality control standards. For half a century it's been part of British life, appearing on products as diverse as window glass and condoms.

When shopping online first began, trust marks provided consumers with assurance about a website's integrity. Most are long since forgotten. New marks are being introduced all the time. TrustMark, TrustATrader and CheckaTrade are three in the UK that supposedly indicate the quality of electricians and plumbers.

Sometimes, they are government-funded but, in the main, they are businesses making money by verifying that companies meet their standards. Well, that's the theory.

Environmental, social, governance, inclusion, diversity and equity are all nebulous terms with no agreed definitions, let alone benchmarks. Helping companies make sense of them has been a gold mine for the consulting industry and has also attracted organisations selling trust emblems. The following is a brief description of the four that have achieved the most notoriety.

Stonewall was founded in the UK in the late 1980s, drawing its name from the 1969 New York Stonewall riots. The organisation played a pivotal role in challenging and ultimately overturning legislation that prohibited the 'promotion' of homosexuality. That was in 2003, the year it was recognised as a charity championing the rights of gays and lesbians. One of its significant milestones was achieving the recognition of same-sex marriages in 2014.

In 2001 Stonewall entered the trust mark business when it launched its Diversity Champions programme, which validated organisations' recognition of gay and lesbian rights. At its peak, 900 organisations displayed the Stonewall logo, proving their diversity credentials. A major change occurred in 2015 when Stonewall announced it was also working for trans equality and apologising for its past failure to do so.

For trust marks to remain successful, their principles and standards must be easy to understand and valued. Stonewall went from promoting gay and lesbian rights to representing something much more complicated and contentious. By 2021 it was attracting criticism from the media and its original founders, who believed it had diverted from its original purpose.

Stonewall's future depends on how the controversy over trans rights is resolved. When a trust mark becomes a divisive symbol with vocal activists and detractors, it has a problem. That many of those who feel threatened by its actions are gay and lesbian only adds to its difficulties.

B Corp claims to define social, environmental and governance best practices for businesses. With over 1,500 members in the UK, it has grown rapidly among small companies – half employ less than ten people.

Coutts Bank, one of B Corp's largest UK customers, has been a certified member for several years. Those working for the bank may already have realised this, but it became headline news once Coutts terminated the account of Nigel Farage.

News outlets highlighted B Corp's website content that encouraged members to confront 'all forms of oppression' and to challenge 'racist systems, policies, practices, and ideologies'. Members were encouraged to take proactive stances on equality, suggesting that silent neutrality isn't sufficient. This vocal advocacy made Coutts Bank and its parent company a headline news story.

B Corp grapples with issues similar to those of the ESG movement, providing a certification process that accommodates budding enterprises and global giants.

Questions arose, for instance, when Nespresso, a Nestle subsidiary, was granted B Corp status in 2022. How could the standards of a mammoth entity match those of a five-person firm? Furthermore, the organisation is now navigating dilemmas concerning certificate holders servicing the fossil fuel industry.

The trajectory of B Corp will be intriguing to observe. With growing scepticism about ESG's relevance, the organisation faces significant challenges. The Farage incident has etched an image in the media of B Corp as championing 'woke' principles. Henceforth, any PR crisis involving a member will inevitably spotlight B

Corp too. A reputation can be painstakingly crafted and then crumble amid a few major controversies.

Conscious Advertising Network (CAN): When five of the UK's largest advertising companies became members, I wondered if they were aware of CAN's links to the Stop Funding Hate campaign that advocates boycotting conservative news outlets and its connection to the Boycott, Divestment and Sanctions movement campaigning to ban Israeli-produced goods. Even worse, some supporters of these groups advocate the destruction of Israel.

CAN's mission statement is full of nice-sounding phrases about 'harmful content' that 'divides communities' and 'undermines scientific consensus'. All the words that attract senior management, anxious to demonstrate their virtue.

When large companies ally themselves with small activist groups, they have to be extremely careful. Searching social media makes it all too easy to find links between supporters who stray away from the fine ideals into much murkier waters.

Badges for everything: Trust marks have expanded into the badge business. You can get one for being 'Carbon Literate' and as an 'ally' working for the NHS. Become trained to be sensitive to LGBT issues and get a Rainbow badge. Mayors of cities subscribing to environmental ideals, like London, Dakar and Lima, wear a C40 badge.

No doubt the badge movement means well; however, their values often conflict with those of a public holding radically different opinions. Then they appear as ways for 'them' to force 'us' to accept their views. Hiding behind the nice words and the complexity of these issues is a battle over control and exercising power.

When trust marks are evidence of a quantifiable and widely valued virtue, like improving quality, they might work, but mostly they don't. The further they venture into contentious areas, where opinions divide along political lines, failure is the most likely outcome.

Intergenerational angst

'Demography is Destiny' is a phrase packed with meaning. The Bud Lite fiasco resulted from attempting to change the brand's appeal by focusing on the assumed values of younger people. That it was clumsily done doesn't mean the objective was wrong, like many of the other faux pas I have described.

The BBC forever proclaims its need to appeal to younger viewers and minority groups by becoming more 'accessible'. Any consideration about how traditional (for that read older) audiences respond is ignored. In the short term, the result is declining audience numbers. I expect the BBC would say it's playing the long game. I have my doubts.

One of the UK's national treasures, the National Trust, has a similar mission. Making their properties more accessible and appealing to tomorrow's customers (the young) is central to their mission. Decolonising its properties and adhering to a strictly ESG investment strategy (which lost money) alienates some existing visitors and volunteers, but that's inevitable.

Neither organisation is managing the transition very well, but I understand why they are trying.

Baby Boomers, the bulge of children born between 1946 and 1964, have determined much of UK life for the past half century, as they have done in the US. They might be leaving the workforce – in 2024 Gen Z outnumber Boomers in work – but their accumulated wealth means they remain a significant group of consumers. In the US, the over-65s account for the highest share of consumer spending (22%); their grandchildren, the 25–34 year olds, a miserly 14% (2023).

Perhaps the most difficult task facing all institutions, especially business, is managing this intergenerational transition. Despite governments pontificating about the implications of demographics, few of the words have translated into actions.

For nearly two decades, I have been imploring companies to face the inevitability of becoming age-neutral, of orientating themselves to succeed with customers old and young. Three books later, numerous conference speeches and thousands of hours of consultancy projects, I can say with some authority it is mighty difficult. Most companies are clueless, not knowing where to begin. It is one of those mega problems that is easy to understand, easier still to shelve and, when attempted, likely to fail.

Those working in media and advertising agencies have always been young, in their mid-30s. Their experiences and values inevitably determine their attitudes and the work they create. This has long been an issue that has worsened as advertising has become as much about parading a company's values as attracting customers. At some stage, the link between advertising spend and the revenue it generates must be re-established.

Those entering the workforce today have more education credentials (and more debt) than their parents or grandparents. If life were fair, they would be achieving a better standard of living. Alas, fairness seems to have skipped this generation, with social mobility stalling and going into reverse. The generational game of musical chairs has left today's young paying the bills incurred by past generations. Delving below the surface reveals a much more complicated situation. The young of some ethnic groups are doing just fine, while others are not, with much of their wealth prospects determined by that of their parents.

When the friction resulting from the generations' different values is combined with a resentment that the old benefited at the young's expense, you get an unhealthy situation made worse by the economic consequences of the pandemic and the economy's transition to higher interest rates. Yet more ominous changes are occurring. Europe's prosperity is declining as the centre of economic focus moves to Asia and India and, of course, there is the mega bill of net zero to be paid.

All of this makes managing the generational change of customers and employees a whole lot more difficult, as witnessed by the bodged attempts described above. There's a lot to learn and not much time to learn it.

Considering the economic upheavals of the past decade, the business world has emerged largely unscathed. It has embraced the changes in social values and used them to its advantage. Despite the accusations of being in the sway of 'woke capitalism', the blunders have been few and mostly soon forgotten.

How will things play out in the coming years? Let's be honest – I haven't a clue. It all depends on the corporate world's response to the problems detailed in the coming pages.

WHAT'S NEXT?

I doubt if any of the four issues I'm about to discuss keep CEOs awake at night. They should and, in the future, they will. Politicians who face a yawning gap between their rhetoric and voters' priorities should also take note.

So should the folks at Davos who claimed they were 'Rebuilding Trust' (the 2024 theme). Their solution of 'focusing on transparency, consistency and accountability' sounds just more corporate speak.

A mismatch of priorities

The era when DEI and ESG was all about grand announcements and photo opportunities, with politicians and CEOs showcasing their moral standing, is rapidly ending. We have reached 'action time' when the masses must embrace the elite's values, pick up the tab and be grateful. Well, that's the theory.

Speaking from a management consultant's perspective, this task is set to be 'challenging'. In other words, it is going to be exceedingly tough, if not impossible.

Whenever the priorities of the great British and American public are canvassed, they answer: coping with the messiness and difficulties of daily life. Worthy notions like 'transparency and reporting ESG' and 'balancing corporate profits with purpose' are at the bottom of their worry list (PwC research). As much as the media obsesses about climate change, the war in Ukraine, the Capitol Riot, Covid and all things LGBTQQIP2SAA, it's articles about rising crime, energy prices and inflation that grab reader interest (Rasmussen Report).

I think most people are considerate and want to do the right thing. They are tolerant and adopt a 'live and let live' attitude to life. They consider it a personal matter when somebody wants to declare their preferred pronouns (she/her, they/them, he/him and others that are less familiar to many people). Young people favour the habit, the old rationalise it away as a 'passing fad' and keep their fingers crossed it will soon end. The media mostly pours ridicule on the practice. But, when it becomes compulsory, it forces employees not only to change behaviour but to accept the underlying theory of gender identity.

Attitudes harden when customers and employees are expected to change their long-held beliefs and behaviours. Just 6% of Brits favour gender-neutral toilets, with half preferring them to be single-sex. The remainder sit on the fence, thinking both should be provided – the perfect British compromise. Acceptance that male athletes can become female athletes is reducing. Gallup's 2023 study indicates that 70% of Americans believe that gender at birth should dictate sports participation. Whereas Republican voters have consistently expressed this opinion, it's now the predominant view among Democrats too.

The UK consistently holds more liberal views about sexual freedom, except for transgender rights. Less than a third of people believe a person's sex on their birth certificate can be altered, down from 53% in 2019 (British Attitudes Study 2023). Sadly, I expect this reaction will worsen the louder the activists scream.

Something similar is happening with the rules about environmental sustainability. If they are simple to understand, cost nothing to obey and don't impinge on personal freedoms, they are widely accepted. When they breach any or all these conditions, they generate opposition.

Waste recycling is a 'no-brainer' (whoops, another banned phrase). Being forced to install heat pumps and replace the plumbing is a whole different matter. The same reaction occurs when car drivers' freedoms are curtailed. Opposition increases further when the rules are only loosely related to environmental improvements and more about raising additional taxation.

This is stating the blindingly obvious but global warming is a global problem, meaning that all the costs and changes that one country accepts make no difference unless the same is done by all the others, especially those creating the most CO_2 (carbon dioxide).

China creates more greenhouse gases than all the G7 countries combined and is still ramping up its use of coal. During the first three months of 2023 more power stations were sanctioned than in the whole of 2021. And don't forget that 40% of all the nuclear power plants being built are in China.

Some of this power is enabling the country to dominate the world's markets for electric cars (66% of the total in 2022) and produce more than three-quarters of the world's solar panels and lithium-ion batteries.

It is a feat of international diplomacy that China has captured the world's markets for so many 'green products' while increasing its production of CO_2.

Against this backdrop, how do you explain to German and American car and steel workers that they must accept changes jeopardising their jobs and increasing their cost of living while the major competitor nation becomes ever stronger using fossil fuels? As the US and EU impose annual tariffs on the percentage of electric cars sold the problem gets even worse.

Where to stop recounting this farce? Net zero policies have resulted in the UK closing its last steel production facility with the loss of 2,800 jobs. If anything, this will increase the amount of CO_2 in the atmosphere since the steel will now be made in countries with less stringent environmental standards.

Most people believe in equal opportunities regardless of race or gender. Issues arise when the focus subtly shifts from 'equality' of opportunity to 'equity' of results. Instead of ensuring fairness and uniform treatment, corporate processes must be modified to address perceived systemic inequalities, and this means overtly treating people differently. There's much debate about the most deserving, oppressed groups, but a consensus has emerged that it's not white middle-aged men. That said, it doesn't appear that the equity concept has percolated to the composition of company senior management teams.

These examples of grand visions floundering when translated into policies have a common theme. As long as beliefs demand little change and are ensconced in warm supportive language about fairness, inclusivity, sustainability, preventing harm and all the other 'blah' words, the public nods and smiles. They are even easier to accept when they don't take effect for a decade or two. Although the overall objectives might be valence issues (meaning there's an overall consensus), the tactics for achieving them are definitely not.

People are expected to accept changes to their lives that are manifestly ill-conceived. Worse still is the expectation that newly acquired moral values are blindly accepted. Naïve and arrogant in equal measure.

When those dictating the new rules are insulated from their implications, the latent cynicism of the masses turns to anger – the perfect introduction to the next section.

Elites and 'the rest'

The mega-rich have always flaunted their wealth in the pursuit of doing good. I have often wondered how Mr Frick acquired the wonderful works of art in the gallery named after him in New York (the production of coke – the black, not the white stuff). His one-time partner Andrew Carnegie built over 2,500 public and university libraries funded by his steel-making business. John Rockefeller founded the University of Chicago and spent part of his fortune, made in the oil business, eradicating nasty diseases.

Some of today's billionaires have used their wealth for the good of mankind (personkind). Bill Gates and Warren Buffett have spent billions of dollars funding programmes to eradicate small-pox. Like their predecessors, you can argue their benevolence is done to relieve their guilt for making so much money. Whatever the rationale, their legacy delivers tangible benefits.

There is a much larger group of wealthy, influential people who devote their energies to promoting their virtue but expect others to pay.

During the week of the 2022 World Economic Forum in Davos, the elite gathered to ponder the world's problems. I have *The Guardian* newspaper to thank for this amusing description of the event: 'The capitalist version of Lourdes, where the rich try and whitewash their sins.'

According to Greenpeace, over 1,000 private jet flights arrived and departed the airport serving the Swiss luxury ski resort. I wonder if the irony of this occurred to the passengers as they gathered in seminars condemning the evils of air transport on the environment.

News coverage of the annual COP conferences always includes counts of the private jets and the commercial flights ferrying attendees (97,000 in 2023) who board planes to decide why we all should fly less. These events are spectacularly successful in providing forums for the great and good to parade their commitments to reducing global warming. Alas, there's scant evidence of their success but they certainly consume a lot of jet fuel.

Following BLM's demands to defund the police Mark Zuckerberg's charitable foundation contributed $5 million to sympathetic activist groups. At the same time, disclosures by his company (Meta) reveal $42 million spent on his personal protection. Lots of 'security personnel' and the 'procurement, installation, and maintenance of security measures for his residences'.

Nobody blames Meta's founder for protecting himself and his family. But what about those left vulnerable to the record levels of crime in Meta's home city (San Francisco) and the other flashpoints of BLM riots? Sadly, it's the poorest in society, many of them black, who have suffered from declining police numbers.

Groups funded by the billionaire founder of eBay (Pierre Omidyar) were patrons of the activist groups demanding police resources be cut. At the same time, Omidyar was investing in start-ups serving the rising demand for private security. The amount he spends on his personal security is unknown, but I would guess it's considerable.

Michael Bloomberg is a regular user of private air transport and has pledged $500 million to lobby US states to close their coal power stations. It's unlikely that Mr Bloomberg will be inconvenienced by the additional costs and disruption resulting from his actions. Dale Vince, with an estimated wealth of £100 million, funded the protest group Just Stop Oil that caused chaos for Londoners by disrupting traffic. No doubt he has basked in self-righteousness while ambulances are delayed, hospital visits missed and working-class Londoners' lives disrupted. Come October 2023 he decided their protests were pointless. I guess, better late than never. Paul Getty made a fortune from the oil industry and now his granddaughter, a beneficiary of his success, funds protest groups wanting it banned.

These are examples of 'luxury beliefs' that enable the privileged to signal their virtue, knowing their position and wealth insulate them from the consequences. That's bad enough – but when they blatantly break the rules they expect others to respect, it is infuriating.

Politicians are enthusiastic exponents of luxury beliefs. They benefit from a wonderfully generous pension scheme (funded by the taxpayer) and opine on why it's necessary to reduce the state pension that is the only source of income for many people.

Occasionally, the public is roused to anger with a sense of indignation that there is one set of rules for 'them' and another for their leaders. The infamous drinks parties in 10 Downing Street during the pandemic led to the demise of Boris Johnson. The health secretary embracing his lover (who was not in his bubble) resulted in his departure.

There is a delicate balance of trust between employees and their employers and citizens and the government. In exchange for paying taxes and obeying the rules, people expect to be treated fairly and equally. This trust is highly durable, but it has limits and, when it breaks, it is impossible to repair. Those proposing to lead should be very worried as all the measures of trust are in free fall.

A Western-centric view of the world

The words 'imperialist' and 'colonialist' are anathema to Europe's politicians and corporate leaders. Ironically, these people assume the rest of the world shares their values and priorities, and, if they don't, they should.

Back in the day, when European nations and America ruled the world, it might have been that way, but those days are fast disappearing. Europe's economic trajectory is one of decline compared with the world's powerhouse economies. Dreams of equality with the US are long since gone. In 2008, the EU and US economies were about the same size; now the US is a third bigger. China and India threaten America's ability to project its influence through military and technological prowess.

Of course, corporate leaders and politicians (well, some of them) understand that there is a 'changing of the guard'. How could they not – the economic statistics are irrefutable. However, there is a huge difference between understanding the numbers and accepting the consequences. I have another, more pressing concern about the ruling elite's unwillingness to engage with two other global trends – population ageing and migration.

As I write this section, 11,000 migrants have arrived on the Mediterranean island of Lampedusa. By the end of 2023, Italy, and consequently the entire EU, had to accept around 180,000 people from Africa. In 2022, the UK admitted 50,000 illegal immigrants who crossed the Channel from France. Only 2% of illegal immigrants have been removed in the past five years.

Theories abound to explain why so many people are fleeing to Europe. Environmentalists blame it on the famines caused by climate change; others cite wars and unstable national governments. These may be contributing reasons and, certainly, the chaos in Syria and the war in Ukraine have swelled the numbers, giving substance to the term 'the weaponization of migration'. But the long-term driving force is the staggering difference between the social and economic conditions experienced by Western nations and those experienced by much of Africa's population.

The statistics are terrifying. Every two years, Africa adds a population the size of France or Thailand. Half the nations in Africa will double in size by 2050 – the magic date when net zero should be achieved. Yet today, half a billion Africans — more than the EU's population — live on less than $2 a day, with 600 million lacking access to electricity. If this wasn't bad enough, Africa's largest economy (Nigeria) depends on oil and gas for 70% of its export earnings and government revenue, and we all know what is happening with oil and gas. South Africa, the second-largest economy, is in a dire economic state with over half the population living in poverty – lots of reasons to move north.

Throughout the rest of the world, populations are stabilising or declining. Italy, the landing point for Africa's young, has Europe's oldest population (23% are aged 65+). Compared with Japan (30%) that's relatively youthful.

Africa, with its abundance of young people, is only 10 kilometres away from Europe, but its demographics are light years away. Europe's population is shrinking, with each native generation only two-thirds the size of the last.

The cup-half-empty interpretation of these facts is that population ageing will destabilise Europe's economies, made worse by the uncontrolled influx of economic migrants aided by a sophisticated criminal transport network. An optimistic view says, as many do, that Africa's abundance of young people is the perfect solution to Europe's declining numbers. My optimistic side would dearly like to embrace the hopeful outcome but I fear the first scenario is the most likely.

America's problem of illegal immigration is a foretaste of what Europe faces. In 2022, just under 3 million undocumented immigrants arrived, many from Mexico but also from Venezuela, Cuba, Colombia and as far afield as India and China. This has become highly politicised, with Democrats accusing Donald Trump of callousness and crazy ideas about building a wall. Republicans shout back that President Biden's policies (or the lack of them) are disastrous, increasing illegal immigration fourfold – over 10 million have crossed the border during his presidency.

At one time the problem was confined to the border states, but a busing programme, taking new arrivals to Democrat 'sanctuary' cities, changed all that. New York and Denver have declared a state of emergency, Washington requested assistance from the National Guard and Chicago says it's facing a humanitarian crisis. Suddenly, the luxury belief of the metropolitan elite that illegal immigration was a moral duty has become a horrible real problem with thousands of people sleeping on their streets.

The scale of the problem is enormous. Approximately 40% of the populations of Latin America and Sub-Saharan Africa said they would like to move, permanently, to another country if they had the opportunity (Gallup, 2024).

Western nations think the solution is more effective barriers or unlimited kindness. Currently, the policies result in a mix of cruelty and chaos. Rarely is the problem framed by understanding the forces driving the exodus of thousands, soon to be millions, of people. Even discussing the problem results in accusations of being a populist, right wing and the ultimate silencing word, racist.

During my lifetime, we have increasingly viewed the world through the prism of our culture and values. Once upon a time, the plight of Africa was headline news. These days unless it experiences a catastrophic event, it is rarely reported, yet its importance to Europe's stability can't be overstated.

I can attest that few corporate leaders are considering how population ageing will change their business.

The economic repercussions of these events are happening now, causing problems now and revealing the ineffectiveness of the political establishment, now. And this is merely the start. Defending this position, for those who think it needs defending, the retort would be that climate change trumps everything else. As I will explain in the concluding chapter, this is a dangerous and wrong assumption. The relative decline of Western values and economies is a reality. Population ageing and mass illegal migration are realities. All are increasing in importance and visibility. The sooner they are viewed as global emergencies the better.

Are free markets history?

My beloved old car has gone to car heaven, resulting in many long chats with car salesmen. I expected much enthusing about electric vehicles (EVs) but not a word, despite their showrooms stuffed with them. Starting in 2024, at least 22% of cars and 10% of vans sold in the UK must be electric-powered. By 2030, 80% of new cars and 70% of vans must be battery-powered.

These figures aren't expectations or forecasts; they are instructions defined in the Zero Emissions Vehicle (ZEV) mandate. I asked the car salesmen how they would sell so many EVs. Some smiled, some laughed – more of a giggle – and changed the subject.

Normally, government interventions in the market are part carrot and part stick. Dictating which products consumers will buy is all stick. What if customers don't want to buy EVs? I have spent my life in marketing trying to understand consumer behaviour and concluded it's impossible. I am fully behind Mr Toyoda, the chairman of Toyota, the world's largest car manufacturer, who thinks 'customers – not regulations or politics – should decide what car they buy'.

When governments intervene in the markets, it invariably results in unintended consequences. For instance, the ZEV mandate is likely to make European car companies subsidise their

Chinese competitors. Surely that's not what the bureaucrats intended? Plans are already being brewed to create a 'level playing field' – that's code for more intervention and complexity. And of course, the hesitancy of consumers has nothing to do with the limitations of EVs, that's yet more disinformation, says the US's envoy for climate (John Kerry): 'They've been trying to scare people about the range of vehicles, so there's range anxiety out there.'

When forced to decide between increasing the number of EVs on the road and protecting the US domestic car industry, the later easily won – it wasn't a contest. A 100% tariff was placed on the inexpensive, high-quality Chinese cars.

Governments have always dabbled in dictating (or guiding?) the market. Mostly the reasons were obvious to customers and concerned the safety of products. It seems to me the regularity and intensity of these interventions are increasing and being justified for their ability to achieve arbitrary targets and fight ill-defined threats rather than benefit the customer. It seems we are witnessing the demise of the 'customer is king' mentality that determined markets throughout my lifetime.

During the pandemic, I was astonished at the willingness of people to accept bureaucratic interference. Government diktats were accepted with minimal resistance with a collective shrug of the shoulders and the reaction that 'they know best'. Despite now learning that they actually 'didn't know very much' the response remains muted. Most want to treat it all as a bad dream and move on with their lives.

My opinion (maybe it's a hope) is that the pandemic was a one-off and not a good guide to my fellows' willingness to obey institutional directives. As we will see, governments think differently, believing controlling consumer preferences is part of their role.

The Economist calls this move to protectionist government policies 'homeland economics'. Others have named it 'global resilience' or 'economic statecraft'. Whatever the name, it heralds more government intervention in the markets.

Why is this happening, other than the government's instinctive desire for more power? I am sure there are numerous factors involved. The ones topping my list are the:

- Economic turmoil following the 2008 meltdown and the 2020 global recession when governments intervened in the financial markets.
- Disruption and inflation resulting from the pandemic's closure of Asia's factories and energy disruption caused by the Ukraine war.
- Global threats to society, real and imagined: global warming, generative AI, inequality, fake news (I am sure you can complete the list)...
- Belief that only governments can fix complex problems.

The foundation of state safeguarding is legislation. One thing nobody contends is the ability of bureaucrats to create rules and regulations. National and supranational agencies have been busy. I will spare you a mind-numbing comprehensive list and provide some examples.

The EU's Digital Services Act, antitrust policies (Articles 101 and 102) and General Data Protection Regulation (GDPR) are saving you from drowning in a sea of fake news and misinformation, protecting your personal details and safeguarding you from the big bad bullying Google, Meta and X. Well, that's the theory. Europe might have failed to compete with US technology companies, but it can influence them by using its legislation tendrils. Fining Apple $540 million for supposedly operating 'unfair trading conditions' is the latest example.

Just as the illogicality of ESG metrics is being exposed, the Corporate Sustainability Reporting Directive, the Sustainable Finance Disclosures Regulation and the Science-Based Targets initiative mandate companies to collect and report them.

My assistant ChatGPT reminds me the EU has been busy creating legislation to protect consumer rights, ensure equality between online and offline commerce, plot the move to green energy, stamp out commercial unfairness, protect food safety and a lot, lot more.

National governments are prolific creators of new rules. The UK's Energy Security Bill defines how homes should be heated and insulated, supported by the financial services rules limiting lending to energy-inefficient properties. The Online Safety Bill is intended to keep us all safe from Russians and paedophiles and hold back the torrent of fake news.

This is not the right place to discuss the need for or practicality of any of this legislation. What it does illustrate is the expansion of the state's authority to curtail the freedoms of companies and citizens. It also shows the bias it creates, favouring large companies that can afford to navigate these legislative minefields.

There's no doubt that commercial success is increasingly determined by satisfying the needs of the state rather than those of customers. I wonder how much that is appreciated by corporate management. Knowing the fallibilities of the state when it comes to governing effectively, I doubt if this is a sustainable position.

The business community has brilliantly navigated society's changing values and employed them to continue making money – lots of it. By adopting the language of environmental and social justice, its leaders have been able to amass wealth and power. Mistakes have been made but, until now, they have been quickly forgotten.

I believe this Faustian pact is quickly unravelling. As the priorities of business and its customers diverge there is only ever one winner – the customers.

The pandemic and, to a lesser extent, the excitement about AI have diverted companies' attention from the megatrends changing how they operate. Managing demographic change and the shift in the world's economic centre of gravity away from the West can't be ignored.

We will look back at the early 2020s as a time of business stability. A period before business had to grapple with problems of its own making.

LANGUAGE – FROM BEAUTIFUL TO BRUTAL

But society cannot be indiscriminate where the pacification of existence, where freedom and happiness themselves are at stake: here, certain things cannot be said, certain ideas cannot be expressed, certain policies cannot be proposed, certain behaviour cannot be permitted without making tolerance an instrument for the continuation of servitude.

Herbert Marcuse, *A Critique of Pure Tolerance*

The great enemy of clear language is insincerity. When there is a gap between one's real and one's declared aims, one turns, as it were, instinctively to long words and exhausted idioms, like a cuttlefish squirting out ink... Political language is designed to make lies sound truthful and murder respectable and to give an appearance of solidity to pure wind.

George Orwell, *Politics and the English Language*

Consider how challenging life would be if, by my calculation, two plus two resulted in five, but your arithmetic produced seven. Fortunately, transcending race, age, gender, politics and wealth, we universally concur that the sum is four. If only this level of accuracy were mirrored in our use of language. Just think of all the arguments and misunderstandings that would be avoided. No more confusion over the meaning of words, no more 'I thought you meant XYZ not ABC.'

A study by Harvard and Google identified over a million words in the English language – the *Oxford English Dictionary* (OED) has 600,000 entries – yet the breadth of our vocabulary is 'only' 20,000 to 35,000 words. This is a guesstimate, but it's the number most often quoted, probably because it first appeared in the prestigious *Economist* magazine. We might hazard a guess at what these words mean, but I doubt if we employ them all in our everyday conversation – I certainly don't.

It's inevitable that the popularity of words changes and their meanings evolve. The March 2023 update to the OED had 1,400 revised and updated entries, and over 700 new words and phrases. New technology and social media accounted for many of these entries. Do you impress friends by slipping 'deepfake', 'antigram' and 'groomzilla' into your conversations? The smartphone gave us many more, including 'selfie' and 'app'.

What about the OED's 2022 word of the year – goblin mode, as in: 'During lockdowns lots of people embraced goblin mode, getting up late, eating too much and pretending to work.' Perhaps goblin mode is the standard dress for those WFH – another term destined for the OED.

A rich and evolving language, a 'living language', is one of the joys of life. However, there are things about its evolution that concern me. My perception is that, instead of enjoying an expanding richness, our use of language is being stifled and contorted. It seems as though word meanings are being manipulated and converted into tools for control and conflict. Is our shared comprehension of the language dissolving as it divides into silos defined by our beliefs?

George Orwell was fearful that words could be used to limit and corral thinking and behaviour. In this essay, I want to investigate the parallels between his concerns and what's happening today. Is the language really being captured and used as a weapon to silence, mislead and manipulate? No doubt this has always occurred but, in my view, not to the same extent or happening so fast. As much as I resist blaming social media for all of society's ills, I am sure it shares the guilt, as does academia's obsession with identity politics. However, I sense there are other more powerful and calculating agents involved.

It's all too easy to jump to conclusions, naming the culprits and speculating about their methods and motivations. I would hate to reinforce the dominant narrative without attempting to understand what's happening. Having struggled to pass O-level English doesn't make me an obvious candidate for the task, but I intend to try. The result might not be the truth, but it will be 'my truth'.

THE NATURAL EVOLUTION OF LANGUAGE

Mr Collins in *Pride and Prejudice* is forever using the word 'condescension' as an expression of praise, especially when describing his patron, the Lady Catherine de Bourgh, who 'is all affability and condescension'. In the bible, the word expresses a similar meaning: 'Knowest thou the condescension of God' (1 Nephi 11:16), as it does in the OED: 'affability to one's inferiors, with courteous disregard of difference of rank or position'. Today, it's a word of criticism about a patronising attitude.

Samuel Taylor Coleridge, the philosopher–poet, invented the word 'clerisy' to describe a secular group of learned individuals who could 'diffuse through the whole community knowledge which was indispensable'. After an initial period of popularity, the word all but disappeared. Recently it came back to life, however, describing the same group of people but with very negative associations. When a *Wall Street Journal* headline says, 'The public-health clerisy rediscovers a principle of immunology it derided throughout the pandemic,' it is criticising, not praising.

The word 'literally' has literally performed a somersault in meaning. The classical use of the word meant exactly as stated – 'The cat saw the snake and its fur literally stood on end.' I used it in a figurative way, not expecting the word to jump from the page and do a backflip.

'Awful' originally meant arousing or inspiring reverential respect, mixed with wonder or fear. Today the positive meaning has disappeared, leaving something unpleasant or terrible.

When Shakespeare used the word 'bully' in *Henry V* it was as a term of endearment: 'From my heart strings I love the lovely bully.' We all know that today, being called a bully has nothing to do with loving feelings. The word's meaning is again in transition. Following the resignation of a government minister accused of bullying, it now seems to mean 'unreasonably and persistently aggressive conduct' with 'aggressive' meaning anything from a punch on the nose to a mild rebuttal.

I am sure an English scholar can explain how each of these changes occurred. There was no 'hidden hand' involved; they happened spontaneously. They are examples of passive change, as are the words in the next section.

Words come and go

Words slip out of use for no obvious reason. My mother often referred to somebody as being 'dapper' to signify their stylish appearance, as in 'why can't you [me] be like your cousin who is always so dapper?' My first cars were always 'jalopies'; another phrase describing their age and poor state of repair was 'rust buckets'.

Dredging my memory provided lots of other retired words. 'Swell' – something that was excellent or first-rate. 'Fiddlesticks' – a word expressing nonsense or disbelief. 'Balderdash' – senseless talk or writing. Somebody foolish was called a 'wally' or a 'berk'. When did you last hear somebody referred to as a 'geezer' or a 'duffer'? I can't remember when I last used the word 'chubby' or 'stout' when describing somebody's body shape. All gone to word heaven.

Then some words suddenly reappear after periods of repose. Young people spray the word 'epic' about with gay abandonment. (We will come back to 'gay' in a short while.) Once 'epic' implied something heroic or grand in scale; it now is applied to the smallest of events – 'thanks for the beer – epic'.

'Hipster' started life in the 1940s in the world of jazz, transitioned to a fashionable item of clothing and has burst into general use as a person wanting to appear outside the cultural mainstream yet following the latest trends and fashions. Would they be 'cool' or maybe the opposite of 'cool'? Whatever, they would be prime customers for anything preceded with the word 'artisan', as in artisan bread and artisan cheese. Why did 'curate', once used to describe an assistant to the parish priest, start appearing in the context of digital 'content', both words redefined by digital technology?

Like plants and animals, when words are stranded on an island they often develop their own evolutionary path. When I talk with my Australian friend, he uses words that are extinct in the UK. If they ever made it to America they are long since gone.

I no longer use 'blimey' and 'crikey' when expressing surprise, or excitement – he often slips them into a sentence. 'Brolly', used as an abbreviation for umbrella, is more commonly used in Australia – yes it does rain 'Down Under' (now a rarely used phrase). I remember saying, 'I had a quick squint at the cricket results'; he would say 'squiz'. I would say 'mosquito', he would say 'mozzie'. 'He's a good bloke' is now associated with Australia, not where it originated. Never ask Australians for 'thongs' unless you intend to wear them on your feet.

Sometimes, words find their way back home. 'Strewth' (surprise or dismay) and 'no problem' (that's OK) – often followed by 'mate' – have been re-imported and added to the richness of the native language. Where would we be without words adopted from

Hindi and other regional languages – bungalow, chutney, avatar, guru, yoga, jungle, pyjamas, shampoo and veranda? No doubt, some would say they are examples of colonial language appropriation. I find the idea of language evolving in a Darwinian way fascinating and uplifting. What I am not so happy about is when this evolution is manipulated to serve the purpose of specific groups of people. Let's begin with the mostly harmless but annoying way academics use words to impress rather than communicate.

Words used to impress

In the essay 'Academia – the trashing of a priceless brand' I detail the infuriating way academics employ complicated and specialised language to flaunt their intellect.

I understand that certain disciplines, especially the sciences, have their own words. If you are a physicist, you must use words like entropy, fission, fusion, quantum and anabatic because they have exact meanings. Medicine has thousands of words naming diseases and parts of the body with no everyday language equivalent.

But why do academics need to use 'pedagogy' rather than 'teaching methods' – 'othering' rather than 'making somebody an outsider' – 'epistemology' when 'the theory of knowledge' would do just as well? Then there are terms like 'intersectionality' that are currently very popular and have something to do with the concurrence of multiple types of 'inequality'. Watch out for 'solastalgia', a form of emotional or existential distress caused by environmental change that's rapidly gaining popularity. In my experience, social scientists are the worst offenders, a view shared by others.

Michael Billig, himself a social scientist, explained why this occurs in his book *Learn to Write Badly: How to Succeed in the Social Sciences* (2013). He believed technical terminology is often less precise than simpler language and was infuriated with nouns like 'reification' or 'nominalisation' rather than the corresponding verbs 'reify' or 'nominalise'. Specialist terminology, in his view, was primarily about signalling membership of the academic club.

Fifty years ago, Stanislav Andreski's book *Social Sciences as Sorcery* said much the same thing but in even more forthright language, claiming the discipline had an 'abundance of pompous bluff and paucity of new ideas'. He thought much of the published research was 'pretentious and nebulous verbosity, interminable repetition of platitudes and disguised propaganda'.

It would seem the 'academicisation' of language – another dreadful word – isn't new. Some researchers recognise the problem and provide plain-language summaries of their findings. Most do not and leave it to the reader to decipher the text.

Words used to insult

The old and young have always exchanged jibes. I know the phrases 'old fogey' and 'old codger' were part of my vocabulary. My parents often accused me of thinking of them as old 'fuddy duddies' and 'stick in the muds'.

When the old criticised the young it was for their attitudes and beliefs. I have recollections of being called 'idealistic', 'naïve' and 'utopian' by my parents. I cringe when I think how right they were.

Today's banter between the generations uses harsher and more venomous words that are more about beliefs, class and race. One of the ritual foods eaten at Xmas is the smoked joint of a pig called a gammon. In 2018 it was *Collins English Dictionary*'s word of the year – and not because of its culinary popularity. First appearing with this meaning in Dickens' *Nicholas Nickleby*, it describes the character becoming 'a little too fervid, or perhaps even hyperbolic'. The term was adopted by the young to describe older people wanting to leave the EU, who they perceived as being angry, white and presumably red in the face because of their fury, bigotry and nationalism. My memory of the EU referendum was that remain voters were the most furious and emotionally fraught group – young and old – especially when they lost!

Karen was once a popular girl's name but has morphed into an insult for a stereotype of middle-aged, middle-class women oozing white privilege. In the US, they would be assumed to be Republicans; in the UK, a leave voter.

Undoubtedly the most popular insult about the young is the word 'snowflake'. First used in the 2010s, it's still the go-to term when young people do the things young people do. Over time its meaning has expanded from the young's fragility to include their sense of entitlement, ease of being offended and inability to deal with opposing opinions.

Even the words used to describe generational age groups have become charged with meaning. Boomers (a shortened version of the phrase 'Baby Boomers') are people born between 1946 and 1964. Now the term means older white people who are angry, closed-minded (especially to technology and all things gender-related) and out of touch with contemporary life. To boot, they are probably living in expensive houses, preventing the young from joining the property ladder.

Millennials, born between 1981 and 1996, were the first group to be labelled snowflakes. As they have passed into early middle age, the insult is hurled at Gen Z, born 1997–2010. Hopefully, we are seeing the end of these age group caricatures. Pew Research, a major US market research organisation, is stopping its use of them, citing a 'growing chorus of criticism about generational research and generational labels'. Maybe it will extend the rationale and drop the term 'boomer'.

Now here's the strange thing. I never hear parents using these terms about their own children, or vice versa. They are sneering insults directed at faceless stereotypes. I don't for an instant think this coarsening of the language is being manipulated. The media adopted the terms because they make for good clickbait headlines that increased in ferocity during the EU referendum, which had a clear generational divide in the voting.

Shortly we will see how words used to insult other groups in society have become even more venomous – not by accident but by intent.

Words that signal our virtue

Once you become conscious of 'blah words', words tossed into sentences to signal the writer's progressive credentials, you see them everywhere. Perhaps media style guides now set a minimum number of mentions for 'renewable', 'inequality', 'inclusion', 'socially engaged', 'diversity', 'sustainability', 'evidence-based' and that most precious of commodities 'agency'.

The half-life of blah words is short. For a month or two they are everywhere and then a new one appears. Is 'allyship' soon to take the top spot? Certainly, North Face, the outdoors clothes supplier, thinks so, having launched its 'Allyship in the Outdoors' training course. Spend an hour taking the online course and you are equipped to make the outdoors more diverse and along the way you get 20% off your clothes purchases.

The World Health Organization's digital health tool is to be based on 'principles of equity, innovation, transparency and data protection and privacy' and will uphold 'sustainable development'. Wow – aren't you impressed? But hold on a minute, what do these words mean?

Why does the latest report from the UN about the evidence of climate change need to be peppered with the words 'equity' and 'inequity'? As in 'social equity', 'global equity', 'equity and justice', 'patterns of inequity' and the report's intention to 'deliver, progress and advance equity'. Astonishingly, nowhere does the report define this precious and much sought after 'equity'.

I can guess what it means, and no doubt so can you. Our chances of reaching the same answer are slim.

Other words that sound good but are hard to define are 'society' and 'communities', although I sense these are going out of fashion. My old profession of consultancy is guilty of littering sentences with vague, impressive-sounding words. Let's be honest, my reports often contained 'synergy', 'synergistic', 'paradigm shift', 'disruptive', 'bandwidth', 'scaleable' and advice to focus on 'low-hanging fruit'. I shudder to remember this linguistic diarrhoea!

Organisations are often 'committed to' and 'embracing' something or another – that's when they are not 'championing' and being a good 'corporate citizen'. How many emails have you received (hopefully not sent) using the term 'I am reaching out'? A sure sign it will be consigned to the bin.

In 2007, HP wrote, 'Acting as a responsible corporate citizen is embedded into our company culture, our management philosophy and business principles.' Time has moved on, and so has the popularity of blah words. Now HP declares, 'Our focus on diversity, equity, and inclusion not only fuels our culture, innovation and growth mindset – it makes a difference in the workplace, the marketplace, and our communities.' What a pile of – very short words associated with defecation.

Politicians are experts at using blah words to distract the listener from the abject nonsense they are speaking. Without a doubt, Biden's vice-president of the US leads the field in this peculiar skill. Here are her insights about the meaning of culture:

> *Culture is – it is a reflection of our moment and our time. Right?* [Long pause.] *And present culture is the way we express how we're feeling about the moment, and we should always find times to express how we feel about the moment. That is a reflection of joy. Because, you know,* [long pause and giggles] *it comes in the morning. We have to find ways to also express the way we feel about the moment in terms of just having language and a connection to how people are experiencing life. And I think about it in that way, too.* [More giggles.]

More examples of her linguistic gymnastics appear in 'Politics – more showbiz than statesmanship'. A word of warning: reading her missives can become addictive. Politicians in the UK are no better – well, a bit better. The leader of the Labour Party launched a 'bold new initiative' wanting all children to learn 'oracy' so they become 'empowered' and valued members of their 'community'.

Finally, there is the trick of concatenating (perhaps I should say adding) blah words together to increase their importance:

> *In the face of stark inequality, the pursuit of equity and inclusion becomes a socially-engaged, evidenced-based initiative that empowers individuals with a sense of agency, acknowledging diversity as an essential ingredient in fostering a society where everyone feels included and in control of their destiny.*

Even better:

> *In a society marred by inequality, the feeling of agency becomes vital: it's through our commitment to evidenced-based strategies, fostering diversity and inclusion, and actively promoting equity, that we can empower individuals to be socially-engaged, thus increasing their sense of control and mitigating societal disparities.*

I must give ChatGPT credit for these sentences that would enhance the missives of any politician, government department, charity or not-for-profit, plus a lengthening list of 'virtue signally' companies.

Words that inflate in value

Inflation in the value of words is no different from the blight that plagues money, halving its value in the past 25 years. Words that once were reserved for extreme conditions have become commonplace.

A 'revelation' was a disclosure or communication by divine or supernatural means. Now it means the latest thing a journalist discovered. Feeling 'exhausted' is to be drained of strength or resources; now it means feeling a tad tired. Covid is to blame for the word 'epidemic' soaring in popularity. Rather than referring to an acute disease affecting many individuals, it's used to describe a few instances of something occurring.

Once you become conscious of word inflation you see it everywhere in how people write and speak. These words are tossed around like confetti with no thought to their proper meaning: survivor, vulnerable, toxic, poverty, blunder, disaster, chaos and catastrophic. Yesterday's *Financial Times* told me that 'Wildfires bring apocalyptic scenes on New York Streets'. Today's forecast is sunny and clear skies.

No event or prediction is worthy of mention unless it can be tagged with 'nightmare', 'crisis' or 'breakdown'. If this isn't enough there is always 'awesome', 'epic' and 'genius' to accentuate the meaning. 'Emergency' was once the 'state of exception', but has become unexceptional. Nobody is ever right- or left-wing; they are always ultra-right or ultra-left.

The proliferation of online content, vying for our attention, is one of the reasons extreme words have become the default. It's like how the noise level in restaurants keeps increasing as customers raise their voices to be heard. If you want to be read, then use shouty words.

There's another, more manipulative reason that explains what's happening. In the manual 'How to be an Activist', the first chapter is about getting attention. Those wanting to 'Stop XYZ' (your choice of good cause) know that disrupting events – at no risk or cost to themselves – generates media attention. That most of it is negative and derisory doesn't seem to matter. Their justification and defence is they are preventing an imminent 'crisis', 'epidemic', 'nightmare', 'extinction', 'Armageddon' or whatever. If these sound a tad extreme, then military analogies are employed. They are involved in a 'battle', worse still, a 'war', or trying to defuse the 'time bomb' that's about to engulf humanity.

XYZ can be climate change, drugs, poverty, terror, inequality, inflation, loneliness, suicides, housing shortage, mental health, hate speech and a host more apocalyptic problems. Is it any surprise that the *Collins English Dictionary*'s word of 2022 was permacrisis? The authors of the Davos *Global Risk Report* (2023) went one better and labelled our condition a polycrisis.

Are we really lurching from crisis to crisis, petrified we will disappear down a mega pothole, perpetually terrified of 'unsafe' words?

Those trying to remould society, the army of activists, have brilliantly exploited catastrophising their messaging, ensuring it is always laced with words expressing the most extreme outcomes. They know that policymakers are terrified of being blamed for catastrophes and the media adores using the word in its headlines because it generates oodles of clicks.

The most worrying aspect of word inflation is how governments justify their actions by portraying them as necessary to 'fight' (yet more war language) the enormity of the problem. The pandemic soon became a 'battle' that governments could win only if their citizens followed a strict set of instructions. I don't intend to discuss the justification for Covid restrictions, but there's no doubt that hyping the language was intentional, not an accident. A similar strategy is being adopted to 'fight' climate change.

Our lives are being lived under the continual threat of disaster that justifies government action. From nowhere, artificial intelligence (AI) has become an existential threat to mankind, demanding strict control. The crisis in healthcare delivery justifies radical changes to primary care. Car pollution is threatening the health of young people, resulting in traffic restrictions and charges.

As a lifelong marketer, I understand why words are captured and used to manipulate our behaviour. However, it can result in horrible unintended side effects. When our earphones are always at maximum volume, our hearing is damaged. I think the same is happening with our sense of wellbeing, which is suffering from continuous bombardment with imminent dangers.

Inciting fear is something to be done sparingly. Used to excess, it leads to a sense of hopelessness and inaction. This is my armchair psychologist's explanation for the 'plague' (now I am using extreme language) in mental health issues, especially among the young. A global study by *The Lancet* reports that three-quarters of young people believe the future is frightening, giving them feelings of sadness, helplessness and guilt. I know this is a complex condition, resulting from numerous factors. I am certain that word inflation is one of them.

Words that confuse rather than explain

In the film *Too Big to Fail,* Hank Paulson (secretary of the US Treasury) is grappling with the 2008 financial crisis and talking to an aide about a bank bailout. His PR director interjects that it's not a bailout but a 'very large purchase assistance plan (VLPAP)'.

The US Department of Defense recently announced that the Airborne Object Identification and Management Synchronization Group (AOIMSG) was renamed the All-domain Anomaly Resolution Office (AARO). These are the people who look for UFOs, so why not just call it the UFO Department? You will be relieved, maybe disappointed, to know that its director 'stated clearly for the record that it hasn't found any'.

Using words, abbreviations and euphemisms to confuse or mislead isn't new. For ages, staff haven't been made redundant but 'let go'. Companies are never in the business of war and destruction but 'defence'. Selling to countries with dubious human rights records is 'bridging East and West'. Being 'race conscious' has long since replaced 'positive discrimination' and nobody ever dares use the term 'negative discrimination'. And when did 'second-hand' get discarded and replaced with 'pre-owned' or, worse still, 'pre-loved'? My current favourite appeared in the document Coutts Bank produced justifying it dumping the politician Nigel Farage. They suggested he was put on a 'glide path' to being removed from the bank. That sounds so gentle, conjuring up images of fluffy white clouds.

These are all amusing and easy to understand. What concerns me are phrases like 'gain of function' to disguise the true meaning – manipulating microorganisms to increase their transmissibility and virulence. It seems 'patient zero' (the first person with Covid) was a gain of function researcher at the Chinese Wuhan Institute working on a SARS-like coronavirus, not somebody gutting fish in the local market.

Increasing the money supply or 'printing money' sounds a tad dodgy (my term for suspicious). Much better to give it a name with positive connotations (quantitative easing). 'Quantitative' sounds precise and 'easing' sounds harmless and pleasurable. Before 2008, the term 'subprime' was rarely mentioned. Prime means 'of first importance' so being sub – next, lower or beneath – cannot be that bad – can it?

When it emerged that $12 trillion of subprime loans had been made and the true meaning was that these loans had gone to 'borrowers with poor credit records' it nearly destroyed the global financial system. Then came the 'solution' – quantitative easing – $25 trillion dollars of new money magically created by the central banks. If you have wondered why property prices have doubled since that time, there's your answer.

Putting 'smart' in front of cities, motorways and utility meters raises our expectation that they will be transformed like our phones. The term sounds positive and exciting and raises expectations of improved performance and functionality. Smart motorways have ended in failure. As smart cities become a reality, they mean a rationale for restricting drivers and a way of generating taxes. Smart meters haven't been so smart. Costing £13 billion to implement, six years behind schedule and still beset by problems.

As I am writing, politicians and technologists are in a terrible tizzy about AI and, for reasons I don't understand, want to impose regulations and restrictions. Of course, they don't say this but talk about the technology needing to be made 'more responsible' and have 'guardrails'. This makes it sound more caring, like putting stabiliser wheels on a child's bicycle or mobility assistance for the elderly. And, of course, the technology must be made sustainable.

Some words sound as if they have a precise meaning but are meaningless. All self-respecting organisations work with their 'stakeholders' and ensure their decisions are 'evidence-based', always guarding against 'systemic' or 'institutionalised' XYZ (all the words ending with an ism).

Being 'carbon neutral', 'net zero' and 'sustainable' are the most frequently used environmental claims in advertising, according to the Advertising Standards Authority. Their research discovered that the Great British Public had only the scantiest idea of what they meant. That's not surprising since they don't have universally agreed definitions. But they do sound like good things and 'must haves' for an environmentally conscious organisation.

Back in the day, applying to university was a simple affair, relying on your A-level grades. Today's applicants must contend with the harmless-sounding 'contextual admissions' process. It really should be called 'admission by privilege', but that doesn't sound so friendly. The admission dice are stacked against you if your parents went to university, you attended private school and you live in a prosperous neighbourhood. Until the US Supreme Court made positive discrimination illegal, Chinese Americans' numbers were limited at Ivy League universities.

Then there is the minefield of selecting the words to use when talking about race. Is the phrase 'people of colour' still appropriate or should it be BIPOC (black, indigenous and people of colour)? Can we use the word Black or is it black? You can hear eggshells cracking the instant you start the sentence.

How do we cope when the language contains so many words that don't mean what they say or don't mean anything at all? For most of the time I think we ignore them by using the equivalent of the noise reduction feature in earphones. We press the button and filter out the noisy background chatter.

I wonder what horrors are disguised by words we are currently filtering? Among the chatter, there are words that slip past our conscious mind and only when it is too late do we understand their true meaning.

Words that get hijacked

My personal trainer's son is in the GB elite gymnastics squad, a member of a select group, the best in the country. But, when 'elite' is attached to the metropolitan, it's anything but praise; it describes a self-selecting group of pretentious people. Captured by the media, the word has been turned into a term of abuse. This is a benign example of changing a word's meaning. There are many others where it has been far more calculating.

For years, the word 'gay' meant homosexual men. Later, it included women who were lesbians. Then, in the 1990s, the term LGBT started appearing. Like Topsy, it kept growing, first to LGBTQIA+ and now to LGBTQQIP2SAA, and includes the word 'queer', once a derisory word for gay. This all gets very confusing for those not part of this 'community'. The *Trans Journalists Association Styleguide*, all 14,000 words, helps the unwary avoid making a gender faux pas.

Even my gay and lesbian friends are confused by the ever-changing terminology. More than that, they are livid that activists – they use more abusive phrases – have taken control of their language.

At the beginning of this book, in 'What's the book about?', I explained why the word 'woke' so irritates me, arguments I am not going to repeat. It is worth mentioning its rarity as a word that has undergone a meaning reversal, shifting from positive to negative and, in the process, losing all precision while evoking exceptionally strong emotions.

During my twenties, climate science was predicting global cooling. A decade later, it reversed and global warming was the concern. That's science for you – it keeps changing and is not 'settled' as some politicians claim. During the early 2000s, a new term appeared, 'climate change'. An adviser to the Bush administration is said to have popularised the term, believing it was less alarming. The renaming had begun a decade earlier when the UN published its first report with 'climate change' in the title.

In 2019, *The Guardian* newspaper advised its journalists to stop using 'global warming', replacing it with 'global heating' or 'climate emergency'. Occasionally the publication goes one step further and slips in a comment about 'climate terror'. I assume that 'warming' was too passive, lacking drama, not threatening enough. Who doesn't like being warm? This beautifully illustrates the intentional use of emotive words to heighten the impact of manipulating behaviours rather than communicating.

So far, we have looked at language's power to suppress or generate attention. Mostly this has been light-hearted, although some of the consequences have been dreadful. We now consider how words are captured and used as weapons to attack or silence opposition. This is a territory Orwell would recognise and warn against. It is something I find deeply disturbing.

USING WORDS AS WEAPONS

Fifty years ago, Saul Alinsky published his book *Rules for Radicals* (1971), which is described as a 'pragmatic primer for realistic radicals' and sets out the theory and techniques to become a successful activist. He wrote the book out of desperation, believing the new generation of radicals was idealistic, disorganised and set to fail.

Does the following description sound familiar? These are his opening words about the state of activism in the late 1960s.

> *Today's generation is desperately trying to make some sense out of their lives and out of the world. Most of them (activists) are products of the middle class. They have rejected their materialistic backgrounds... They have seen the almost unbelievable idiocy of our political leadership – in the past political leaders... were regarded with respect; today they are viewed with contempt.*
>
> *This negativism now extends to all institutions, from the police and the courts to 'the system' itself. We are living in a world of mass media which daily exposes society's innate hypocrisy, its contradictions and the apparent failure of almost every facet of our social and political life.*

Today's young and angry appear to have read the book, since much of his theory is seen in their campaigning. Those coming to his work in the turbulent years of the 1970s are now the establishment. They also seem to have remembered his advice.

I want to consider two of his rules associated with the power of language (my underlining).

> _Ridicule is man's most potent weapon. It is almost impossible to counterattack ridicule. Also, it infuriates the opposition, who then react to your advantage._
>
> _Pick the target, freeze it, personalize it, and polarize it. The opposition must be singled out as the target and 'frozen'._

I imagine when activists muster for combat training, their first lesson is about owning and deploying words as weapons. This begins by wrapping yourself in warm-sounding words – think of it as body armour. Being a progressive, passionate about equality and sustainability and the rights of minorities is a good starting point. None of the words means much, but they sound reassuring and virtuous. Now, you are ready to use the language to attack.

Memories of the pandemic are still fresh in our minds, so it's a good place to start. The efficacy of vaccinations was probably the most contentious issue, closely followed by the usefulness of face-masks. The narrative about Covid rapidly solidified as the science became 'settled' – I am sure you don't need me to remind you about the details.

Most people, especially during the early months, obediently accepted government instructions. As the restrictions to civil liberties unfolded, stories began appearing of fanciful conspiracy theories. For example, the pandemic was manufactured to extend the aims of the Davos elite orchestrated by Bill Gates. Soon, anybody doubting the official narrative was attacked with the words, 'covidiots' and 'covid deniers'. Those believing the government's intentions weren't all benign were labelled as members of the 'tin foil brigade'.

This statement from a California state senator (the underlining is my emphasis) illustrates the escalation of the language directed at those questioning vaccinations:

> *These extremists have not yet been held accountable, so they continue to escalate violence against the body public... We must now summon the political will to demand that domestic terrorists face consequences for their words and actions.*

The word weapons had been deployed and adopted by willing supporters, including most of the mainstream media (MSM). Alinsky's advice to ridicule and personalise the attacks worked well.

Within months of the lockdown policies being enacted their scientific legitimacy was being questioned by highly credentialled scientists and established journalists. Yet they were met with the same ridicule. Question any aspect of the narrative and you were fair game. When three highly acclaimed scientists issued a statement proposing an alternative to the blanket lockdown strategy, they were attacked with a firestorm of abuse. A director of the National Institutes of Health demanded 'there needs to be a quick and devastating published takedown of their premises'. Journalists meekly obliged and, as by magic, the media was teeming with accusations about the flawed science of 'three fringe epidemiologists', a term that mysteriously kept appearing.

The US administration picked its target and attacked with ridicule – Alinsky would have been proud. This might have achieved the short-term aim of silencing dissent, but its long-term effects are frightening. An editorial in the *Wall Street Journal* concluded: 'The legacy will be that millions of Americans will never trust government health experts in the same way again' (2022).

It's clear that much of the pandemic narrative was wrong. That's not a criticism; it's inevitable. The circumstances demanded decisions be made on incomplete research and in a rush. Rather than admit to the mistakes, the authorities and their media allies have adopted a policy to minimise the magnitude of the errors or to ignore the fact that they occurred.

The more extreme transgender activists deploy a similar use of language to target and ridicule. Opponents are 'homophobes', 'gender critical', 'transphobic' and the much-used term 'trans-exclusionary radical feminists (TERF)'.

Those questioning any aspect of the net zero narrative are immediately labelled climate 'sceptics' or 'deniers' – as in Holocaust deniers.

When in June 2023 the US Supreme Court stopped colleges from using a person's race to determine their admission, it was called 'an affront to democracy and equity' (governor of New York) and the work of 'right-wing activists' (governor of California) despite it being supported by the majority of Democrats and Republicans.

All these examples follow the same pattern of pigeonholing your target as being '-phobic', an '-ist' and negative, being 'anti'-something. Attacking the person and painting them as untrustworthy, better still evil, means you don't have to engage with their arguments. In addition to these subject-specific words, there are numerous generalist terms of abuse – 'bigoted', 'Fascist', 'xenophobic', 'hysterical', 'fantasist', 'authoritarian', 'popularist' and 'zealot'.

Where to stop? Disagree with the rules? – label them 'arcane'. Dislike a person's view of history? – accuse them of supporting 'colonialism'. Accusations of 'racialist' have been replaced by 'racist', perhaps because it's easier to spell, shout and write on placards. Anybody who disagrees with your economic mantra must be a 'neoliberal'. For good measure, the multi-purpose insult 'privileged' can always be used.

Next time you hear these words remember their purpose is (almost certainly) not to communicate, not to convey information but to 'target the opposition and attack with ridicule'. Saul Alinsky would be proud.

You can't say that

I still remember my mother telling me 'you can't say that' and my instinctive response 'why not?' I know she meant well yet it still bugs me when told what and I can and cannot say.

Long ago, I was lecturing and used the word 'brainstorming'. Before I could finish the sentence, a student said it was wrong to use the word because it's hurtful to people with epilepsy and I should use 'thought shower'. Instinctively I asked if the student had epilepsy – she didn't – did her close family? – they didn't. Then I asked if anybody in the class had the illness – nobody did.

A cardinal rule of teaching is never to belittle a student. Alas, the 'why not' response got the better of me, something I still regret. I couldn't resist saying, 'so I am the only person in the room with epilepsy and I think brainstorming is fine, as does the British Epilepsy Society'. As they say, 'the toothpaste was out of the tube'.

I remain unsure if 'you can't say that' words are to protect the vulnerable or about grabbing power and enhancing the speaker's virtue. As you will see, I favour the second explanation.

The attempt to control the language has increased greatly since this incident and is something I discuss in the essay 'Academia – the trashing of a priceless brand'. The NHS, charities and government agencies have all adopted the practice with gusto. Their attempts are regularly featured in the MSM and ridiculed along the lines 'haven't they got anything better to do?' Rather than deterring them, this criticism seems to lead them to make even more bizarre demands.

For example, during the past week, London's City Hall directed its staff to stop using 'ladies and gentlemen' because it excludes non-binary people. 'Men and women' should be replaced with 'people' or 'Londoners'. Illegal migrants are 'undocumented' or 'those with insecure immigration status'. Never use 'non-English speakers' because it positions them as flawed or defective; they are 'Londoners with English Language needs'.

The 'you can't say that' diktat of the week came from Johns Hopkins University in the US, which defined 'lesbians' as 'non-men attracted to non-men'. This was a step too far, even in the febrile atmosphere of American academia. The online glossary of LGBTQQIP2SAA terms in which it appeared was rapidly removed for 'further consideration'.

Publishing is on the front line for the word wars. Books have always been edited, but now they face the red pen of the 'sensitivity editors' looking for, as the name suggests, 'sensitive' words. A few authors believe this improves their work; others think it is crazy; and most keep quiet.

It's not just new books that are being checked for sensitive words. The new edition of the James Bond novel *Live and Let Die* by Ian Fleming has been changed. Gone are the words 'Bond could hear the audience panting and grunting like pigs at the trough. He felt his hands gripping the tablecloth. His mouth was dry', replaced with 'Bond could sense the electric tension in the room.' I assume the changes were made because the incident occurred in Harlem, which was then the black area of New York.

ChatGPT's suggested text omitting the reference to pigs is as good, I think better. Be careful, Sensitivity Editors; AI will be taking your jobs:

 Bond could hear the audience breathing heavily and making gruff noises, much like a windstorm blowing through a dense forest. He noticed his hands involuntarily tightening their hold on the tablecloth. The sensation in his mouth was reminiscent of arid desert air.

It was the changes to Roald Dahl's books that riled the British media. Why does Augustus Gloop, a memorable character in *Charlie and the Chocolate Factory,* go from being 'fat' to 'enormous'? Oompa Loompas are no longer 'small men' but 'small people'. In *James and the Giant Peach,* the 'Cloud Men' become 'Cloud People'.

Sensibly (in my view) the publisher realised their 'improvements' weren't receiving universal acclaim and announced they would also keep the original version of Dahl's books in publication. I suspect this was a tactical retreat rather than a surrender.

Sir Trevor Phillips, who was head of the Commission for Racial Equality, has definite views about word censorship. He and his brother are publishing an updated version of their book *Windrush*, a subject close to his heart since his parents came to the UK from British Guiana. He is adamant they will not replace any of the book's language that was used to insult his parents' generation. I am sure you can guess the words he means.

> *It may offend some; but what should offend is not the six letters on the page but the actions and attitudes that once lay behind them. They should hurt and they should sting.*

Such a sensible sentence shouldn't need to be written. Alas, it does.

Lucy Kellaway related a sad example of word censorship in her book *Re-educated*, her story of becoming a schoolteacher after a career as a *Financial Times* journalist. She was known for detesting politically correct language but found herself nervous using the terms 'black mark' and 'whiter than white' when teaching a class with few white faces.

> *Should I acknowledge that some of them were offended and explain that 'whiter than white' came from a Persil advertisement from the 1970s, and for me had no racial subtext? Or might this open an entire Pandora's box of grievances?*

An old colleague at the newspaper was aghast at this story. I had a similar reaction, but now I am not so sure. Her predicament is one that white people face but shouldn't. Perhaps she was being too sensitive? When I was talking with a friend of Jamaican heritage who was fuming about something not being a 'black or white' choice, he seemed perfectly relaxed about the phrase.

Claiming words lead to distress, even to being a crime, has become part of our culture. We live in a time of 'disfavoured speech', 'hateful speech', 'hate crimes' and 'hateful content', all resulting in 'harm', 'trauma' or worse. Attempting to get a precise definition of these terms is impossible, leading to a tautological impasse.

California is leading the way in 'supporting individuals and communities targeted for hate'. Their meaning of hate is that something may not violate the law but 'causes significant harm in a community', a definition dependent on three blah words, 'significant', 'harm' and 'community'. Are you enlightened or confused? Does this rationale have any substance for banning words, for banning free expression?

The underground stations in London are decorated with posters stating Transport for London takes a stand against hate crimes. In the press release explaining its stance, 'hate crimes' appears 30 times but not a single word defining what they are.

Surely the Crown Prosecution Service (CPS) must have a definition. They did, and they didn't. A hate crime is 'any criminal offence which is perceived by the victim or any other person, to be motivated by hostility or prejudice'. It goes on that there is no legal definition of hostility; however, it includes ill-will, spite, contempt, prejudice, unfriendliness, antagonism, resentment and dislike. In 'Justice − teetering on a slippery slope' I delve deeper into the murky waters of hate and hurt.

The vagueness of this definition allows anybody to become a victim of 'hate' language for a long list of subjective reasons. Alongside the term's vagueness is its potential to be used as a 'false binary' weapon − unless you are against 'hate' − as vague as it is − you are for it. Are you confused?

Here's my dilemma. Some people are clearly distressed by the words and beliefs expressed by others. In my experience, most people do their best not to offend, yet some do and some are easily offended. I think we have moved to a point where tagging actions with the label 'hate' has become a tool of censorship. Censorship in the name of kindness, censorship with a smile but censorship all the same. Sadly, it works all too well. Three-quarters of people said they had refrained from expressing their views in public amid fear of being harassed (UK government-commissioned poll, 2024).

Fake news

This journey through the evolution and application of language ends with words that could only have originated in the bureaucracies of governments and large organisations. Using the lovely term we learnt during the pandemic ('gain of function'), they are words intentionally manipulated to serve a specific purpose. This is the mystical, scary world of fake news.

When Mark was only a glimmer in Mrs Zuckerberg's eye it was much easier for the state to control the media. The UK government had the D-notice system to constrain newspapers in the interests of 'national security' – a catch-all term for what the government didn't want you to know. In the US, the Espionage Act governs media controls, the legislation used to prosecute Donald Trump for possessing confidential papers. Its powers are limited by the First Amendment, which protects the freedom of speech.

Today we have Facebook with 3,000,000,000 users and X/Twitter 400,000,000, all with the power to say what they want 24/7. Yet, the machinery of the state and the judiciary is built for a pre-internet age, something governments have been attempting to rectify. China's approach has been simple, banning Facebook in 2009. Twitter/X suffered the same fate, although it's accessible by the technically adept. The democracies of the West have found other, more 'progressive' ways of exerting control.

Social media is used for some very nasty purposes, like recruiting terrorist supporters and paedophiles grooming their prey. Few people question controlling these odious practices. The internet's flexibility and global access deliver wonders and horrors – hopefully much more of the former. Even so, according to the UK's Children's Commissioner, by the age of 13, half of children have seen online pornography. Heaven knows what goes on in the depths of the Dark Web.

How the state intervenes in its citizens' internet use is a non-trivial question with no easy answers. With their billionaire owners portrayed as the oil barons of yesteryear, some argue social media companies are too big and powerful and should be 'broken up', whatever good that would do. Most of the establishment favours legislation forcing them to protect users from the most extreme content. Attempting to placate their critics and fend off government legislation, the companies have restricted permissible content.

Like so many things, the pandemic changed everything, including the ferocity of suppressing content and its originators. Authoritarian states imposed the binary condition of designating content good or bad, approved or censored. What happened in the Western democracies was more subtle. Like taxation rules, the complexity of 'disapproved' and 'disfavoured' content keeps growing, spawning a lexicon of new words. Here are the most popular, with their definitions, collectively known as MDM:

- 'Misinformation' – Facebook says, 'there is no way to articulate a comprehensive list of what is prohibited' and then does. Among the items is 'content likely to directly contribute to interference with the functioning of political processes'.
- 'Disinformation' – Facebook's definition: 'false or misleading posts shared intentionally to deceive people'.
- 'Malinformation' – The Council of Europe defines this as true information shared intentionally to cause harm.

Facebook invented another term, 'coordinated inauthentic activity' (CIA). For obvious reasons, this had unwanted connotations, so the 'activity' was changed to 'behaviour' (CIB). The best definition I could find was 'groups of pages or people working together to mislead others about who they are or what they are doing'. Are you any the wiser?

If none of these applies, there's the catch-all category 'problematic content'. Something that doesn't violate social media's community standards 'but might still be problematic or otherwise low-quality'. It's a term that is appearing in all sorts of strange places. For example, the Archbishop of York thinks using the term 'Our Father' in the Lord's Prayer might be 'problematic' for victims of abusive parents. If that sounds too judgemental, then it could be 'offensive', 'unhelpful', even 'inappropriate'. The University of Cambridge's national library has asked all the university's 31 colleges to identify books that might be problematic for reasons 'not just in connection with decolonisation'.

Such language appears sensitive, thoughtful and 'inclusive'. That's another word that masks a doctrinal impulse, really meaning 'don't say anything that might hurt someone's feelings'. All such words are ostensibly non-judgemental, but all hide a profoundly judgemental impulse. You don't have to be a conspiracy theorist to wonder if they are employed by saints or people who want to censor and silence others.

To add oomph to these phrases, they are often preceded with 'truly toxic', 'shocking' and of course 'harmful'.

We are not done yet. The World Health Organization has another new word – 'infodemic'.

Too much false or misleading information causes confusion and risk-taking behaviours that can harm health. It also leads to mistrust in health authorities and undermines public health.

I wonder if the fears expressed by governments about fake news are not so much about the consequences for their citizens but for themselves. Certainly, that's the tone of this statement from the EU:

> *The spread of false and misleading information, as well as information manipulation, often parallels distrust in public institutions, political leaders, and governments. Misinformation poses a threat to social cohesion and democracy and, as such, it should be a concern for all policy areas.*

I find this potpourri of vague terminology confusing and disturbing. Who gets to decide what's true and false and what's misleading? Where is the justification that we are sinking under a deluge of MDM? Fighting a war on fake news sounds suspiciously like justifying yet more censorship.

BENIGN PROTECTION OR MALIGN MANIPULATION?

It has been fascinating seeing how words evolve and become stranded in time and space, then emerge in a new guise. Spotting how often writers use blah words and inflate the language becomes a game, albeit a frustrating game. Squirming at how the terms ultra-right, fascists and toxic are drained of meaning and employed as ways of stifling debate. Worst of all, seeing words used to confuse rather than explain and honed into weapons.

Accessing the truth is still possible once you realise what's happening and are prepared to fight through the babble. Communicating becomes frustrating and hard work, but remains possible. As soon as you spot the 'weapon' words, you can ignore or discount the content. And yes, I understand the dangers of polarising content into good or bad, believable or suspect. This is the rocky road to confirmation bias that continually erodes trust.

It's when my freedom to use words and to communicate is constrained that things turn nasty, and things get worse still when the state and its supporters are the culprits. Let's be clear: during the pandemic we witnessed good old-fashioned censorship. Sure, it was dressed up in quasi-scientific language, but the aim was to silence people deemed undesirable and dangerous. Attempting to make sense of why and how this happens concludes this essay.

Let's start with the 'why question' and begin by discarding the conspiracy theory that a handful of megalomaniacs, the attendees at Davos, disciples of Bill Gates or the 'dark state' want to rule the world. I don't believe they would be so well organised. There isn't some worldwide conspiracy at work.

No, I think the cause is wrapped in good intentions and we all know where good intentions lead. I deal with these topics in more detail in the essay 'Beliefs – my moral compass is busted'.

In my view, the justification for this systematic tampering with content has its origins deeply embedded in the mindset of progressives, folk who think of themselves as liberal and advocates of free expression. They believe the human condition can be improved through political action to ensure the fairness and progress of society. It's their mission to protect the vulnerable by fighting back the regressive forces. Forces that succeed by telling half-truths and lies.

The good guys are an alliance of those needing support (the vulnerable of society) and those intent on improving their lot. Always an unstable relationship – the aims and priorities of these two groups have long been diverging. I contend that the election of Trump and the Brexit vote shockingly crystallised how far apart they had become. Progressives could not comprehend how these events occurred, events they saw as fundamentally and obviously wrong, events that directly affected their lives in ways they detested.

Surely no sane person, no educated person, no reasonable person could vote in this way? Other forces must have been at work to mislead these poor souls who were duped by populist propaganda. Another factor that has increasingly divided progressives from the vulnerable is educational achievement. The educated class, those with a degree, were firmly anti-Brexit and anti-Trump. It was the 'uneducated' who had been duped into these horrific blunders. This introduces yet more complexity since it's the young who are dripping in credentials that weren't available to their parents. Age and educational credentials are two factors that make this such a disturbing story.

Stick with me – I am nearly finished explaining the 'why question'.

A dominant narrative quickly emerged to explain these two events. Malicious forces must have influenced the results, with Russia being the chief suspect. Somehow social media was being used to mislead Brits and Americans with fake news. Closer to home, populist politicians peddled fake promises. Crowd-pleasing had replaced rational debate. It didn't matter how many experts explained their mistake, the populists triumphed. Simplistic slogans like 'Take back control' and 'Make America great again' drowned out the voices of sane, well-meaning people. These were regressive and destructive, nothing like the inspiring progressive mantras of 'Black Lives Matter', 'Extinction Rebellion' and 'Occupy Wall Street'.

Bewilderment was replaced by anger at those who had made such terrible decisions. This wasn't like the usual rough and tumble of politics. By installing a tyrant as president of America and severing the UK's membership of the EU the masses had shown they could no longer be respected or trusted. Democracy itself was (and still is) under threat when elections, decided by the smallest margins, by the decisions of swing voters, are so easily influenced by malign forces.

And then came Covid.

During the pandemic's first few months, there was no questioning of governments as they imposed increasingly restrictive rules. As more was learnt about the virus, a few people started doubting the scientific rationale. In addition to the anarchist fringe, there were scientists and journalists with genuine concerns. When vaccinations were introduced and their use enforced with mandates, the dissenting voices became louder, as did the need to ensure they were silenced.

The masses had made two mistakes, and now there was a danger of a third that involved life and death.

Although the protesting voices were few, they could, like the virus, infect the larger population who could so easily be misled. Being vaccinated was not a decision for the individual; it was for the good of society. The success of the vaccination campaign must not be threatened by questioning voices; exceptional times demanded exceptional actions. Removing personal freedom was a small price to pay. It was the right decision for thinking, educated people to make.

Distilling the narrative about vaccinations into simple sound bites divided the population into those doing the right thing and being socially minded and Covid deniers. Exactly the same applies to the climate change 'debate', where you're either a net zero devotee or a denier, zealot or worse. And where have you heard the term before? The much-used criticism of Holocaust deniers. I believe the technical name for this technique is 'smearing by association'.

The 'elite' (now I am using a pejorative term) has become guided by the thinking of Dietrich Bonhoeffer – stupid people are more dangerous than evil ones – and Dunning-Kruger – unknowledgeable people overestimate their expertise and ability to make reasoned decisions.

Armed with this new perspective and having witnessed the consequences of the ill-informed masses, the narrative about censorship morphed into a force for good. Of course, this is not the old-fashioned right-wing nasty censorship, detested by the progressive left. This is about protecting and guiding those susceptible to making the wrong decisions. For heaven's sake, even things that are true can be interpreted incorrectly. Given time and exposure to the correct narrative, 'they' would understand it's in their best interest.

Explaining 'why' it was necessary to tamper with free expression was relatively easy. The 'how' it was done is far more complicated, with the details still emerging. No, not so much emerging as being extracted.

The simplest and probably the most powerful mechanism was that those working for and controlling communications channels thought it was the obvious and right thing to do. Most of those determining the content of legacy and social media would identify with the progressive left. I doubt if there are many Republicans working for Google and Facebook and probably fewer still leave voters at the BBC. We know that Twitter's staff were adamant that

Trump be banned from the platform. Measures to silence dissent were pushing at an open door with these right-thinking people.

During the early months of the pandemic, the government was the only source of information. The legacy media acted as an echo chamber, not a forum for analysis and debate. As the language became more war-like, with the 'war against the virus' and daily 'battles' being fought by hospitals, dissenting voices were silenced.

Now we move to another explanation you might well discard as a fanciful conspiracy theory. When I ask friends their views about the 'Twitter files' I mostly get a vague look and a 'what are they' response. Occasionally I hear, 'isn't that something to do with Elon Musk' and very rarely, 'they are terrifying'. The last comment is my starting point for this story.

Everybody knows that Elon Musk – the guy behind SpaceX and Tesla – bought Twitter (which he later renamed X) and immediately sacked most of the management and staff. In December 2022, he invited a group of journalists to interrogate the company's historic emails and Slack channels. His only condition was they publish the results on Twitter. To date, 19 sets of files have been published, totalling many million words. What they revealed would fill another book. Here is an ultra-summarised account.

Many parts of the US government, including the FBI, CIA and the Department of Homeland Security, had direct access to the major social media companies and instructed them on what content was permissible, who could use the networks and how their content was to be published. Initially justified as part of 'the fight against terror', this was expanded to include threats caused by MDM (mis-, dis- and malinformation).

The mission creep of these agencies and the vagueness of the MDM definitions gave the government control of free speech in direct contradiction to the American First Amendment. Since the first Twitter files were released, the mainstream media has done its best to ignore these stories. The BBC thought it only worth a short mention in its technology section.

Due to a court ruling in July 2023 (*Missouri v. Biden*), the media was forced to cover the story, and the subsequent release of emails confirmed the extent of the government's involvement. Needless to say the reporting of the case varies depending on the political perspective of the media.

The New York Times says:

> *The case, which could alter how the government battles disinformation, is a flashpoint in a broader effort by conservatives to document what they contend is a liberal conspiracy to silence their views.*

The *WSJ* reports:

> *Discovery in* Missouri v. Biden *revealed extensive evidence of government coercion and encouragement of censorship. It is the most massive assault on free speech in the nation's history.*

In a majority decision (6–3), the Supreme Court found in June 2024 for Biden on the technicality that the plaintiffs lacked 'legal standing'.

Even the executives running the social media companies were questioning what they were instructed to do. Mark Zuckerberg admitted that Facebook had removed 18 million posts containing misinformation about the virus. With time to consider the implications of his action, he has subsequently said (June 2023), not in the most succinct language:

> *So misinformation I think is has been a really tricky one because there are things that are kinda obviously false but they may be factual but may not harmful can you censor somebody for being wrong when there is no harm implications for what they are doing? There are bunch of real issues and challenges there.*
>
> *Just take some of the stuff around Covid earlier in the*

pandemic, where there were real health implications, but there hadn't been time to fully vet a bunch of the scientific assumptions. Unfortunately, <u>I think a lot of the kind of establishment on that kind of waffled on a bunch of facts and asked for a bunch of things to be censored that, in retrospect, ended up being more debatable or true. That stuff is really tough, right? It really undermines trust</u>. [Underlining is my emphasis.]

'It really undermines trust' – indeed it does, Mr Zuckerberg.

In Facebook emails released by the House Judiciary Committee, Facebook's president of global affairs – Nick Clegg, the one-time deputy prime minister of the UK – asked the question:

> *Can someone quickly remind me why we were removing – rather than demoting/labelling – claims that Covid is man-made?*

A good question, Mr Clegg, now that its origins in the Wuhan laboratory seem 95% certain.

The reason, according to the VP in charge of content policy, was 'we were under pressure from the Biden administration and others to do more' followed by 'we shouldn't have done it'. That's a sentiment I would echo. Remember that President Biden accused Facebook of 'killing people' – like many of his outbursts, it was soon retracted.

Facebook should be commended for fighting the White House's demands for censorship. The director of strategic response argued that vaccine censorship would '1/ prevent hesitant people from talking through their concerns online and 2/ reinforce the notion that there's a cover-up' and that research showed the importance of 'an open and safe space for people to have vaccine-related conversations'.

It was to no avail. Facebook was forced to do the White House's bidding. The punishment for not acquiescing was likely to be an antitrust proceeding and revoking its legal protection from being treated as a media or publishing company.

If we dive deeper into this morass of censorship we discover that the 50 or so arbiters of the truth – the fact-checkers – aren't as neutral as they proclaim, having links with government, wealthy sponsors and large corporates – especially the pharmaceutical industry.

And there we have it, a tale of the state's involvement in limiting free speech.

Before you discount it as an America-centric distraction, take a moment to understand what's happening in Europe, Australia and Canada. The UK has its own Counter Disinformation Unit monitoring social media and is trying to pass legislation giving government agencies the right to interrogate all encrypted communications. On a lighter note, working away in the bowels of Whitehall is Prevent, a group tasked with safeguarding citizens from terrorist attacks. It also monitors social media and decided that certain online spaces, frequented by 'terrorist, extremist influencers and susceptible audiences', regularly mentioned the TV programmes *Yes Minister* and *Great British Railways*. For non-UK readers, these are two of the most popular TV family shows. Not surprisingly, when Prevent's effectiveness was audited, it was found wanting!

It doesn't require new legislation for the state to restrict speech. The Communications Act of 2003 provides jail time for anyone sending a 'grossly offensive' or 'indecent' message via a tweet or on WhatsApp.

It was only by accident that a UK news website (UnHerd) discovered it had been put on the exclusion list operated by UK-based non-profit company the Global Disinformation Index (GDI). This resulted in it receiving much less online advertising revenue than would be expected, because companies were told it was unsafe for their brands. After much effort it learnt this ranking was because it had published an article by Kathleen Stock, the prominent defender of women's rights who happens to believe that biological sex differences exist and are important. They categorised this belief as disinformation.

Further research revealed that GDI received funds from the UK government, the European Union, the German Foreign Office and the US State Department.

Once the UK government's involvement was discovered the issue escalated, both in the media and in Parliament, and the foreign secretary declared the company was no longer being used.

This didn't answer the question of what was so terrible about Kathleen Stock's writing, somebody who regularly writes for other UK publications, including *The Times*.

Further research revealed that GDI's definition of disinformation is so broad as to include just about everything they find objectionable. For them, disinformation 'transcends overly simple false dichotomies like true vs false'. Instead, they view disinformation 'through the lens of adversarial narrative conflict'. Are you still with me?

So, reader, you are having the content you read determined by an organisation you have probably never heard of, funded by your government, to prevent you reading material their obscure filter determines might cause you harm.

Ireland is passing legislation (Incitement to Violence or Hatred and Hate Offences Bill) giving the police the right to search electronic devices on the suspicion that they contain 'hate material'. Ownership is enough for criminal proceedings to be initiated. And you thought 'pre-crime' was science fiction from the film *Minority Report*!

The EU is passing the Digital Services Act to protect its citizens from drowning in MDM and giving itself powers to administer enormous fines on large, internet-based companies – 6% of their annual global revenue. These Byzantine rules and regulations will apply to companies reaching 10% or more of the EU's population, or around 45 million people. A cursory reading of the Act shows it could be a bureaucratic minefield with new agents censoring content (Trusted Flaggers) and dangers to be navigated (Dark Spaces).

The infringements on personal privacy get worse, if that's possible. Legislation is being enacted to enable the monitoring of all text communication on email, WhatsApp and other text messaging services. Messaging services like Signal that provide guaranteed end-to-end encryption would no longer be possible.

This trend of governments wanting control over digital communications is spreading fast. X is threatened with legal action by the authorities in Brazil, India and Australia to remove content they perceive as being illegal and harmful. Elon Musk sees this as attempts by nation states to dictate what content can be published on the global internet.

And so it goes on. In response to the existential threat of MDM, this awful fate that's never quantified, our rights to free expression are being curtailed, or do I mean stifled?

This essay concludes with a question to you, the reader. Is this all a storm in a teacup and proof the state is doing its best to protect us from the idiocy of the many and the criminality of the few? Do you believe it's essential we clean up the cesspit of social media and if a few innocent voices are silenced, then so be it? We are living in exceptional and fearful times – like the election and possible re-election of Donald Trump – that require exceptional actions. When normality returns, all will be well.

Or do you think this a frightening overreach by the state? No doubt, it started with the best intentions of protecting citizens from ISIS terrorists and Russian propaganda, but it has now become the way of enforcing the elite's version of the truth. A version of the truth that seems so inherently right to society's good guys that questioning it is tantamount to endorsing the evils of MDM.

Before reaching your decision, ponder for a moment what George Orwell would have made of it all.

JUSTICE – TEETERING ON A SLIPPERY SLOPE

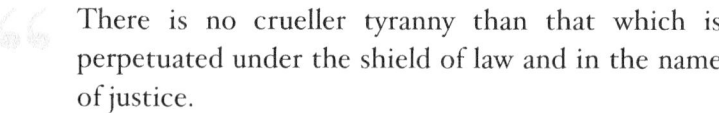 There is no crueller tyranny than that which is perpetuated under the shield of law and in the name of justice.

Charles-Louis de Secondat, Baron de La Brède et de Montesquieu

For all the talk of the 'weaponization of justice' we hear of late, this has been a reality of our politics now for decades – a ruse whereby we give a patina of neutrality to a process that is inevitably political.

Gerald Baker, *The Wall Street Journal*, 2024

All the research – and I mean all – highlights the public's unhappiness with policing in the UK. It is a similar picture in the US – trust is at an all-time low. Not surprisingly, His Majesty's Chief Inspector of Constabulary suggests he is a worried man (June 2023):

> *There are clear and systemic failings throughout the police service in England and Wales and, thanks to a series of dreadful scandals, public trust in the police is hanging by a thread. We have a small window of opportunity to repair it.*

Defining trust as a 'belief in the reliability of the police to behave fairly and effectively', the UK parliament concluded that between 2018 and 2022, it fell from 62% to 52%. The World Values Survey has slightly different statistics, with 67% of Britons having confidence in the police in 2022 – down from 87% in 1981.

Yet the data from the Office for National Statistics Crime Survey (2023) tells a different, upbeat story. Compared with 2022, many types of crime decreased in 2023 – theft from the person (33%), criminal damage (33%) and homicides (16%). This good news didn't convince the CEOs of the UK's largest retail stores, who told the government they are suffering an epidemic of theft and violence aimed at their employees. In the 12 months to August 2023 there were an astonishing 16,700,000 incidents of retail theft (British Retail Consortium).

The mainstream media (MSM) isn't convinced things are improving and publishes a daily drip feed of clickbait headlines about the police's failure to solve crimes. Here are some recent examples: 'Just one in 20 car thefts result in a conviction and in two-thirds of cases, police fail to identify a suspect' – 'More than a million thefts and burglaries go unsolved as just 4% lead to a charge' – 'In nearly half of England and Wales, not a single break-in was solved in the three years to March 2023' – 'Police give up on four crimes a minute' and so on and so on.

The original aim of this essay was to interpret these crime statistics and evaluate the effectiveness of law and order in the UK. How naïve could I be to think that was possible?

What seems beyond doubt is that over the long term, crime has soared. During my lifetime, reported crimes have increased twelvefold. I am not even sure about the accuracy of this stark statistic. The TV series *Dixon of Dock Green* moulded my generation's ideas about policing. Each week, the dependable George Dixon solved the crime, the criminals received their comeuppance and all would be well with the world. The reality was much darker. This was the era of the Kray twins and gangland violence, when villains openly mixed with celebrities, politicians and, yes, the police.

During the past few decades, things have become much more complicated. Sometimes, the police are portrayed as heroes, sometimes as fallible and sometimes as eviller than the villains. The TV series *Police Interceptors* puts today's George Dixon behind the wheel of a supercharged BMW, apprehending drug runners and joy riders. *Happy Valley* revels in the human side of policing, and *Line of Duty* reveals the evils of 'bent coppers'.

Perhaps this more critical and complex portrayal of the police results in the erosion of trust. Maybe they are suffering from the wave of scepticism that has enveloped all the institutions. Surprisingly, faith in the court system remains relatively high – something I don't think is deserved, and I will explain why later. The first question I cannot answer is whether the distrust in the police is deserved or a symptom of a nation suffering from an evaporating trust psychosis.

Judging police effectiveness is nigh impossible. Records kept by the police tell a very different story from the public's response when surveyed. Both have huge opportunities to introduce inaccuracies. For instance, the types of crime and how they are recorded keep changing, as does the public's willingness to report unlawful incidents. Do the statistics reflect fluctuations in the volume of crimes or the effectiveness of the police?

Has the public accepted that certain types of crime are so common that they don't involve the police? Three-quarters of Brits say they wouldn't expect the police to investigate if their phones or bikes were stolen, despite costing thousands of pounds. If the police are involved, it's to provide a crime number to assist with making a claim with the victim's insurance company.

Much of police and court time is spent on drug-related crime – drug consumption, supply and associated offences. This isn't surprising when a quarter of young people aged 16 to 24 use drugs (2022). With an appreciable percentage of the population complicit in these crimes, do the statistics tell a story about the faults of the police or society?

Does the rising awareness of hate crimes and the ease of reporting them account for their increase, or is the country suffering from a hate epidemic? When the threshold for committing such a crime is using the wrong pronoun or interpreting the expression of disagreement as 'hate', should we be surprised?

If these weren't enough difficulties, crime statistics have become a party-political battleground and weapons used by pressure groups, resulting in prejudiced reporting and obfuscation of the data. It would be nice to think that academics with more time and resources than me are beavering away, making sense of the numbers. However, as explained in the essay 'Academia – the trashing of a priceless brand', I would be sceptical about their findings.

For all these reasons, I abandoned my original aim of writing about the qualitative changes to law and order. The best answer I can give is that the nature of crime is changing, as is our tolerance towards it.

Instead, I want to consider the role the law plays in our lives, how it relates to the other parts of the state (especially elected politicians) and how it is enforced and neglected.

It all begins with an implicit agreement between the government and its citizens that we obey the rules and support their enforcement in exchange for security and a fairly administered justice system. My sense is this belief is hanging by its fingertips. The impartiality of the law and its enforcers is foundational to our legal system. Delving into this belief is a logical starting point. While many of my illustrations are from the UK, I'll also cite examples from the US, where confidence in the judiciary is at record lows, tying with Italy as the G7 country with the least faith in its judiciary (Gallup, 2024).

THE MESSY REALITY OF POLICING

Before becoming qualified, UK police officers must commit to the 'Peelian principles', much in the same way doctors take the Hippocratic oath ('first, do no harm').

> *The police are the public and the public are the police, the police being only members of the public who are paid to give full-time attention to duties which are incumbent on every citizen in the interests of community welfare and existence.*
>
> *To seek and preserve public favour, not by pandering to public opinion, but by constantly demonstrating absolutely impartial service to law, in complete independence of policy, and without regard to the justice or injustice of the substance of individual laws.*

These are fine ideals but, in practice, they are the only way the police can operate. 'Consent of the majority' is essential if 140,000 police officers are to maintain order among a population of 50 million adults, even with the assistance of 6 million CCTV cameras.

I would like to think that most of the time, the 'majority' are instinctively law-abiding and make few demands of the police and justice system. Most of us would settle for living an ordered life, free from violence and robbery, travelling in safety and knowing the police will sort out the mess when accidents occur. Occasionally, we stumble into the world of the minority, where the police spend most of their time, and are frightened and appalled.

Magistrates' courts process 95% of UK crimes (1.2 million cases) and, for over a decade, I regularly witnessed their workings, gazing into a parallel universe that coexisted with the cosy one I, and maybe you, inhabit.

Let's spend a few moments in this bizarre and frightening world:

- Abuse within families and the subsequent family breakdowns consume 20% of police time.
- Many offenders aren't equipped to live constructive lives, with poor education and mental health problems. Half of those in jail are functionally illiterate.
- Drug abuse accounts for two-thirds of shoplifting offences and half of burglaries. Over half of prisoners are addicted to drugs.
- The administrative systems for recording and processing crimes are not fit for purpose. They consume 440,000 police officer hours a year and contribute to the 200-day backlog in processing crimes.
- Prisons are chronically overcrowded and do little to avoid reoffending. The chief inspector of prisons is gloomy about their future: 'we can expect more deprivation, squalor and risk of further violence' (2022).

Something that is impossible to measure, yet accounts for increasing amounts of police time, is their job of being social workers in uniforms. They are expected to sort out the mess when other parts of the social care and justice system fail. With record levels of mental health problems and a failing NHS, emergency calls get directed to the police. For instance, when a patient is so mentally distressed that they need to be sectioned, police officers spend, on average, 14 hours in hospital accident and emergency departments. With skyrocketing numbers of people with severe mental health conditions, this consumes more and more police time.

In addition to tackling this background noise of crime, much police time is spent on 'prolific offenders' who are responsible for half of all criminal convictions. Each of these people commits over 20 offences – eight times more than the average. Worse still, the 'elite' among this group are convicted 45 times over their lifetime. You might think they spend most of their time in prison but, because of overcrowding, only half of their offences result in a custodial sentence.

Politicians of all political persuasions treat the justice system as having infinite capacity and as a vehicle to demonstrate their moral priorities. The Labour Party proposes to make repeated misgendering an 'aggravated offence' that could result in a two-year prison sentence – applause and nods of agreement from their LGBTQQIP2SAA supporters.

The Conservatives want the police to investigate every single burglary – applause and nods of agreement from their 'get tough on crime' supporters. Irrespective of your views about the proposals, the practicalities of implementing them are immense and ill thought through.

What I am describing is one almighty mess. Like so much of the machinery of government, it's busted.

Let's return to the world of the majority. We sense this chaos but don't want to know the detailed reasons. What we see reported in the media are instances of police actions (or inactions) that seem absurd and blatantly unfair, doing nothing to address our day-to-day concerns.

It's as if the police have a secret agenda intended to confuse and anger the public. Here are some of my 'why' questions about recent police activity.

Why should I receive a fine for my car stopping for 30 seconds in a yellow box at a roundabout when demonstrators intentionally cause traffic chaos by slowly walking in the road?

Why did six police officers raid a pub to seize six golliwog dolls, yet no action was taken when thousands of demonstrators marched through London shouting racial abuse? The police explained that these protests 'went without issue, and thousands were able to express themselves'.

Why are people allowed to disrupt sporting events and deface works of art on the pretext of saving the planet, then arrested and immediately released?

Why are those who broke Covid restrictions still being prosecuted when most of the rules were ineffective and ignored by hoards of the political class?

Why, when there are so many domestic demands on their time, are they investigating war crimes in Ukraine and Israel?

Why is somebody arrested with a sign saying 'Hamas are terrorists' – as they are under the Terrorism Act 2000 – while a few yards away demonstrators carry placards celebrating the sinking of UK shipping by Houthi insurgents?

The answer to all these questions is that 'it's the law' decided by our elected politicians or 'in the interest of public safety'. Police officers aren't supposed to question the law; they are duty-bound to enforce it: 'not by pandering to public opinion, but by constantly demonstrating absolutely impartial service to law'.

Dissatisfaction with the police might diminish if we had an annual referendum in which we expressed our priorities for which laws the police should uphold and which to ignore. That's never going to happen. The sausage factory of parliament creates the laws and the police have no option but to enforce them. Of course, this is grossly unfair since, like most things in society, the loudest, most organised voices have a disproportionate influence.

Policing has many similarities to the UK's health service. Both are understaffed and expected to operate at full capacity, all of the time. Both are dealing with random acute incidents. Both are dealing with the public in their most distressed state.

That other countries are just as dissatisfied with their law and order systems isn't much comfort, but it suggests the problems are more global than national. A staggering 90% of the French believe crime has increased in poor neighbourhoods and three-quarters say they have lost confidence in the state to maintain law and order. Just 14% of Americans say they have confidence in the criminal justice system, the lowest level ever recorded. Canadians are a little happier, but not much.

For the remainder of this essay, I want to look at why the bond of trust with the public is under such stress. Not surprisingly, many of the reasons are the same as those described in the other essays.

THE UNFAIRNESS OF HATE

Two people are being treated in a casualty unit after being savagely attacked. Their families are distraught. One was beaten during the theft of his £10 lookalike Rolex watch. The other for reasons of 'hate'. In both cases, the offender was caught and punished. The victim of the crime motivated by hate will, in 80% of cases, receive the more severe prison sentence.

How would you explain to the partner of the victim attacked for reasons of greed or malice that society valued their injuries less than those because of 'who they were'?

The Crown Prosecution Service (CPS) explains the difference in sentencing as depending on 'aggravating factors'. 'Hate' is deemed to be one such factor:

> *The purpose behind this approach is to recognize the severe harm caused by hate crimes, not only to the individual victim but also to communities and society at large.*

To my mind, the terms 'severe harm' and 'communities and society at large' are the sort of blah phrases you write in the absence of words of substance. However, that's the law the police must enforce.

Perhaps the victim's partner shouldn't read the next part of the CPS's reply: 'Evidence of the hate element is not a requirement.' Yes, you did read that correctly and it gets worse:

> *You do not need to personally perceive the incident to be hate related. It would be enough if another person, a witness or even a police officer thought that the incident was hate related.*

We are halfway into the Mad Hatter's Tea Party so we might as well take a seat at the table. If the injuries had been caused because of the watch-owner's actual (or perceived) race, religion or sexual orientation or for being transgender then the sentence would be increased.

Can you understand the weeping partner's reaction when she learns that because he wasn't in a 'protected group' the UK justice system discounts the value of his injuries and her resulting fury?

Personalising the differential sentencing of hate crimes forces us to confront their human consequences. I wonder if 'society at large' does benefit from the artificial division between the 'protected' and the rest. My guess is that it doesn't and that most people are unaware of this distinction until it affects them. That's not the case with activists, of course, many of whom shout 'hate' at the first opportunity.

Now, back in the real world, how do the police actually deal with things when crimes of hate are committed? What happens when huge crowds march through London with some carrying emblems of hate towards Jews? How do the police respond? As explained by a former senior officer with London's police force, their priorities change to 'maintaining order and/or prevent violent disorder – everything is subservient to that'.

Maybe we haven't left Alice's world because what this means is that if large enough numbers of people commit hate crimes the law isn't enforced. Worse still, because large demonstrations receive media attention, they broadcast the act of hate to a large audience, making it more visible to 'society at large'.

During the time of Covid restrictions the police were seen to be ignoring the rules during the Black Lives Matter demonstrations that were all about hate crimes and the police. When groups of people gathered for other reasons, the police intervened.

No doubt some can rationalise these anomalies in enforcing the law, but for many people they break the fundamental rule of 'being fair'. And so trust in the police falls a little further. For sure, it would decline even more if the UK followed Ireland's lead, which allows imprisonment for those refusing to give their computer passwords if they are suspected of committing hate speech. Worse still, England could be like Scotland where the Hate Crime and Public Order Act takes crimes of hate to farcical extremes.

If the victim of hate feels too harmed to talk with the police, they can use third-party reporting centres to report the crime. I guess in the name of inclusivity these are located in unthreatening settings, like a Glasgow sex shop (I am not kidding) and a mushroom farm. As Kathleen Stock commented: 'Snitch on someone you dislike and pick up a dildo at the same time – isn't modern life wonderful?'

Getting tough on hate has turned into a global competition. Just after one country raises its punishments another increases the severity. Canada's Online Harms Act (Bill C-63) has taken the lead. Anybody who commits an offence under this Act or *any other act of parliament*, if it is motivated by hate, is liable to *imprisonment for life*. Yes, it does say 'imprisonment for life' and for committing an offence under any other act of parliament. Where do we go from here? The death penalty? Being hung, drawn and quartered?

RACE HAS DISTORTED THE JUSTICE SYSTEM

Between 2011 and 2022, two-thirds of murder victims in the UK, aged 16–24, were black. Other than their loved ones, few will remember any of their 369 names. That's not the case for one black youth (Stephen Lawrence) whose murder in 1993 set in train events that branded London's police as 'institutionally racist'.

Following Lawrence's murder, six suspects were arrested. None of them were charged. His family pursued the case, using a private prosecution, which also failed to secure convictions. After four years of sustained pressure by the family and supporters (including the Labour Party), his case was investigated by a commission headed by Sir William Macpherson. Two years later (1999), the 350-page report was presented to the home secretary.

Those people who can recall the incident have probably forgotten its 70 recommendations but will remember the accusation that London's police force was 'institutionally racist' – a term that dates back at least to 1967, when it appeared in the book *Black Power* by the radicals Charles Hamilton and Stokely Carmichael. During the commission that investigated the Brixton riots (1981) its chairman (Lord Scarman) had been critical of the police but rejected using the term to describe their behaviour.

Macpherson thought differently and defined it as:

> *The collective failure of an organisation to provide an appropriate and professional service to people because of their colour, culture or ethnic origin. It can be seen or detected in processes, attitudes and behaviour which amount to discrimination through unwitting prejudice, ignorance, thoughtlessness and racial stereotyping.*

You might wonder how you prove such a conclusion. What collection of metrics, when processed, produces the result 'institutionally racist'? More importantly, how do you know when the actions you have taken have reversed the condition? The report was long on claims but short on tangible evidence.

That an organisation, or indeed all of society, can be found guilty of 'unwitting' prejudice has had long-lasting effects. The word 'institutionally' has been joined by 'systemic' as terms to accuse groups for their perceived beliefs about race and sexual behaviour. Two more of the report's conclusions dramatically altered the unwritten contract between citizens and the state. The first of these resulted from the conclusion:

A racist incident is any incident which is perceived to be racist by the victim or any other person.

The objective evidence that a crime had been committed was extended to include the emotional reaction of the victim. Today, we know these incidents as non-crime hate incidents (NCHI). Since 2014 the police have recorded details of people whose speech is perceived as 'motivated by a hostility to race, gender, or other protected categories'.

I have already mentioned this, but it's important to emphasise it again: when the police are involved in investigating a 'hate incident' they are instructed that:

The victim does not have to justify or provide evidence of their belief, and police officers or staff should not directly challenge this perception. Evidence of the hostility is not required.

I am sure NCHIs were introduced with the best of intentions, but they are now being used as a weapon for the perpetually angry in society to attack and silence their adversaries. There is no evidence they have done any good but much to suggest they have undermined the belief that the police act fairly.

Another Macpherson recommendation was that the police adapt their behaviour to account for the accused's background:

Colour-blind policing must be outlawed. The police must deliver a service which recognises the different experiences, perceptions and needs of a diverse society.

These are nice, warm words, but how do they translate into actions late at night when the police are called to a violent domestic incident where one of the people is black, the other white? Macpherson strongly condemned the police for treating black people as stereotypes rather than as individuals. To my mind this means 'colour blind' is good policing, not something to abandon.

There's no doubt that the death of Stephen Lawrence resulted in some fundamental changes in the process of policing and their relationship with the public. It's impossible to judge whether these have been positive or negative. What we do know is that since Macpherson, the rate of deaths of black teenagers has increased, standing at a record high compared with murders of white people – in two-thirds of cases, the assailant is also black.

Another black person's death resulted in another massive appraisal of policing. In May 2020, George Floyd was killed during an arrest by a policeman in Minneapolis, USA. The event was videoed, which showed the policeman using excessive force, resulting in Floyd's death. A year later, the policeman was found guilty of murder (2021).

Within days of the death demonstrations raged across the US. The deaths and damage resulting from these protests are hotly contested. At least nine people died and numerous buildings were burnt and looted. Black Lives Matter (BLM) became the focus of the demonstrations, which rapidly spread to other countries. 'Defund the police' is what BLM is most remembered for demanding. To date, 22 US cities have adopted the call, including New York, Los Angeles, San Francisco and Portland.

The budget cuts, estimated at $2 billion, were soon headline news. What has taken longer to emerge has been the damage done to police morale. It has become harder to recruit police and those close to retirement have left. The New York Police Department had more resignations in 2022 than any other year. San Francisco's policy supervisor said: 'We are on the precipice of a potentially catastrophic police staffing shortage, and there are too many public safety problems we'll be helpless to solve.' Other large US cities have similar stories.

Perhaps it's too early to judge whether the experiment in reducing police budgets has worked. Like the UK's, American crime statistics are difficult to interpret. What is beyond doubt is that violent crime is an important issue for voters. During the mid-term elections in 2022, two-thirds of the electorate said violent crime was a very important factor in determining how they vote. This figure increased to 81% among black voters. Ironically (and sadly), it's black people who have been most affected by the reduction in policing.

These two events altered the functioning of UK and US policing and their perception by the public. That the police are institutionally or systemically racist remains the view of many people, especially among non-white groups.

In 2021 Dr Tony Sewell chaired a commission to look at the evidence for the race and ethnic disparities in the functioning of the UK state, including the police and criminal system. This statement from the report sums up his conclusion:

> *The police service is imperfect, like all major services and organisations. However the challenges they face when dealing with both victims and perpetrators of crime are complex as the causes are beyond their control. Great strides have been made towards becoming a service that can fairly police a multi-ethnic society. It is important to recognise and acknowledge this.*

His report echoed some of the facts I have already mentioned. In over 80% of cases of homicides, the victim and suspect were the same ethnicity. Half of all black homicides are under 24 years old, compared with 10% for whites. Black youths aged 16 to 24 are 11 times more likely than their white counterparts to be a victim of homicide.

Social deprivation and the difference in the demographics of the black community were, in his view, the reasons for these high rates of murder among young black males. As with most areas of difference in the outcomes between races, Sewell's report identified structural reasons, not a pervasive bias by the white establishment.

I think it is fair to say that the response to Sewell's report was less than enthusiastic. Human rights experts from the UN believed it was an attempt to 'normalise white supremacy' by not recognising the ugly systemic racism affecting UK institutions. A little after this, another black man, Trevor Philips, expressed the view that the higher rate of Covid deaths among different ethnic groups resulted from structural reasons, not racism. He was shouted down for denying the institutional/systemic explanation.

In the final chapter, I will return to these reactions because they are important in explaining the mindset that is common among today's young (and many old). In the context of policing, they demonstrate the depth of belief that racism and policing are inextricably linked.

It seems large sections of society are convinced the police are irredeemably racist, while others believe they are overly lenient to minorities at the expense of protecting the majority. Perhaps being perceived as unfair by all is a measure of being fair?

We must not forget the police enforce the law our democratically elected representatives define. I am sure they would love the ability to ignore parts of it and emphasise others, but that's not their job and they don't have that power. As I have explained, most of their time is spent in the messy part of society, doing messy jobs that the rest of us do our best to avoid.

Of course they make mistakes, and the acts of some individual police officers are reprehensible and illegal. But surely that's the same for all parts of society? Why should the wrongdoing of one policeman be any more representative of the police than the evils of a doctor or nurse be of the NHS?

A notable failing of the police that is invariably overlooked, however, is their abysmal failure to promote their brand, something I will discuss in the next section.

WHO SPEAKS FOR THE POLICE?

Take a moment to consider the breadth of services provided by the police. They send an officer to the parish council meeting to talk about local speeding problems and thefts from garages. They are expected to keep order when hundreds of thousands of people demonstrate in London. With a quarter of a million employees and a budget of £25 billion, they are one of the UK's largest and most complex organisations.

Organised geographically, England and Wales have 43 police forces. Scotland and Northern Ireland are separately managed. In each geographic area, an elected police and crime commissioner is responsible for planning, finance and appointing the chief constable. In corporate speak, the commissioner is the chairman, and the chief constable is the managing director. Sitting above all these organisations is the Home Office, which is under parliamentary control, although this lever of power seems more theoretical than actual. If you are getting confused, you are not alone.

Where I live in the UK, just 17% of the electorate could be bothered to vote for their crime commissioner (I wasn't one of them). Throughout the country, it is a little higher, about a third. I suspect most people just want and expect the law to be applied efficiently and consistently and don't care about the intricacies of the hierarchical organisation.

However, this complex structure means that on each level, there's a media office promoting 'brand police' to the legacy and social media. There's no central control over the quality and messaging. Understandably, when the national media reports about the police, it treats all representatives the same – they are 'the police'.

Something unique among the police is the profusion of 'staff networks' that officers join and that focus on their special needs, including gender, sexuality, ethnicity and religion. Since 2010, these networks have increased by 80% and now stand at 200. There is the National Black Police Association, the National

Association of Muslim Police, the Christian Police Association and the Disabled Police Association. There is even a Vegan Network.

Many of these appear to be small self-help groups, supporting their members with coaching and mentoring. The larger networks claim to have a broader remit, including 'community engagement and outreach' and influencing government policing policy. Most networks are active on social media, claiming to speak for their special interest group.

So, who among the 43 police forces and 200 police networks speaks for the police? They all do, and none of them do. This results in a cacophony of messages, some of which are contradictory, that does nothing to promote a unified police brand, leaving the loudest voice, saying the most controversial thing, to determine the public's attitudes.

While law enforcement (the order part of 'law and order') is the most visible part of the justice system, it's the accessibility, fairness and efficiency of the law that ultimately shape our trust in its ability to serve us effectively. This essay concludes by looking at the features of the legal system that most concern me.

THE LEGAL SYSTEM: EXPENSIVE, INEFFICIENT AND UNFAIR

It is much easier to reduce the budget of the justice system than those of the NHS and schools, and that's what's happened. Since 2010, the justice system's budget has been cut by a quarter, resulting in 43% of courts being closed, leaving two-thirds of parliamentary constituencies without an active local court. The legal system has been under relentless pressure to cut costs, achieved by lengthening waiting times. There's a record 65,000 cases waiting to be heard by the Crown Courts. When cases eventually get to court, over a quarter are classed as 'ineffective', being cancelled at the last moment.

For most Brits, their tangles with the justice system begin with the arrival of a fixed penalty notice letter informing them they have broken the law and must pay a fine to the courts. Most of these 40 offences relate to cars and driving (speeding, nuisance parking, not having insurance...). Anti-social behaviour misdemeanours make up the remainder, such as noisy and disorderly behaviour and discarding waste. Nobody knows how many of these are issued. My guess is it's measured in the tens of millions a year and likely to increase given that they not only act as a deterrent (theoretically), but they also generate revenue.

If you decide to contest or ignore these fines, you are summoned to a magistrates' court, at which point it's prudent to seek legal advice. The more serious the case, the more important it is to have legal representation.

Individuals with limited financial resources receive state assistance with the costs, although the criteria for receiving state-funded legal aid have become increasingly stringent. Like so much of the justice system, its budget has been repeatedly cut and is only a third the 2005 level, adjusted for today's currency value. The Bar Council doesn't mince its words about the consequences: 'cuts to legal aid have been catastrophic in their impact on the ability of people to access justice for their legal needs'.

Hiring legal representation is costly. Solicitors charge between £150 and £350 per hour, and barristers' rates are higher, ranging from £250 to £500, varying with their experience level. High-quality legal advice is a luxury like vintage champagne that few can afford.

These high costs undoubtedly distort the fairness of the legal system. This is amplified by the rewards given for a guilty plea, which supposedly reduces the costs of the justice system. We might all be equal in the eyes of the law, but the wealthier you are, the more likely the 'eyes' will see your innocence. If you can afford high-quality legal representation, your chances of acquittal increase – it's as simple as that.

In other words, because the legal system is so complicated and costly, the wealthy can buy protection from justice. It's like playing poker that favours those who can afford to lose the most money by allowing them to 'buy the hand'. By raising the cost of remaining in the game, it intimidates other players into folding (giving up), even if they might have better cards.

I am certain those working in the legal system do their very best to deliver justice, but the cards are stacked against them. It's a complicated and costly branch of government to operate, and repeated cuts mean it is limping along at best. As for 'we are all equal before the law' – forget it.

I will leave the final words about this crisis to the Law Society, which represents UK solicitors:

> *Victims, witnesses and defendants are having to wait years with their lives in limbo before cases come to court. This is unacceptable and many are understandably losing faith in the criminal justice system.*
>
> *Urgent investment is needed across the entire criminal justice system to prevent it from collapsing. There are crumbling courts, overwhelmed prisons, vast legal aid deserts and a shortage of lawyers and judges.*
>
> *Years of neglect of our criminal justice system can't be put right overnight but continued inaction will only result in its collapse.*

THE LAW HAS BECOME A POLITICAL WEAPON

Back in 2016 there was speculation that Donald Trump would use the law to punish his adversaries. Now he is facing multiple legal actions and appealing his felony convictions, it's the Democrats who are accused of weaponising the law to destroy his chances in the next presidential election. The more conspiratorially minded believe it's to divert attention from President Biden's legal and cognitive 'issues' and the misdemeanours of his son.

Views about the legitimacy of these charges divide along party lines. Irrespective of who is right, this means approximately half of America's electorate believe the legal process has been compromised for political purposes.

Using the law to intimidate or obstruct an adversary is often referred to as 'lawfare'. Although mostly discussed in the context of Donald Trump, it is widely used.

When climate activists use the European Court of Human Rights to force governments to change their environmental policies, you either think it's an abuse of human rights legislation or a much-needed action to save the planet. With lots of funding from the eco-friendly billionaire community, the court found in favour of a group of older Swiss ladies that the state had violated the Human Rights Convention right 'to have respect for private and family life'. The lawyer representing the ladies commented that 'in Switzerland it's particularly problematic because they have referendums'. In 2021 the Swiss voted against stronger environmental regulations. Much better to let the judges decide these matters than ask the public.

When the law is used to stop the UK government from implementing an asylum policy, it's viewed as either a victory for the compassionate or another example of lawyers usurping the democratic process while indulging their luxury beliefs.

Geoffrey Robinson's book *Lawfare* is in no doubt about those exploiting the law. The subtitle reads: 'How Russians, the Rich and the Government try and prevent free speech'. Those with the deepest pockets are the culprits. So what do we call the practice of politicians using the law to discredit their opponents? Tom Watson, who later became deputy leader of the Labour Party, became a vocal supporter of a massive police investigation into members of the establishment, all of them his political opponents. Fourteen months after it began the investigation was abandoned, with the only witness being prosecuted. A judicial review followed that was scathing about the police's actions, saying that Watson's intervention adversely affected the investigation. In 2022 he was awarded a life peerage (Baron Watson of Wyre Forest). Our trust in politics and justice declines a little further.

This seems as much a case of lawfare as a rich Russian oligarch using the law to silence criticism from the media. The same with activists stopping government policies by employing legislation for reasons other than originally intended. In the UK, the Habitats Regulations about nutriment neutrality, a leftover from the UK's membership of the EU, are currently stopping the building of 140,000 new homes.

The innocuous-sounding Climate Judiciary Project has a mandate to: 'provide the judiciary with authoritative, objective, and trusted education on climate science and the ways climate science is arising in the law'. Then you discover that it is funded by William and Flora Hewlett. Yes, that's the same Hewlett as in your HP printer. Their foundation is politically left of centre and funds environmentalist causes. Yet more no doubt well-intentioned wealthy people, using it to influence our lives.

You can portray this tension between the law and the elected government as healthy and necessary, as something that's in the best interests of citizens, protecting their fundamental freedoms. Perhaps that's true, but perhaps it's more visceral and about battling over exercising power. Whatever the explanation, it's not limited to the UK and US but is happening in Brazil, France, Germany and Israel, before the 7 October Hamas attack.

Prosecuting the law is expensive but there are many wealthy philanthropists willing to use it to impose their vision of society.

Events in the US fill me with concern. If the willingness of students at the premier US law schools to take direct action is indicative of how they will conduct themselves when practising the law, then we can expect a more radical judiciary. The same can be expected in the UK, with advocates wanting to abandon the 'cab rank rule' whereby lawyers accepted cases irrespective of their personal beliefs. Like the police, the UK's legal profession has enthusiastically embraced DEI policies, which is testing its impartiality.

It's probably a naïve idea that the law has ever been a bastion of fairness. Today it looks like a battlefield between the powerful. Sometimes, this might be to protect the best interests of the majority; mostly, it's just about winning.

PANDERING TO THE FEW ALIENATES THE MAJORITY

Have the repeated accusations of institutional 'isms' resulted in the police overcompensating and confusing their role as enforcers of the law with visibly embracing all the tropes of the DEI culture? Are they so anxious to appease their critics that they ignore their natural supporters, the boring law-abiding public? I think the answer to both questions is more yes than no.

After the awful murder of Sarah Everard (2021) by a serving police officer, a review was highly critical of London's police force, concluding that it was failing women and children and unable to police itself. Naturally, the evergreen accusation of institutional racism, sexism and homophobia was one of the conclusions. In 2023, a neonatal NHS nurse was found guilty of murdering seven infants. In another incident, a maternity unit was accused of 1,700 cases of inflicting harm on newborn babies. Each year, the NHS pays £2.5 billion in compensation for mistakes and damaging patients.

Why are the faults of one institution always treated as an example of institutional failure and those of the other as a series of tragic but isolated events? Platitudes are used to explain away NHS horror stories about 'always one bad apple in the box' and the 'results from working under stressful conditions'. Mistakes by the police are met with boilerplate cries of 'rotten culture', 'bunch of bully boys' and demands for 'root and branch' changes.

You might think I am being complacent and too forgiving. Perhaps I have witnessed too much of the nasty world where the police work and feel thankful it's them, not me. One moment they are dealing with the worst sides of human nature; the next pandering to noisy activists, desperate to become martyrs and stars on TikTok. We want them to protect us from society's baddies, using the correct inclusive language. On a dark, rainy Saturday night in Stafford, as the clubs empty and trouble breaks out the police must remember never to use 'mixed race' instead of 'mixed heritage', to substitute 'neurodiverse' for 'mental health disorder' and to avoid at all costs the terms 'man up' or 'grow a pair'.

These examples are taken from Staffordshire Police's language guide, one of the numerous documents resulting from the National Police Chiefs Diversity, Equality and Inclusion strategy, which believes: 'Embedding diversity, equality and inclusion into all that we do is an essential ingredient for success.' For the life of me, I cannot understand why calling me an OAP or pensioner is so bad and why I would prefer the title an over 65, 75 or 80s. Guessing my age incorrectly is much more likely to result in offence!

I dare not think how much time has been consumed producing the hundreds of DEI strategies and reports for each police force. Certainly, if word count was a measure of success, then the police get top marks. Similar comments apply to the part of the justice system that prosecutes suspected criminals – the Crown Prosecution Service – which is knee-deep in guides to dealing with ethnic minorities and transgenderism.

The Lammy Review of 2017 into *The treatment of, and outcomes for, Black, Asian and Minority Ethnic individuals in the Criminal Justice System* stopped short of finding institutional racism. Still, it concluded there should be more focus on tackling 'unconscious bias'. All of its 35 recommendations were about processes, most of them about the type of data to collect and how it's published.

Hopefully, all this effort, all these reports, all the strategy meetings and all the hours of sensitivity training are delivering results. Alas, it would seem not; it would seem it is getting worse.

The number of black, Asian and minority ethnic (BAME) children in prison, four years after Lammy's report's publication, has increased by 10%. In London, 91% of young people on remand were from BAME backgrounds. Ironically, the police are now instructed not to use the term BAME. How fast times change.

There comes a point where irrespective of how many changes the police make, whatever words they use, however they are trained, they can't affect all the ills of society that result in crime. What's risked by this overt focus on processes and achieving equity is the trust of the majority, that group that doesn't shout, that isn't in the statistics other than when they become the victims of crime.

BEND PATIENCE TOO FAR AND IT SNAPS

During my schoolboy physics lessons, we had great fun bending metal strips. I was amazed at how far they could be distorted yet return to their original shape. Then comes a point when they undergo 'plastic deformation' – they snap, permanently busted, with a loud bang.

Something similar is happening with policing and the system of justice. The fundamentals of what they are supposed to be doing are being bent out of shape by another set of values that aren't necessarily shared with the majority. This is a common theme that appears in my other essays about academia, business, politics and the media.

The term 'silent majority' is much overused but, for most of the time, they are silent, having no structures to channel their anger or approval. Saying they have the democratic right to change things is little comfort when, as we have seen, politics is a ritualised stage play that is more comedy than serious drama. My views on the political farce are described in the essay 'Politics – more showbiz than statesmanship'.

Only when the anger and disillusionment of the majority become so intense that it erupts as an issue that cannot be ignored does change occur. Policing is at the threshold where the actions of the vocal and visible minorities threaten the tolerance of the majority. Memories of the Vietnam War demonstrations, the coal miners' strike, the Brixton riots and the IRA bombings prove it's not a comfortable place to be. Most recently, there have been the anti-Israel demonstrations, with their mix of genuine concern for the Palestinians and a large dose of hateful antisemitism.

I don't know how far we are away from the loud bang, when plastic deformation occurs. The pessimist in me says the anger and polarisation fuelled by social media make it inevitable when significant parts of society believe the narrative that the police and justice system are inherently biased. Gazing on in disbelief, the majority increasingly thinks the police no longer care about them.

My optimistic side says that the durability of the bond between the public and police, although tested, is deeply embedded in society. Perhaps it's an age thing, but my optimistic side is fighting a losing battle.

FINANCIAL AUTHORITIES – INCOMPETENT REGULATORS DON'T PROTECT US FROM GREED

Only when the tide goes out do you discover who's been swimming naked. Monkeys could do as good a job investing as Wall Street financial advisors.

Warren Buffett

Act as if you're a wealthy man, rich already, and then you'll surely become rich. Act as if you have unmatched confidence and then people will surely have confidence in you. Act as if you have unmatched experience and then people will follow your advice.

The Wolf of Wall Street

W hat a difference a year can make. At the start of 2022 Sam Bankman-Fried was hailed as a financial genius. He was the epitome of Gen Z, with oodles of social conscience, brimming with progressive beliefs and a master of the digital universe. By December, he was extradited from the Bahamas to the US on fraud charges with the prospect of decades, if not centuries, of jail time.

I am intrigued and more than a little envious how this 30-year-old MIT graduate apparently amassed so much wealth, so fast. I can't help being amused at how he bamboozled the 'great and the good' and how easily they were bribed and manipulated. Photos of him sitting (in shorts and tee shirt) with Tony Blair and Bill Clinton (in suits, no ties) still amuse me.

I am appalled at the regulator's impotence as they stood by and did nothing.

This essay investigates why incompetence and stupidity keep permitting financial disasters to occur and why individuals and institutions keep behaving in an irrational and idiotic way. By looking at the most notable financial scams we will understand why the unwary and their money are so easily parted and why you must **never** trust the regulator to protect your interests.

As the saying goes, 'the jury is out' – but in the case of Mr Bankman-Fried, it soon returned. We will wait until the end of the essay to learn what it decided and what we can learn from his case.

PERSONAL EXPERIENCES

I want to start with a couple of tales of financial deception involving me, thankfully not as the victim, but as an observer.

My first story started in the late 1990s with a solicitor duping his clients. Despite being investigated by the legal authorities, he retained his legal licence but was banned from practising in the UK. He moved his business to mainland Europe, where he committed multiple frauds totalling £20 million in today's pounds, by promising loans for businessmen with poor credit records in exchange for an upfront fee. The loans never materialised, and he pocketed the fees.

His deception relied on portraying the image of a successful entrepreneur, flaunting a luxury lifestyle as evidence of his success. All he required to complete the act was a glamorous wife. That's where our paths crossed, when he met and quickly married a close friend. She ticked all the boxes. Well-educated at a top US business school, a successful career and very attractive.

They dined at the Ritz, holidayed in Barbados and jetted to New York for long weekends of shopping. Once married, however, her world fell apart. It started gradually, when he separated her from family and friends. Then he began to control every aspect of her life, what she wore, where she went. All I could do was watch from afar as her life imploded.

No doubt he was charming when capturing new clients, but his default demeanour was arrogant and aloof. But then lots of successful people have these traits.

I will cut to the end of the story with him being declared bankrupt and jailed. After a prolonged legal tussle, they divorced, but it was years before she recovered from the experience. Like those who funded his lavish lifestyle, she had been duped.

Finally, a story that is literally close to home. Soon after moving to the country, I learnt that a neighbour, living in a far grander house than ours, was wealthy and a budding politician. We never met – he only mixed with his supposed social equals. The village gossip told of his good deeds and him being 'something big in the city' and a major contributor to the Liberal Democratic Party. Nobody was surprised when he became their parliamentary candidate. Anxious to project his commitment to his constituents, he funded the town football team and supported local charities.

This man was in a hurry, destined for high places – until he wasn't. In 2011 he was declared bankrupt, with millions of pounds of outstanding debts. Despite his being an insolvency practitioner, his numerous business interests collapsed – including the football team.

After he disappeared from the village, unsavoury stories surfaced about his personal and business life, including past troubles with the accountancy authorities. Only then did it emerge that he had a long history of bending the rules for his financial benefit.

There are some common themes linking these very different stories. The perpetrators of the fraud all appeared to be wealthy and successful. In two cases, and probably the third, the authorities should have protected the investors but failed in their duty. Most worryingly, they demonstrate our gullibility when faced with a determined fraudster.

FRAUD AND ITS CAUSES ARE ETERNAL

I'm sure that fraud has existed since humans first started trading with each other. We can imagine unscrupulous individuals trying to overcharge for building the pyramids in ancient Egypt, and speculators bidding up the price of wheat.

For centuries, bad investment decisions have parted people and their money, but mostly due to human fragility and ignorance, not fraud. The unpredictability of the financial markets is why most people lose money. If only more people paid attention to the warning that 'financial assets can go down as well as up in value'.

When the link between an asset's intrinsic worth and its price becomes ridiculously disconnected, it's called a 'bubble'. Invariably, there's some make-believe rationale for why this is occurring. During my lifetime, it has been that the asset is special and defies the laws of economics, that it's valued in a new, unfathomable way and, the most common, that it harnesses a new technological innovation causing a 'paradigm shift' in business. Whenever anybody suggests 'It's different this time', it should set alarm bells ringing.

Most recently, cryptocurrencies appeared to defy financial

logic. In 2008 the decade-long rise in house prices went into reverse, causing mayhem in the financial markets. During the late 1990s, the stock market valuation of internet-related companies soared and then plummeted when the 'dot.com bubble' burst.

Further back in time, the 'South Sea Bubble' (1720) resulted in a catastrophic financial crash. What started as a way of reducing Britain's national debt by creating a company to manage the country's trade with the Americas ended in disaster when its stock price plummeted. Perhaps the weirdest bubble occurred in the Netherlands. This country's sophisticated financial markets traded the future value of tulip bulbs. During 1637 the price of certain varieties rose to ridiculously high values and fell just as quickly.

In all of these cases, some lucky and some unscrupulous individuals profited at the expense of ordinary investors. However, these were not frauds but instances of human frailty that readily suspends logical judgement and believes the impossible is possible. We now label this behaviour 'groupthink' or the 'madness of crowds'. This weakness and the impotence of the regulatory authorities can't protect investors against the worst excesses of their greed.

Like asset bubbles, unscrupulous individuals have preyed on the unwary for centuries. Two of Charles Dickens' characters provide timeless descriptions of fraudsters and their illegal shenanigans. In *Martin Chuzzlewit* (1844), Mr Montague bamboozles the public by selling worthless life insurance. His Anglo-Bengalee Disinterested Loan and Life Assurance Company has long been the role model used by the unscrupulous.

Symbols of success and opulence are the bedrock used to sustain its wrongdoings. At the entrance of Montague's company stands a finely attired porter radiating evidence of its success and stability:

A wonderful creature, in a vast red waistcoat and a short-tailed pepper-and-salt coat who carried more conviction to the minds of sceptics than the whole establishment without

him. When he sat upon a seat erected for him in a corner of the office, with his glazed hat hanging on a peg over his head, it was impossible to doubt the respectability of the concern.

When Montague is asked the value of the company's paid-up capital, he laughs and answers: 'A figure of two, and as many oughts after it as the printer can get into the same line.' Like all fraudsters, he has contempt for contracts, verbal and written. And, rightly, believes he is surrounded by the gullible.

Montague and his thieving enterprise are trivial compared with the antics of Mr Merdle, who appears in *Little Dorrit* (1857). Here is another villain oozing wealth, success and influence:

> *Mr Merdle was immensely rich; a man of prodigious enterprise; a Midas without the ears, who turned all he touched to gold. He was in everything good, from banking to building. He was in Parliament, of course. He was in the City, necessarily. He was Chairman of this, Trustee of that, President of the other.*

Theoretically, his victims should have been protected by 'the authorities', in this case the wonderfully named 'Circumlocution Office':

> *The most important Department under Government. No public business of any kind could possibly be done at any time without the acquiescence of the Circumlocution Office. Its finger was in the largest public pie, and in the smallest public tart.*

As so often happens, the 'authorities' were toothless and incompetent, failing to protect investors. Dickens scholars believe his Circumlocution Office ridiculed the incompetence of the UK's

Treasury. Perhaps it represented his disdain for the ineffectiveness and corruption of all government institutions.

The stories of the most notorious real-life fraudsters are perhaps even more dramatic than Dickens' fictitious characters. If you were to list frauds by their magnitude, then Charles Ponzi would barely make the top ten, yet his name has become synonymous with the simplest of get-rich schemes.

'Rob Peter to pay Paul' means discharging a liability using somebody else's money. We often use the phrase, light-heartedly, when describing the disorganised management of personal financial affairs. Before 1920 it also referred to scams that promised to provide an abnormally high investment return by using some impressive-sounding financial scheme. In practice, the 'profits' were paid using funds from new investors. Thanks to the antics of Charles Ponzi this type of fraud is now always called 'a Ponzi scheme'.

In 1920 the rate of interest in the US was 5%, much the same as in 2024. Ponzi began issuing notes that paid 50% interest on investments in 45 days. How could he achieve such a staggeringly high rate of return?

His scheme was masterful in its simplicity. To help the international exchange of mail and parcels, the International Universal Postal Union provided an 'International Reply Coupon' that was purchased in one country and exchanged for postage stamps in another. It was a type of international funds transfer and operated in over 60 countries.

WWI had just ended and the exchange rates of European countries had plunged against the US dollar. For instance, between 1918 and 1920 the Italian lira–dollar exchange rate went from 8 to 21. Ponzi discovered that the coupons didn't reflect these changes. Theoretically, he could buy coupons abroad, bring them back to the US, exchange them for postage stamps and make a significant profit.

This was a perfectly legal way of making money that provided the financial argument justifying his sky-high interest rate. The logistics of making this scheme work would be extremely difficult, but it was a superb argument to convince the unwary to part with their money.

Ponzi exuded charm and the air of a wealthy and successful man. He was also the consummate salesman and an accomplished organiser, establishing a network of agents selling his investment notes.

In little over a year it all ended in tears. No postage stamps were ever purchased and all the interest was paid using new investors' funds. When his scheme failed, investors lost approximately $130 million in today's dollars, a trifling amount compared with modern-day frauds. Ponzi had lived well and bought all the baubles that rich people buy, but most of the money had been returned to the early investors or lost through bad investments.

These were the components of Ponzi's scheme that made it so successful (for a while) and a model for future lookalike frauds:

Personal qualities: Accounts of the time describe his easy-going ways and personal charm. He was a natural salesman. More than that, he instinctively understood human nature and how to exploit its greedy side.

Radiating success: He had the possessions of a wealthy man, a fine house and travelled everywhere in his luxury car (a Locomobile) that cost over $400,000 in today's dollars.

Convincing story: The postage stamps scheme was a wonderful tale containing enough elements of truth that investors persuaded themselves that it was possible to receive a sky-high rate of interest.

Echoing the times: This was the 'roaring 1920s' when everything seemed possible. People wanted fun, and fun cost money. Ponzi was one of many exploiting the optimism of the times.

Partly legitimate: By the time the scheme failed, he had multiple investments in Boston banks that he used in his sales pitch to gain 'credibility by association'.

Unsavoury backstory: Ponzi had a history of failed business ventures and had been imprisoned in the US and Canada.

Impotent authorities: It was a concerted campaign by the *Boston Post* newspaper that ended Ponzi's business, not the financial authorities.

If Ponzi gave his name to such schemes, it was Bernard (Bernie) Lawrence Madoff who made them infamous and a symbol of all that was, and probably still is, rotten with the financial markets.

When he was arrested (2008) it was estimated that Madoff's liabilities were $25 billion – that's 200 times larger than the losses of Ponzi's investors. The similarities between the two men are scary, despite being separated by over 80 years.

Personal qualities: When his business crashed, most of Madoff's investors had never met the man. Some didn't even know their money was invested in his funds. At the start of the scheme, it was his charm and persuasiveness that got friends and family to trust him with their money. These same qualities deterred the authorities from mounting an investigation even when they had reliable evidence proving it was a fraud.

Keeping numerous plates spinning and living in continual fear of being found out was something both men could do. Neither of their wives knew anything about their husband's deceit. Ponzi managed this for a year, Madoff for decades.

Radiating success: Connections with prestigious organisations and flaunting their wealth, symbolising their success and credibility, came naturally to them.

Times had changed since Ponzi, and success meant owning a yacht, an Upper East Side apartment and homes in The Hamptons and Palm Beach. Madoff had all of these and more. Ponzi was a major shareholder in Hanover Trust, a Boston bank – Madoff had been chairman of NASDAQ and chairman of the National Association of Securities Dealers.

Convincing story: Madoff's astonishing ability to buy and sell stocks at just the right time made him a legend. Investors' trading statements showed the wonderful performance of their blue-chip stocks that were bought and sold just at the right time.

These were bogus documents, however, constructed retrospectively after knowing how the markets had performed. The mechanics of sustaining this fantasy were astonishing. No shares were ever traded. It was all a gigantic confidence trick.

Partly legitimate: At the time of his demise, Madoff's sons were running the legitimate side of his business, a major market-maker on NASDAQ. Visitors to his offices in the Lipstick Building, in mid-town Manhattan, would be impressed by the bustling high-tech finance office. All the illegal operations were conducted on a floor that no visitors and few staff were permitted to visit.

Impotent authorities: Peter Madoff, Bernie's brother, was the company's chief compliance officer and his niece, Shana, its compliance lawyer. Friehling & Horowitz was a tiny firm of accountants and Madoff's auditor. At best they were ineffective and they were probably involved in the scam. The SEC was told on numerous occasions about suspected fraud. It kept going through the motions of investigating and declaring Madoff to be legitimate.

A sustained exit of investors is what causes Ponzi schemes to collapse. That's what happened to Madoff during the chaotic market conditions of 2008. You could say that he was a victim of the market crash, just like the investment bank Lehman Brothers.

Some people, fortunately not many, can lie and knowingly defraud even their closest friends, without any sense of guilt. They are missing the moral gene. When this 'skill' is combined with the charm to convince and dominate others, it's seriously dangerous.

A few such people can also convince themselves of their rightness, that they are on the side of the angels. Ponzi and Madoff knew what they were doing was illegal but found ways to justify their actions. These lines from the musical *Evita* about Eva Peron's Foundation describe this power of self-delusion:

When the money keeps rolling in you don't ask how.
Think of all the people guaranteed a good time now.

You can tell you've done well by the happy grateful looks.

Accountants only slow things down, figures get in the way.

The device used to deceive always reflects the values of the time. Fraudsters in the 1980s convinced themselves (and investors) that they were exploiting the workings and morals of the market economy in a better way than their competitors. Everybody was doing something similar; they were doing it more and better.

Ivan Boesky (1986) was convicted for making trades using information unavailable in the public domain ('insider trading'). When you are fighting takeover battles with voracious competitors (T. Boone Pickens and Sir James Goldsmith), the line between legal and illegal gets very blurred.

Michael Milken (1989) pioneered a new way of financing takeovers using high-risk, high-return 'junk bonds', making a fortune for himself and his employer Drexel Burnham Lambert. These were the heady days of takeovers funded by weird-sounding financial instruments. I remember listening to business school colleagues convinced that reshaping companies by acquisition and restructuring was a natural evolution of market capitalism. Those doubting the long-term benefits just 'didn't get it'. Milken strayed over the boundary of legality and was found guilty of illegal securities trading.

All the major fraud cases of this period were committed in the US, except for the case of Nick Leeson, a Brit operating in Singapore. His escapades resulted in the collapse of a pillar of the UK merchant banking industry (Baring Brothers). In the early 1990s the global financial services industry was thriving. Gone were the days of the 'gentleman banker'; this was the era of brash young men (mostly) trading complicated financial products.

The Leeson saga had many twists and turns, but the crux of the story was the huge losses he incurred and concealed trading on Japan's Nikkei stock index. There's no doubt he acted illegally but Barings must shoulder responsibility for its lack of oversight and controls. As the song from *Evita* says 'when the money keeps rolling in you don't ask how'.

He was a star trader and appeared to be making the bank a fortune. Following the Kobe earthquake, the Nikkei index collapsed and not long after so did Barings. Ironically, a hundred years before, it had narrowly avoided bankruptcy after Argentina defaulted on its debt, something the country makes a habit of doing.

Leeson was living the lifestyle of a successful trader but didn't amass significant wealth. He committed the fatal error of gamblers, believing his next bet would recoup his losses. I wonder how many traders would do the same if it were not for their bank's compliance and audit controls?

Leeson's story also shows the opportunity for illegality that new and poorly understood technology provides. Back in the US it was happening on a far grander scale.

During the late 1990s two companies (Enron and WorldCom) appeared to epitomise the new world order of technology companies that were changing the fabric of American business. Enron was a supplier and trader of electricity, natural gas and communications. From 1996 to 2001 it was titled 'America's Most Innovative Company' by *Fortune* magazine. It took the traditional, some would say boring, activity of energy supply into the dot.com era and was valued accordingly.

When the company's accounts were discovered to be make-believe, it was forecasting that it would become the world's largest energy company. Surely this fact alone should have alerted investors that something was horribly wrong?

WorldCom was an also-ran among US telecommunications companies. Then it adopted a policy of acquiring its competitors at a ferocious rate, with its revenues and profits soaring (supposedly). The company convinced the markets that it would prosper by supplying the telecommunications capacity needed for the thriving dot.com economy.

WorldCom's rise and fall had many parallels with Enron. Its accounting was fraudulent. Disguised by its rapid growth, it redefined the terms 'revenue' and 'profit'. Both companies could perpetrate these illegal actions because investors, consumers and the authorities were blinded by the rhetoric that 'the Internet changes everything'.

I must admit to being one of those who believed this story. During this period, I published my first book *Internet Strategies,* which supported the notion that the rules of business were being rewritten. My mistake, shared with everybody else, was misjudging how long it would take for these new rules to become a reality. Eventually, the bubble burst. The NASDAQ stock market index that had risen by a staggering 400%, between 1995 and early 2000, plummeted 80% by the final quarter of 2002. Talk of 'paradigm shifts' and 'technology revolutions' ceased, and the world returned to normal, for a while.

INSTITUTIONAL INCOMPETENCE

What happened next is not so much about corporate fraud, although that undoubtedly continued; rather, it is a period when financial and government institutions lost all semblances of control.

America had just suffered a medium-sized stock market bubble and mini-recession, yet the average price of homes kept rising, an anomaly that went unnoticed by all but a handful of people. Michael Burry was one of those people and didn't believe this 'normal' would last for long; he used his investment fund to bet the housing market would collapse. Nobody working on Wall Street had been around when this last happened.

His story is the basis of a wonderful film (*The Big Short*) that documented this period. In this exchange he is talking to a potential employee and asks: 'Didn't you find it odd that when the tech bubble burst in 2001 the housing market in San Jose, the tech centre of the world, went up?' After a puzzled silence, the answer comes, 'Huh. I guess. I mean, no. It's housing. It's always AAA-rated, low-risk.'

The assumption that property is always a low-risk investment proved wrong and nearly collapsed the world's financial markets. Disaster was avoided, but at a cost that is still affecting lives two decades later.

When the story is recounted, the natural reaction is surely everybody could see this happening. All financial disasters seem so obvious after they have occurred. Burry couldn't understand how the price of an average American home, which had been unchanged from 1992 to 1997, kept rising despite all the economic turmoil. Between 1997 and October 2006 the average home price increased by 50% in real terms. It was too good to be true. Something else that defied logic was the doubling of the S&P 500 index between March 2003 and the end of 2007. Also too good to be true.

The reason was that Wall Street investment banks had discovered a solution to what seems an unsolvable problem. There is an inexhaustible supply of families wanting homes but a finite number who can afford the mortgages. A new way of lending was created that enabled these people to buy homes – it was called subprime loans.

Laying in a bubble bath drinking champagne, Margot Robbie in *The Big Short* provides a memorable (and accurate) explanation of subprime lending:

> *These risky mortgages are called 'subprime'; any time you hear subprime, think shit.*

An earthy explanation but true. Wall Street packaged these loans together and then, as if by magic, they became AAA-rated. The theory was that putting thousands of these loans together would spread the risk.

Of course, these new homeowners needed to pay a higher interest rate, but this was delayed for a few years. Called 'teaser loans', for obvious reasons, they gave the appearance that all was well until the higher rates were charged.

This is an ultra-simplified explanation of what happened. The full account contains even more bizarre shenanigans of the financial authorities and the bankers. Both the long and short versions of the story have the same ending. Financial carnage erupted in 2008, resulting in the US government injecting an astronomical sum of money into the finance sector.

What is missing from this accepted narrative is the role played by politicians, especially during the Clinton presidency, in 'encouraging', some say forcing, banks to reduce their lending requirements. In today's parlance, this was done to create 'racial equity'. For the best of reasons – and also to boost their popularity – politicians distorted the affordability of housing. The bankers duly obeyed and exploited the opportunity.

When reality and the markets collided, chaos ensued. Estimates of the bailout vary. It's safe to say it was at least half a trillion dollars. Let's write that out in full – $500,000,000,000. What happened next is even more extraordinary and permanently distorted the value of financial assets. Readers unable to buy a property because of their ultra-high prices, pay special attention. The world's central banks slashed interest rates. In January 2008 the US Fed rate was 3.5%. Come December, it was 0.25% and there it stayed until 2015. For *seven years* the cost of buying assets was next to nothing.

You don't need a doctorate in economics to realise that asset prices rise when interest rates are effectively zero. That's what happened, big time. Property prices and the world's stock markets rocketed. Again, this is a simplified version of events that misses out the advent of the magical process of quantitative easing, more commonly known as printing money. *Too Big to Fail* is a great film account of these events; remember, the part that describes our close brush with financial Armageddon is not fiction.

The bubble in asset prices continued to inflate until it was popped by the Covid pandemic, which brings us to the present day. Undoubtedly, politicians' extraordinary actions in their 'fight against the virus' have triggered a new bubble but that's a subject somebody else can tackle.

Before returning to tales of individuals and their dastardly deeds, it must be said that the machinery of government, all those zillions of people employed to know what is going on and to protect the unwary from the dangers of the markets, failed and kept failing on a monumental scale. Ronald Reagan isn't famous for many quotes but this one will last for ever: 'The nine most terrifying words in the English language are: I'm from the Government, and I'm here to help.'

The latest episode of governments distorting the markets is the pursuit of ethical investing. Rather than seeking unbridled success and its rewards, companies are to be tempered with concerns about environmental, social and governance (ESG) issues. Making money is OK, but not at the expense of others and the planet. The 'simple' question of whether an investment makes money has a caveat that it meets ESG conditions.

I have to admit to finding this all very confusing. Why was Tesla, the electric car company at the forefront of establishing the industry, not considered an ESG investment, but Northrop Grumman, the developer of the B-2 Spirit stealth bomber, was? There is much more about the rise and fall of ESG in the essay 'Business – charting new paths or losing direction?'

WRAPPING FRAUD IN PROGRESSIVE-SPEAK

Dubious business practices have excelled at adapting to new social norms. A perfect example was the company Theranos, founded by Elizabeth Holmes, which was once valued at $10 billion (2014). She persuaded Silicon Valley venture funds, Rupert Murdoch, Henry Kissinger and George Shultz that Theranos would revolutionise the blood testing industry.

Soon to be gone were the days of sticking a needle into the arm. Holmes' device needed only a few drops of blood from the finger. Instead of waiting days, her device promised the results in minutes. She talked and dressed like Steve Jobs and promised to create the Apple of the blood business.

Holmes' mantra was that faster, easier and less threatening blood tests would save lives. Saving lives was her purpose in life, not making money – or so she said. Sadly, the product didn't work.

An adage in Silicon Valley is 'fake it until you make it' but the Theranos product could never be made; it was scientifically impossible. Holmes went from being a deceitful entrepreneur to a criminal who lied about the product's deficiencies and intentionally misled the healthcare authorities. In 2022 she was sentenced to 11 years' imprisonment. The film *The Inventor: Out for Blood in Silicon Valley* gives a gripping account of this financial and personal disaster.

Adam Neumann is not a fraudster but is a perfect example of how to lose shedloads of other people's money making the world a better place. He is the founder of WeWork, a name you must have seen plastered over offices around the world. Renting shared office space isn't a new idea. Somehow, Neumann convinced financiers it was possible to transform it into a glamourous, life-enhancing business.

His first venture Green Desk (2008) was an 'eco-friendly coworking space'. Two years later, WeWork was launched and by 2014 it was the US's fastest-growing company, leasing new office space. Fuelled by money from blue-chip lenders, it expanded into the world's major business centres. 'The money kept rolling in' and by the time reality caught up with the rhetoric, WeWork was valued at $47 billion and far from profitability.

Neumann joined the list of people who claimed to have found that elusive Philosopher's Stone that could transform an established business model into a tech empire. To this day, I don't understand why so many people believed his story. Of course, he was brimming with personal charisma and energy, but it was his claims to be making the world a better place, to be embracing all the progressive nostrums, that made the difference.

These fatuous words peppered the documents WeWork used to raise more cash:

> *Our mission is to elevate the world's consciousness... philo-*
> *sophically, we believe in bringing comfort and happiness to*
> *the workplace... we are a community company committed to*
> *maximum global impact.*

Playing fast and loose with accounting standards was never mentioned, but that's what the company did.

You might be wondering, 'surely investors did their due diligence?' You might well wonder this about all of these ventures. In most instances, they didn't – or if they did, they did it very badly.

By 2019 hopes the company was the new Google or Amazon were in tatters and Neumann was forced to resign. Things kept deteriorating and in October 2023 WeWork filed for bankruptcy. Somebody far from bankrupt is Mr Neumann, however, who *Forbes* estimated walked away with $800 million.

Another entrepreneur who persuaded investors that his business could simultaneously make money and alleviate poverty and suffering was Arif Naqvi. His company, The Abraaj Group, was feted by the world's great and good as an 'impact investor', another wonderful term that sounds impressive but is impossible to define. He was supposedly making profits and simultaneously doing good in the world. Naqvi failed on both counts but managed to increase his personal wealth, significantly. Eventually, two of his investors, the World Bank and the Bill and Melinda Gates Foundation, demanded an audit to understand what had happened to their investments. This revealed fraud of epic proportions. Naqvi is currently under house arrest in London pending extradition to the US for trial on 16 counts of alleged fraud and money laundering.

Finally, two stories that sound like works of fiction. Part farce, part tragedy with lots of excitement.

Thanks to an Apple TV documentary (*The Big Conn*) a crime that took place in rural Kentucky USA has achieved worldwide exposure. Eric C. Conn was a US lawyer and a larger-than-life character at the centre of a scheme that defrauded the Social Security Administration (SSA) of half a billion dollars. In cahoots with crooked judges and doctors he processed tens of thousands of claimants, some legal, most not.

What made this fraud so extraordinary was that despite the weight of evidence about his wrongdoings, he was allowed to continue. Although it was never proven, it seems certain that employees of the SSA were involved in the deception. Either that or they did their damnedest to prevent their incompetence from being discovered by mounting repeated coverups. Eventually, two determined whistleblowers forced the FBI to stop the scam. Conn is serving a 27-year prison sentence.

All these examples suggest that financial crime is the preserve of the UK and US. That's far from true, as the saga of the German company Wirecard proves. It was the classic case of a company that seemed to do no wrong that rapidly grew in size and was listed on the country's stockmarket (the DAX). After a prolonged campaign by the *FT*, the company admitted to a $2 billion hole in its balance sheet and the stock price collapsed. The company filed for insolvency, creating one of Germany's biggest corporate disasters since WWII.

Wirecard was a composite of all the corporate financial fraud I have discussed. It was a company with cutting-edge technology, leading the 'fintech' industry that promised investors huge returns. It grew by acquisition, mostly abroad in countries with minimal regulatory oversight. Those running the company seemed to exert a mesmerising control over its auditors and the regulators, who repeatedly failed to act when given evidence proving the company's wrongdoings. At this point, however, all similarities with other frauds end.

According to a headline in *The Wall Street Journal* (January 2024):

 Jan Marsalek, the jet-setting former COO of now-defunct Wirecard, enabled Moscow to fund covert operations around the world. He's Now Suspected of Being a Russian Spy.

It would seem that Marsalek had been a Russian agent for over a decade, using Wirecard not only to steal money but to fund spy agencies around the world, including Yevgeny Prigozhin, the late Russian warlord. We will leave the story here since the full truth about this saga is still emerging. What is crystal clear is the authorities repeatedly failed – maybe we will learn they were involved?

This essay started with the story of Sam Bankman-Fried (SBF), and that's how it ends. On 2 November 2023, he was found guilty on all seven counts of fraud, conspiracy and money laundering. He theoretically could have received 105 years of jail time. The prosecution wanted 50 years, the defence 6 years. The judge decided on 25 years.

During the trial it emerged that SBF and his fellow directors were adherents of the beliefs of Effective Altruism (EF), which sounded more like a cult than a set of rational ideas. This is how its devotees describe their beliefs:

> *Effective altruism is an intellectual project, using evidence and reason to figure out how to benefit others as much as possible. And it's also a practical project: to take action based on this research, and build a radically better world.*

These are commendable aims. It was how they were bent out of shape that made them sound like an excuse for making money by ignoring the rules. To my mind, they seem like an extreme form of the progressive mindset.

When submitted to the forensic analysis of the trial, EF turned out to have subverted all other considerations to saving mankind by 'doing good'. What constituted 'doing good' was an intellectual game played by the super-bright EF devotees. Was preventing malaria in Africa more important than protecting mankind from AI? Should we be reducing inequality or colonising Mars (I am not jesting)? In this world, working in private equity was far superior to being a doctor.

If you extrapolate this thinking, you can easily believe that breaking a few financial rules is insignificant if it helps save the human race. Good intentions morphed into an ugly cabal of arrogant young people with an extreme dose of Messiah Complex. It gets even weirder. Michael Lewis's book *Going Infinite* is the nearest we will get to an SBF biography. He observes:

> *Sam viewed other people, and maybe himself too, not as fixed characters – good or bad, honest or false, brave or cowardly – but as a probability distribution around some mean.*

I will give the final word to SBF. Despite the EA gobbledygook, he retained a presence in the real world and just possibly a sense of humour emerges when he is asked if all his talk of ethics was for real:

> *It's what reputations are made of, to some extent. I feel bad for those who get fucked by it, but this dumb game that we woke westerners play when we say all the right shibboleths, and so everyone likes us.*

NEVER TRUST THE REGULATORS

The most important conclusion of this essay, the single thing to remember, is never to trust the authorities that are supposed to guard against misdeeds. They may be powerless to exercise their role, incompetent, dishonest or all three. A regulator's fancy kitemark and skyscraper offices might impress but they don't guarantee your safety. If the organisation is part of the government, you should be doubly suspicious.

If somebody like me, somebody who is innately sceptical of bureaucracies, was shocked by the pattern of their incompetence, then you should be worried – very worried.

All large organisations make mistakes. For some, incompetence is part of their culture. Nobody is surprised when yet another NHS computer project collapses. The most recent being the failure of the Covid test and trace system (cost £37 billion) and the bankruptcy of Babylon, the company that was to replace GP visits with artificial intelligence. Each time, the same questions are asked: how could so many supposedly intelligent people not see these systems were never going to work?

Over the last decade, three-quarters of large UK companies that went bust did so without alarms being raised by their auditors. In a scathing report about the lack of standards and accountability in the audit industry, Prof Adam Leaver said:

 The UK audit sector is plagued by poor standards, a toothless regulator, conflicts of interests and weak sanctions for malpractice.

When the Bank of England's inflation forecasts are horribly wrong (yet again), a few eyes will roll, heads will shake, but that's it. Are you shocked to read that a government department has failed to meet its target of building houses, returning illegal economic migrants, training nurses, etc? Let's face it, you would be more amazed if the targets were achieved. When dealing with a local authority you expect poor customer service so anything approaching an acceptable response is greeted as a welcome surprise. When you anticipate organisational failure, you are prepared.

My tales of scams describe a failing that is much worse than this run-of-the-mill systemic ineptitude. Organisations that we instinctively trust, whose sole purpose is to protect us from villains, fail to do their job. It has become almost a joke that following an inquest to discover why the public was fleeced, yet again, a glum-faced official will utter the words 'lessons have been learnt' and 'processes have been put into place', and not a soul believes they have. I am talking about company auditors, credit rating agencies, accountancy associations, stock market regulators and the whole panoply of people who are richly reward to spot and stop illegality.

This shocking situation means that your own antennae to fraud have to be all the more sensitive. You cannot trust others to do it for you.

THREE RULES YOU WILL PROBABLY FORGET

Unlike the other essays, I am ending this one with words of advice. Having spent much of my life in the finance world, there are a few truisms that seem so obvious that we ignore and forget them. Let me remind you.

Top of the list is to abide by the age-old saying: '**If something sounds too good to be true it probably is.**' That sounds blindingly obvious, so let's rewrite it in financial speak: 'Nobody consistently beats the markets.' For more effect, in scientific language: 'Perpetual motion is impossible.' Whenever you see claims like 'guaranteed returns', 'market-beating performance', 'limited availability' or 'loss protected' – something is wrong. Perhaps it was an over-enthusiastic copywriter making extravagant claims; whatever, your level of suspicion should jump an order of magnitude.

In 2008, the Icelandic banks offered an interest rate way higher than their UK competitors. How on earth could they do that? If only consumers and institutions had remembered the 'too good to be true' rule they would have saved themselves the nightmare that unfolded when the banks defaulted on $60 billion of debt. Numerous UK local councils, charities, pension funds and thousands of consumers found their funds had disappeared.

Rule number two is to remember **the Philosopher's Stone doesn't exist**. Financial disasters are often preceded by claims that society, technology, the markets are radically changing and the old rules no longer apply. When the claims sound like two plus two equals five then beware.

For instance, many believe that cryptocurrencies are a discontinuity in the world order, and that they don't obey the old rules. It is beyond the scope of this essay (and my knowledge) to refute this belief. However, the odds are that it's wrong, so the safest, most likely outcome is that the old rules will prevail. Bitcoin, Ethereum and numerous other currencies rapidly fluctuate in price so treat them as a gamble with higher odds of failure than success.

Just because an investment is festooned with reassuring words that resonate with the progressive culture doesn't mean a thing; if anything, more reasons to be sceptical.

The final rule concerns the behavioural weaknesses that make us liable to being duped. **Most of us believe we are good judges of human nature, but the evidence suggests the contrary.** We are overly impressed by the trappings of success displayed by individuals and organisations. As we have seen, they count for nothing.

Seeing others profiting from an investment dulls our rational mind – if they are getting richer, why not me? The 'fear of missing out' is a well-documented reaction that invariably ends in tears.

Normally it's hard work to understand an investment opportunity so we rely on others for advice and protection. Let's be honest; most people's eyes glaze over when dealing with financial gobbledygook. That's when we employ our mental shortcuts like 'if all these other people are investing, it must be OK', 'XYZ celebrity says it's a good deal' and, worst of all, 'they say ABC regulator protects it'. Sadly, none of these provides protection when things go wrong. In an advertisement for a crypto exchange, the actor Matt Damon concludes with the words 'fortune favours the brave'. Had you been brave and purchased Bitcoin on the day the advert was released and sold them two years later you would have lost three-quarters of your investment.

It's been a long but hopefully interesting journey through the world of fraud, flawed human nature and regulator incompetence. Hopefully, you feel better informed and protected. When you are next presented with a wonderful-looking opportunity to make money, spend a couple of minutes reminding yourself of these rules.

BELIEFS – MY MORAL COMPASS IS BUSTED

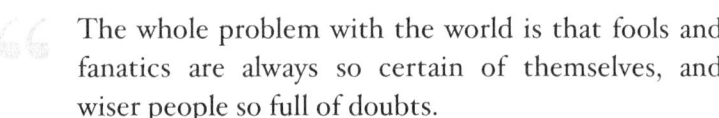

> The whole problem with the world is that fools and fanatics are always so certain of themselves, and wiser people so full of doubts.

Bertrand Russell, *History of Western Philosophy*

> It does not particularly surprise me that people do this kind of thing, nor even that they announce that they are doing them. What does impress me, however, is that other people's reaction to such happenings is governed solely by the political fashion of the moment.
>
> In every case believed in or disbelieved in according to political predilection, with utter non-interest in the facts and with complete willingness to alter one's beliefs as soon as the political scene alters.

George Orwell's diary, 1942, after the Nazis eradicated the Czech village of Ladice

B efore writing these essays, I was confident(ish) about my beliefs and the rules for navigating life. You might say – many people did – that I was 'set in my ways', a trait I valued as acquired wisdom along with that prized commodity 'experience'. Having researched and written these essays, most of my certainties are less certain; many have gone. I can no longer trust the heuristics, the mental shortcuts, that guided my behaviour. My belief compass is busted.

Perhaps my uncertainties are an 'age thing' and result from having the luxury of time to reflect on matters I previously accepted without question. Completing the next consultancy assignment took precedence over pondering the world's problems. If the reports of plummeting levels of trust, along with the pervasive mood of disillusionment, are to be believed, then my unease is widely shared. Perhaps these are the 'interesting times' foretold in the Chinese curse?

My final essay 'So what's going on? Making sense of it all' does what it says on the tin, but before that, I must understand how the old rules have changed and what, if anything, has replaced them.

R.I.P. THE 'LEFT-RIGHT' IDEOLOGICAL SPECTRUM

Back in the day, political beliefs were on a spectrum stretching from the 'left' to the 'right'. Those on the left believed in the power of the state to do good and enable progress; that trade unions improved the lot of the working classes and higher taxes made for a better society. Cooperation always beat competition and making society fairer was achieved by redistributing wealth.

The right's objective was to minimise the size of the state and lower taxation. Markets that responded to the public's cumulative wants and needs were the best way of achieving economic growth. Politics was about improving life for individuals, not the construct of the left called 'society' and 'community'. The state and its intervention in citizens' lives was a necessary evil to be minimised.

These opinions were called 'left-wing' and right-wing'. Socialists held more trenchant left-wing views; more extreme still were
communists. Somewhere out on the farthest reaches of the spectrum were anarchists.

Holders of extreme right-wing views were fascists, something I
could never understand since Stalin, Mao and Pol Pot, all communists, and hence left-wing, had much in common with Hitler, the
archetypal fascist. Perhaps those at the extremes of the political
spectrum are always malevolent psychopaths.

The aficionados of the left proudly described themselves as
liberal or progressive, sometimes both. I think progressives were
more to the left than liberals. Less-used terms – conservative, reactionary and traditionalist – were labels given to the right wing.

In the UK, Labour was the party of the left, the Conservatives
of the right. Democrats and Republicans held these respective
positions in the US.

The Labour Party was mostly working class with a dash of the
well-educated upper classes. Conservative support came from the
professional and middle classes, with a sizeable group of indepen-
dently minded working class. A person's 'class' was an important
thing in the UK, much less so in the US.

Support for the church and monarchy spanned the central part
of the spectrum, turning to hostility at both extremes. Despite
favouring individual choice, the Conservatives publicly frowned on
those with non-orthodox lifestyles, though this was not always
reflected in their private lives. Labour supporters espoused a belief
in economic equality despite many living opulent lifestyles, not so
affectionately known as 'champagne socialists'.

The left believed businesses were run for the interest of their
owners, who were invariably right-wing. Trade unions acted as the
counterweight, protecting workers' rights, and were the bulwark of
the left. The machinery of government, like the mainstream
media, instinctively favoured the right.

There was a rough correlation between age and beliefs, with
the young leaning to the left and their parents and grandparents to

the right. Supposedly, views became more right-wing with age as experience overcame youthful naïvety or, as the elders would say, 'when they grow up'.

Yes, I know, this is a simplified and subjective overview of the political spectrum. The main point is that until recently, economic issues and the role of government were the dividing lines between left and right. Once upon a time, 'harnessing the power of the state' generated nodding heads (the left) and shrieks of disagreement (the right).

Ronald Reagan's comment 'The nine most terrifying words in the English language are: I'm from the Government, and I'm here to help' was the rallying cry of the right and an anathema to the left.

The same split of attitudes extended to supernational organisations, with the left believing the EU, UN, WHO, IMF and the European Court of Human Rights were symbols of collective endeavour to be celebrated and supported. Those on the right thought they were at best wasteful, most likely incompetent and promoting their own agenda free from democratic controls.

The left revered Keynes and his belief that government borrowing could boost the economy and more recently Thomas Piketty with his ideas about wealth inequality resulting in low growth. Economists on the right deployed Hayek's theories advocating laissez-faire capitalism and minimising state controls. This was supplemented with Milton Friedman's theory about limiting money supply to control inflation. If economists are wincing at this point, my apologies.

Remnants of this old model still exist, but the ideologies that now separate people have changed beyond all recognition. Despite the terms 'left' and 'right' still being popular as labels for beliefs, they are no longer fit for purpose; they've become a caricature of themselves.

WORDS DON'T MAKE SENSE

The main reason the left–right spectrum has lost its usefulness is that words that once had a precise meaning are now used as insults. For example, the terms fascist and appending 'ultra', 'far' and 'extreme' to 'right-wing' are tossed into sentences describing anybody not sharing the writer's opinions. The essay 'Language – from beautiful to brutal' explores this in more detail.

As I write this section in November 2023, the winner of the Dutch general election has just been announced, with the leader of the party with the most votes described as:

Hard-right extreme nationalist (The Times)

Far-right figurehead (The Guardian)

Extreme-right (Financial Times)

Hard-right (The Economist)

Earlier in the year, Italy elected its first female prime minister, who was described as:

Leading a right-wing coalition which had its roots in neo-fascism (FT)

A hardcore Catholic politician, the most right-wing leader since Mussolini (Mail)

Leading her hard-right Brothers to power (Times)

A far-right coalition victory (Guardian)

A breakthrough for Europe's Hard Right (The New York Times)

These headlines are not intended to explain but express each publication's opinion and condemnation. *The Economist* is proud of its accuracy of language but couldn't resist slipping 'hard-right' and 'populism' into its description of these politicians and their impact on Europe's political landscape:

> *A fresh wave of hard-right populism is stalking Europe. It could toxify politics, disenfranchise a large share of voters and prevent crucial reforms of the European Union.*

But surely politics is already 'toxic', and voters can't feel any more disenfranchised. I guess the association of the right and its negative attitude to the EU is the thing that annoys the journalist. A similar view was expressed when the former co-editor of *FT Deutschland* talked about Alternative für Deutschland ('a far-Right populist party') wanting 'Germany to leave Nato, they want Germany to leave the EU — and the Euro.'

Scepticism about the EU was once the view of the left; now, it has become associated with not just the right but the 'hard-right'.

The once revered *Economist* abandoned all attempts at objective communications and ranted in its leader article about National Conservatives, who it accused of being:

> *Obsessed with dismantling institutions they think are tainted by wokeness and globalism. Instead of a sunny belief in progress, national conservatives are seized by declinism. Not content with resisting progress, they also want to destroy classical liberalism.*

And so the trashing of the language goes on when the mayor of London describes those protesting about his latest traffic restrictions as 'far-right' and then for good measure 'Covid deniers' and the final insult 'Tories'. When the UK and Italian prime ministers meet with other politicians, it is labelled by the BBC as a 'far-right rally'.

Maybe we should dismiss this as excitable politicians pandering to their supporters and journalists chasing clicks by spicing up the language and believing their sentiments trump objective reporting. What damage is done by prefacing 'right wing' with 'ultra' or 'extreme' other than debasing the language to harangue rather than explain?

There is no consistency in the details of policies that warrant these labels. Critical views about immigration, environmental controls and the EU are at odds with much of the media; however, that could be because journalists are predisposed to be ultra-left. You can see how easy it is to slip into inflating the language to make it meaningless.

This same debasement happens to the term 'left-wing', but according to Google Trends, five times less often.

Many of those who in the late 90s labelled themselves as progressive are horrified that the word now means committing to an ever-changing menu of beliefs. Failure to agree to the whole package results in being labelled a 'neoliberal'. Long gone are the ideals about the basics of improving all of society, protecting free speech and holding the powerful to account.

Perhaps the most abused term is 'populist', defined by the *Oxford English Dictionary* as: 'A person who seeks to represent or appeal to the interests of ordinary people.' This seems a perfectly reasonable political strategy, yet the word has now become a term of derision, especially about those on the right. According to ChatGPT, Mr Donald Trump is the global role model for populist politicians.

The remnants of the political spectrum are littered with other terms, such as 'social democrat', 'social conservative' and 'social liberal'. Does appending 'social' and 'neo' confer some special qualities, or is it done for effect? What's the difference between a democratic socialist and a social democrat? Are libertarians the same as liberals? Would neo-conservatives and neo-liberals be sending each other Xmas cards? Are the two words liberal and democracy inextricably linked, implying that democracy is less democratic if it is not liberal?

Our political language has become devoid of shared meaning. When I claim to be holding a ladder and you call it a bucket, all is lost. Perhaps the words have meaning within small groups of believers but mostly they are deployed to create an emotional response, either elevating the user's virtue or insulting the recipient. What these words no longer do is describe a commonly understood model of beliefs.

EQUITY IN – EQUALITY OUT

In the essay 'Academia – the trashing of a priceless brand' I explained the influence of diversity, equity and inclusion (DEI) departments on the workings of US universities and to a lesser extent those in the UK. In both countries, the 'D' means 'diversity' and the 'I' 'inclusion' but at Harvard and Yale the 'E' stands for 'equity', whereas at Oxford and Cambridge it means 'equality'. These are not typing mistakes; they represent a chasm of difference. Most US universities began striving for equality and switched to equity, a pattern being repeated in the UK. What does it matter that they are jettisoning 'al' from their titles – it matters a lot. It's another reason my moral compass is broken.

Stay with me while I explain the implications of this word change.

Equity has multiple definitions. The *Oxford English Dictionary* lists those relating to law and finance and it's the name of the actors' trade union. What interests me is its meaning related to fairness: 'The quality of being equal or fair; fairness, impartiality; even-handed dealing.' Merriam-Webster, the US dictionary, slips in the word 'justice' as in 'fairness or justice in the way people are treated'.

Back in 2016, Stanford University tried defining the word (*What the Heck Does 'Equity' Mean?*) and concluded it all depended on interpreting the words 'justice and fairness'. Since then, academia has crystallised its meaning and implications. This is how the US Ivy League universities use the word in their DEI mission statements (thanks, ChatGPT):

> *It means emphasising fairness or justice in the way people are treated. It is rooted in the concept of moral fairness and refers to <u>customising the allocation of resources</u>, opportunities, and treatment to achieve <u>equal outcomes</u> for different groups.*

The underlined parts of this statement make me squirm – more about why later.

In addition to this specific meaning, it has become a 'blah' word used to decorate reports. For instance, the latest document from the UN detailing the evidence of climate change is peppered with the words 'equity' and 'inequity'. As in 'social equity', 'global equity', 'equity and justice', 'patterns of inequity' and the report's intention to 'deliver, progress and advance equity'.

The term is a favourite of the US President Biden, regularly appearing on his prompt cards. No wonder the poor man so often looks confused when you read how it is defined on the White House website: 'The consistent and systematic fair, just, and impartial treatment of all individuals'. Having stated it's for 'all individuals' the definition continues:

> *Including individuals who belong to underserved communities that have been denied such treatment, such as Black, Latino, and Indigenous and Native American persons, Asian Americans and Pacific Islanders and other persons of color; members of religious minorities; lesbian, gay, bisexual, transgender, and queer (LGBTQ+) persons; persons with disabilities; persons who live in rural areas; and persons otherwise adversely affected by persistent poverty or inequality.*

The only group not listed are urban-living, straight, able-bodied whites, who must be the 'overserved community', whatever that might be.

I am confused, very confused. It appears that achieving equity requires balancing the outcomes for all these diverse groups. In the final essay, I will unpack the implications of this objective that is at the heart of the social justice movement.

My moral compass was calibrated in the era when equality was society's goal. When the UK established the Commission for Racial Equality (1976) it was to 'give everyone an equal chance to live free from fear of discrimination, prejudice and racism'. That's when equality meant 'the state or condition of being equal, emphasising sameness and uniformity in treatment, opportunities, and rights among all individuals'.

While I was writing this book, an event occurred that starkly contrasted the difference between the words and the anger it generates.

Coleman Hughes is a young black author who writes about culture, politics and race. He was invited to give a TED talk about colour blindness, the subject of his book, which was about to publish. *The End of Race Politics: Arguments for a Colorblind America* is an excellent analysis of the subject.

I have always respected TED and its goal of being 'devoted to curiosity, reason, wonder and the pursuit of knowledge – without an agenda'. I especially warmed to the part about 'without an agenda'.

Hughes believes colour blindness was central to the antislavery and civil rights movement but has now become a dirty word. With the TED curation team, Hughes prepared his presentation, had it approved and delivered it to a crowd of 2,000. It was well received. He was delighted, as were the TED staff – or so they seemed.

At this point, the story becomes one of those tales the mainstream media (MSM) relishes as further proof the world is going crazy. Unfortunately for Hughes, they might be right. Research overwhelmingly shows that most Americans believe race and ethnicity should not influence job applications, entrance to academia or any other competitive part of life. The US Supreme Court concluded the same in 2023. Despite this, Hughes was told his talk had caused 'blowback' from some black TED employees. After much negotiation with TED's founder, the video of his talk was posted on the website. Ironically, it seemed the equality principle didn't apply to him.

Much to his horror, Hughes discovered it received far fewer views than would have been expected or could be explained. There was a 90% difference between his and other videos posted around the same time. The only explanation was TED's social media promotion machine was responsible. That's when the story was widely reported, and his viewing numbers soared.

If you are baffled at TED's actions, join the club. What could be wrong with seeking equality and, in the case of race, being colour blind? Seemingly its list of evils is long and grave. Here are a few: it ignores historical and systematic inequality, invalidates personal and cultural identities, perpetuates the status quo and so on and so on. These complaints are all expressed in impenetrable academic speak.

The next time you encounter an impassioned plea for equity, beware of its far-reaching consequences.

NEUTRALITY IS TAKING SIDES

For much of my life, I have been self-opinionated. I was a textbook case of having a dogmatic, obstinate belief in the correctness of my own beliefs. You name it, I would think it right or wrong, important or trivial, passionately supported by a smattering of facts.

Now I subscribe to the view, 'the older I get, the less I know'. When asked my thoughts about the latest event dominating the headlines my response is most likely, 'I haven't a clue', 'I'm not equipped to answer' or some other neutral response.

Rather than 'I have no opinion' being an honest statement of ignorance, it's now interpreted as being uncaring – perhaps this is a generational thing? It seems that being neutral or uninformed signifies tolerating the status quo. From there, it gets worse, with tolerance equating to supporting oppression. So we go from an honest statement: 'I know very little about the Ukraine conflict' to the accusation 'you must support Vladimir Putin'. Of course, I can recite the MSM's daily messages about who is the good and bad guy, but that is the thinnest of veneers covering an immensely complicated situation.

This capture and redefinition of words and their meaning is like the previous example of equity replacing equality. We have Herbert Marcuse, the German-American philosopher, to thank for this inversion of logic. In his *A Critique of Pure Tolerance* he says:

> *What is proclaimed and practiced as tolerance today is, in many of its most effective manifestations, serving the cause of oppression.*

Outside academia, I doubt many people have grappled with Marcuse's linking neutrality to oppression. Hopefully, they have better things to do with their time. However, this notion has affected society's behaviour and not for the better. Yet another reason my compass is pointing in the wrong direction.

When organisations feel impelled to take sides and involve themselves in issues beyond their control, it often ends in tears, sometimes of pain, more often of laughter. When Islington (a borough of London) declared itself a nuclear-free zone it brought cries of derision. Not that being nuclear-free is a bad idea – the criticism was of the irrelevance and arrogance of Islington's announcement.

Unilever decided that its products must have purpose over and above being safe and good value for money. For instance, Lux Soap was: 'inspiring women to rise above everyday sexist judgements and express their beauty and femininity unapologetically'. Vaseline was far more than skin creams, soaps and lotions – its purpose was:

 Bringing oversight, a racial equity lens, and social impact expertise to the strategy and creative, including advice on authentic community engagement, influencers and partnership, and storytelling.

Other than infuriating some of the company's investors, this dalliance with 'purpose' did no lasting harm and was abandoned when the next CEO took control, saying it had been 'an unwelcome distraction'. I guess you could argue it was a cackhanded marketing strategy to appeal to a generation of consumers who supposedly spend their lives looking for purpose.

What's harder to reverse is when organisations take a stand on moral issues. Then they set a precedent and declare a political and social position. Worse still, is when the views expressed haven't been canvassed; they are those of the senior executives.

Watching the heads of Harvard, MIT and Penn State University testifying before a Congress Committee was excruciating. Given numerous instances where their universities had intervened to stop speakers deemed 'hurtful', they defended their tolerance of the antisemitic demonstrations with the lame excuse 'it depends on the context'. The instant you take a position about one social issue and don't with another, you are being hypocritical, something we all do, all the time, but we are not a world-leading university.

The slaughter of 1,200 Israelis and the taking of 240 hostages revealed the deep-seated bias and hypocrisy that pervades organisations that claim to be impartial and caring. Academia has been the worst but the UN, Amnesty, BBC and Human Rights Watch failed badly on the neutrality test. Yes, yes, yes they must be balanced and take into account all 'sides' of the conflict. What institutions that rely on our trust can't do is make a virtue out of holding double standards.

There is no universe where responses like these can be judged as balanced:

- Human Rights Watch announced it had only verified three deliberate killings by Hamas and was soon calling on the US, UK and Canada to stop arms sales to Israel.
- A month after the attack, Iran, the country that trained and funded the attack, was appointed chair of the UN Human Rights Council's social forum.
- UN Women, an organisation supposedly safeguarding women's rights, issued a paper on the needs of Gazan women. It waited two months to condemn the rape of Israeli women.
- It took six months for the United Nations to confirm there are grounds to believe sexual violence, including rape, occurred during the 7 October attacks on Israel by Hamas.
- Time after time, the BBC misreported events in the conflict. The worst was attributing the destruction of a hospital to the Israeli military without evidence, which was soon revealed as nonsense.
- Amnesty was silent about the 7 October slaughter and eventually issued a statement condemning 'war crimes on all sides'.

Even the Red Cross failed to maintain neutrality in its social media coverage.

I can list a dozen conflicts and repressive acts by the state that have resulted in far more deaths than occurred in Gaza. Why did these not ignite the passions displayed by the passionate condemning Israel? What was it about the deaths of Muslims in China and Syria that only warranted a shrug, if indeed they received that? Somehow the sensitive and compassionate young have aligned themselves with a movement that despises everything they value.

What sense of balance has the UN had to these awful events? Between 2015 and 2022 the General Assembly adopted 140 resolutions about Israel and 68 for **all** other countries (UN Watch).

How these events contributed to the destruction of my moral compass is not that they happened, although even a cynic like me was shocked by the blatant display of bias. I have long suspected these institutions of being prejudiced. What shocked me was that nobody cared.

Those agreeing with my conclusions will shrug their shoulders and accept that's just how it is. Those who believe they were acting responsibly have already redefined neutrality as being a position they support. The majority accepted the behaviour without a thought.

JUSTICE IDEOLOGIES GO GLOBAL

The Vietnam War (1970s) was a proxy war between the ideologies of communism and capitalism. By any measure it was global event. The same with the wars in Iraq and Afghanistan, which also involved the religious dimension of Muslims pitted against the Christian West. Added to this list of bloody conflicts is Russia's invasion of Ukraine and Palestine's attack on Israel (7 October).

All these sparked demonstrations that might be a genuine outpouring of support for the innocent victims or an excuse for expressing hatred of the perceived villains and their allies. My hunch is it's primarily about the latter. No matter – it's understandable why death and destruction generate such strong feelings.

What I find difficult to grasp is why events about social justice receive global attention. A word of caution. Most of the time, the phrase 'global' really means events occurring throughout the Anglosphere or Western nations, at most 10% of the planet's population. This distinction is important because it is so easy to believe the concerns of the Western world are shared by the people of Africa and Asia – mostly, they aren't. Perhaps that's proof of our lingering, Western-centric arrogance.

Arguably, Occupy Wall Street (2011) was the last of the outpourings against the old nemeses of the left: unbridled capitalism, greedy bankers and injustice caused by financial inequality. The Occupy movement began with a demonstration in New York and quickly spread to 82 countries. Supposedly a response to the aftermath of the 2008 financial crash, it was energised by the uprisings in Egypt (part of the 'Arab Spring') and those in Greece and Spain resulting from the Eurozone crisis. The UK equivalent was Uncut, which focused on the age-old practice of tax avoidance.

Young, middle-class, university-educated activists started the US Occupy demonstration. All identified as Democrats, with different levels of disgruntlement at the party's acceptance of the status quo. Lots of angry young people without any objectives other than to demonstrate their disillusionment.

To my mind, this marked the end of the era when demonstrators allowed themselves to express humour. I always smile when seeing pictures of the placard reading 'Dear Capitalism, it's not you, it's us. Just kidding it's you.' In the UK, demonstrators set up camp close to St Paul's Cathedral and had a party. After attracting broad support, the mood changed, and they were eventually removed after allegations of drunkenness and drug taking.

After a few months, the movement ran out of steam and collapsed. Detractors dismissed the events as just another eruption of youthful anger. Supporters believed the movement was responsible for popularising the term 'the top 1%' in reference to those with disproportionate influence and benefits. What's certain is its anger was directed at economic inequities.

Today, rage against social inequities is what galvanises the young. There are lots of reasons for this but one event is often quoted as crystallising the change. During the Democratic primary election in 2016, when Bernie Sanders was performing well against Hillary Clinton, she gave a speech that elevated social issues above economic ones.

Sanders' policies were based on rectifying economic inequality.

He believed the vested interests of the establishment were the root cause of America's problems. Clinton attacked this as being simplistic and one-dimensional:

> *Raising taxes on millionaires and billionaires does little to change the painful reality that African-Americans are nearly three times as likely as whites to be denied a mortgage.*

Was this the point at which American politics experienced a seismic shock? Did this shift politics towards social rather than economic inequality? The irony about her speech that Democrats would prefer to forget is that after she beat Sanders to contest the presidency, many of his supporters transferred their allegiance to Donald Trump (12%). Holding vastly divergent political views, these two individuals were united in their scepticism about the establishment, the thing Clinton represented.

From then on, it's been social injustice that has galvanised mass protest, starting with the #MeToo storm in October 2017. The origins of this movement date from a decade before when a black American social activist (Tarana Burke) used the term Me Too to promote 'empowerment through empathy' among women who, like her, had been sexually abused. When 'Me Too' became the hashtag #MeToo and went viral on social media, it exposed shocking instances of sexual misconduct, especially in the entertainment industry and politics.

The legacy of this movement is the exposure of influential men who believed their positions gave them power over subordinate women. Harvey Weinstein, a former prominent film producer and now convicted sexual offender, was initially sentenced to 39 years in prison; this was reduced to 16 years on appeal in 2024.

This movement marked a shift in societal norms, making it more difficult for men to exploit their position to coerce women, at least in Western nations. The swift and broad impact was remarkable, yet it paled in comparison to the global reaction to the death of African American George Floyd in May 2020.

The circumstances of his death are well known, so I will not recount the story. What I still struggle to understand is the speed and extent of the subsequent protests. Each year, hundreds of Americans are killed in the process of arrest; many, probably most, are black. What distinguished Floyd's death was that it was captured on video and released on social media. The group Black Lives Matter (BLM) then became involved and the use of the hashtag #BlackLivesMatter soared. Between 26 May and 7 June 2020, it was used nearly 50 million times on Twitter (now X).

Anger on social media was followed by demonstrations on the streets in the US and throughout Europe. It's impossible to quantify the costs of the buildings destroyed and lives lost during these riots. The property damage resulting from the riots in the US is estimated to have surpassed $2 billion, making them the costliest in the country's history. At least 25 deaths directly resulted from the disturbances and the looting.

In the UK, the BLM logo and the face of George Floyd were everywhere. It sparked a prolonged period of introspection where it seemed every organisation was atoning for past racial wrongdoings and lack of racial diversity. What I still wrestle to understand is how the death of a black man in Minnesota, USA, affected so many people in the UK. Yet the annual murder of around 50 black teenagers by stabbing barely gets reported.

Both these events have resulted in much good that is to be celebrated. However, I have a lingering unease that's hard to define. It's the speed these social movements spread and the simplicity and conformity of their beliefs. They reduce complex problems to simple battles between good and bad. Perhaps that's how social change now evolves, driven by events that tick all the boxes for success on social media. Let's hope it only works when the social change is for the good and not when it's driven by darker motives. I fear that question may have already been answered by the surge in antisemitism following the 7 October attack.

ONE STRIKE AND YOU ARE OUT

In 2013, a 16-year-old Palestinian girl sent some nasty racist tweets about blacks and Jews. It was a fit of teenage rebellion that she soon regretted and she deleted the messages. Seven years later, she works for her father's food business in Minneapolis. The year is 2020 and the protests about George Floyd's death are raging. Like many other businesses, her father hung BLM posters in his stores and donated food to the demonstrators. His daughter took part in the protests.

Somehow, her teenage tweets re-emerged and triggered a hate campaign against her father's company. Customers and employees were intimidated and the anger turned on his family. A few idiotic tweets by his teenage daughter very nearly ruined his business.

The company survived, although his daughter was forced abroad. This is a graphic example of the intolerant attitude that has developed in parallel with the supposedly caring social justice movement. There are so many things that are disturbing about this story that it's hard to know where to start. The response by the demonstrators was so extreme and unnecessary it defies explanation. What possible good was served by ruining a family business employing hundreds of local people (many of whom were black)?

In English law, those under 18 have their criminal convictions removed from their record after five years – inappropriate social media posts live on forever. You might argue that Floyd's death caused extreme reactions among the protesters, who were so emotional their anger led to unwarranted actions. That much of the rioting that followed involved looting questions that explanation.

Perhaps the same rationale applies to the academic who expressed views deemed to be racist, the author who liked a tweet thought to be transphobic and the comedian whose jokes were seen as harmful. Their wrongs create such feelings of distress, resulting in an unintentional overreaction. There are so many subjects that ignite these extreme reactions, so many easily hurt people and so many defenders of the vulnerable that the link between the 'crime' and the retribution has become horribly distorted.

This extreme reaction of retribution to a perceived wrong has its own name: 'cancel culture'.

I detest the term nearly as much as I do the word 'woke'. In his book *A Heretic's Manifesto: Essays on the Unsayable* Brendan O'Neill eloquently captured how it understates the enormity of what's occurring:

> *It's too soft. Too quaint. Cute, almost. It's like referring to the Inquisition as information management or to Salem as accountability culture. It's too euphemistic. And like all euphemisms, with their embarrassment at bluntness, their discomfort with the unpleasantries of truth, it disguises more than it illuminates. That phrase makes it sound like we are experiencing a mere inconvenience – the bloody drag of occasional cancellation – when in truth we are living through one of the gravest reversals of free thought and of Enlightenment itself of modern times. Sorry to say it so uneuphemistically.*

I don't for an instant believe there is a rational, humane explanation for this extreme behaviour. This 'gotcha' reaction is all about the thrill of exercising power; it's the crazed illogicality once called mob rule. Wearing the mask of standing up for minorities, for righting past wrongs, soon slips to good old-fashioned vengeful behaviour.

Mining social media to discover past indiscretions and then acting as judge and jury over past events, by applying today's transitory moral code, provides an endless supply of baddies to be vilified.

There is no way I can orientate my moral compass to make sense of this lust for instant, disproportional justice.

In the early days of the internet, the Chinese searched for evidence of wrongdoing. It was called *renrou sousuo*, literally translated as 'human flesh search'. If we had been as honest, instead of wrapping it in moralistic language, we might have saved ourselves a lot of pain.

OPPONENTS AREN'T JUST WRONG, THEY'RE EVIL

About half a century ago, I attended my first sales training course. I was learning a new technique to persuade people to agree with my arguments and buy my products. Previously, sales tactics involved either subtly manipulating customers into buying or inundating them with information and aggressively addressing their reservations until their resolve broke and they signed the contract. Back then, selling was akin to engaging in combat.

This new approach was all about exercising empathy by anticipating their objections, admitting they had valid concerns, declaring you shared some of their opinions and then gradually building the arguments, making them part of the team that made the purchase decision, not the adversary that was beaten. Thus, selling transformed into a civilised process, not a battle. Well, that was the theory.

This experience calibrated my moral compass. Bullying adversaries into agreement might seem to work, but it's an illusion. The expression 'I guess you are right' really means 'I am not really convinced but will keep my opinions to myself.'

It seems we are returning to the old school of persuasion but going one step further. Rather than viewing those with different views as being innocently ill-informed, they are now seen as evil. We all too often see activists shouting their beliefs with a passion that's not intended to convince but to silence. The rallying cries 'You need to get educated', 'do the work' and 'check your privilege' set my compass into an uncontrollable spin.

There can't be two words more likely to ignite a tirade of abusive arguments than 'Donald' and 'Trump'. I must admit that I have teased my friends by suggesting that the past president was not as bad as they thought. It's like flipping a switch and watching them explode with expletives about the man. Long ago, I became convinced that Trump's derangement syndrome was a real and serious condition. I am more convinced than ever I was right.

Not only did Hillary Clinton label Trump's supporters as 'deplorables' she believes they need 'deprogramming'. I was surprised she didn't suggest exorcism. Politicians have always exercised the art of hyperbole but those opposing Trump have set new records. He is posed as an existential risk to America's democracy. Such extreme reactions have polarised politics into two factions that don't just disagree; they hate each other. Perhaps I am being melodramatic? I hope so.

According to Pew Research, there's little chance that romance will overcome political differences. Nearly half of single Democrat supporters said they 'definitely wouldn't' date somebody who voted for Trump — about three-quarters said it was 'unlikely' they would. Women were far more strident in their opposition than men. Republican supporters were less phased by having a romantic entanglement with a Democrat. For them, physical attraction trumps political views.

Virtually the same aversion to cross-political dating happens in the UK. Labour supporters are unlikely to date Conservatives, who are far more politically agnostic. Female Labour supporters are the most strident about 'never kissing a Tory'.

A similar divide occurs with views about the EU referendum. Only a third of 'remain'-supporting young people would consider dating a 'leaver'. Those wanting out of Europe weren't so concerned — two-thirds didn't care and would happily date a remainer.

The leftward drift of women keeps showing up in opinion research. Most recently (November 2023) 46% of Gen Z women identified themselves as liberal compared with 28% of their male contemporaries.

It was during the UK's referendum to leave the EU that

debating went from the usual rough and tumble to becoming toxic. Even within political parties, disagreement about the EU turned nasty. Referring to leave supporters as 'mad, swivel-eyed loons' isn't likely to change their minds. This was one Tory talking about another. Eight years after the referendum, I'm still reticent talking about the subject because of the anger it generates.

This demonisation of opponents isn't limited to political adversaries; it extends to those with opposing views on social issues. When a founder of the UK environmental group Extinction Rebellion was asked if he would allow a demonstration to block an ambulance with a dying child from reaching the hospital, he said, without hesitation, 'Yep.'

At a transgender pride rally, the crowd cheer and applaud as a speaker shouts, 'If you see a fucking Terf [slang for traditional feminist], punch them in the face.' After his arrest and release, it was revealed he was a biological male with criminal convictions for kidnap, torture and attempted murder. Ironically, many in the crowd were holding placards declaring #NotSafeToBeMe and other expressions of their vulnerability.

During a lecture at Yale School of Medicine's Child Study Centre a New York-based psychiatrist said:

> *I had fantasies of unloading a revolver in the head of any white person that got in my way, burying their body and wiping my bloody hands as I walked away relatively guilt-less, with a bounce in my step.*

This is one of the more printable quotes from her lecture about racial intolerance.

These are extreme examples; at least, I hope to God that they are extreme and rare. And yes, I appreciate it is dangerous to use them to draw conclusions, but, and it's a big but, they do illustrate a type of behaviour that I fear is spreading. It's as if wrapping oneself in the righteousness of supporting a cause permits unreasonable behaviour. I care so much about XYZ; I am so fearful, hurt and vulnerable (add your own term) that I am permitted to say and do things that would normally be forbidden.

I am writing these words on Xmas Eve and wonder how many Xmas Day lunches will be ruined by fruitless arguments when words will be said that can't be unsaid. Too many, I fear.

AREN'T SMART PEOPLE SUPPOSED TO MAKE SMART CHOICES?

History is littered with examples of bright people, brimming with academic credentials, making stupid decisions. My mother drummed into me as a child that I could be top of the class – something I never achieved – and have no common sense. If anybody doubted this wisdom, then watching the investigations into the Covid pandemic reveals politicians and their advisers, all educated at the finest universities, running around like headless chickens with their hair on fire (excuse the mixed metaphors).

When writing about the antics of academics, journalists, businesspeople, politicians and the great and good of society, I have been spoilt for examples of idiotic behaviour. You are probably thinking that reading any newspaper provides ample proof that the inmates are running the asylum.

And yet it's hard to understand that intelligence, the sort that's rewarded with degrees and doctorates, doesn't necessarily result in intelligent decisions. Achieving academic success was the single objective of my early years. And here I am, gazing at my compass, wondering how it could have been so wrong. My instinctive reaction on hearing Prof XYZ from the University of ABC intoning on the certainty of their beliefs is to disbelieve them.

What makes this revelation even more disturbing is that for most adolescents, achieving academic success is the only game in town. Riding the exam escalator and jumping off clasping a BSc or BA is the default behaviour. Many stay for an additional year to study for an MSc. Brimming with youthful optimism and proudly holding their diplomas, members of Generation Z naturally view themselves as the architects of tomorrow. Lacking practical experi-

ence, their academic qualifications are all that validate the legitimacy of their viewpoints.

Social commentators reinforce the value of academic success
and confer on it a sense of superiority and rightness by differenti-
ating opinions by the respondent's educational achievement. Here
are some recent examples:

- *Adults with postgraduate experience most likely to have
  consistently liberal political values. (Pew Research)*
- *There is an increasing divergence in outcomes based on
  education levels, with Democrats making serious gains with
  college-educated voters while Republicans win far greater
  shares of non-college-educated white voters. (Politico)*
- *If current trends continue, more educated voters will only
  become more electorally important: by 2030, the majority of
  constituencies are set to contain more graduates than school
  leavers. (Social Market Foundation)*

There was more commentary about the educational divide of
Brexit voters than any other variable. I still laugh at the false precision of the research by Leicester University that concluded: 'Had
just 3% more of the population gone to university, the UK would
probably not be leaving the EU.'

The explicit assumption is that those possessing academic
credentials hold the correct views and will make the right decision.
This is such a dangerous assumption. Not only is it wrong, but it is
a driving force for the polarisation that is dividing society.

There have been at least half a dozen research studies showing
social class is inversely related to the exercise of 'wise reasoning',
especially about interpersonal matters. Those from poor or working-class backgrounds seem better able to appreciate the views of
others and reach compromised solutions while avoiding conflict.

We will return to the implications of this blunder in the final
chapter, but first, how is it possible for so many bright people to
believe so many stupid things?

Gurwinder Bhogal, a British-Indian writer, penned my favourite explanation in *Why Smart People Believe Stupid Things.* This quote summarises his thinking:

> *When intelligent people affiliate themselves to ideology, their intellect ceases to guard against wishful thinking, and instead begins to fortify it, causing them to inadvertently mastermind their own delusion, and to very cleverly become stupid.*

None of us like being proved wrong. We will do our damnedest to amass evidence to support our beliefs by erecting barriers to exclude facts that undermine them. The extent to which we defend our opinions may differ, but we all employ techniques to avoid changing our minds. Sometimes called 'belief perseverance' or 'motivated reasoning', it is best known as confirmation bias. The more cognitive reasoning intelligence you have the better you are at doing it.

We view the world through the filter of our 'mind-locked' beliefs, which are reinforced by our selective access to new information. If by mistake we encounter a contrary view, we ignore it or diminish its importance. Can you see the elegant feedback loop this creates?

Being selective about the news we consume strengthens our long-held beliefs and that, in turn, makes us more determined to reject or ignore information that challenges these opinions. Such an elegant arrangement avoids the chore of thinking anew, and bright people have better things to do than re-evaluate their past decisions.

This explains why the supposedly intelligent are good at maintaining silly beliefs, but how did they get it so wrong to start with? This begins with another of the behavioural quirks we mistake for intelligence called the 'bias blind spot'. Most of us believe that biased thinking occurs in others, not ourselves. This belief is more pronounced in those with higher cognitive ability.

Bright people are good at fooling themselves that they aren't biased.

And so we get to the core question of the link between intelligence and the rightness of our beliefs. It would be nice to think we employ our intelligence in the quest for truth. So, the more intelligence you have the closer to the truth your beliefs. There's lots of research showing that's not the case, however. More likely, we employ our intelligence to increase our status and wellbeing, which is known as 'identity-protective cognition'. Put bluntly, enhancing our social value is a huge factor in determining our beliefs, not their intellectual elegance.

Combine all of these factors with the skills many intelligent people have to argue and promote their ideas, and you can see why such dubious and simplistic notions are espoused by those who should know better.

WEALTH OF WOES: THE IRONY OF MODERN UNHAPPINESS

Throughout these essays, two themes have emerged: trust in our institutions is in freefall, and many of us are unhappy and anxious. I will not repeat the statistics that justify these trends and my caveats about the accuracy of the numbers. Despite all my reservations about the difficulty of researching social issues, I must conclude the mood of society is disturbingly bleak.

It's very easy to slip on the rose-tinted glasses and opine about how life in the past was much simpler, more fun and freer from the weight of doom that's crushing so many young people and a lot of their parents. There's no science that allows me to compare the relative highs and lows of different eras, but my trusty moral compass tells me ours is not exceptionally awful.

I am writing these words as the year comes to an end, and the news focuses on the horrible loss of life in the Ukraine war and the Middle East conflict. Irrespective of your views, the death toll is dreadful and another reason to be gloomy about 2023 and apprehensive about 2024. As awful as this is, the total loss of life in these conflicts is less than in a single battle at the Somme during WWI. We watch the suffering on TV and social media; my parents and grandparents were directly involved.

Shouldn't we celebrate that the UK has become the first G20 country to cut its carbon emissions in half and is now at levels last seen in 1879? That's because the average household's energy consumption is 40% less than in the mid-1990s. Along the way, the air quality in UK cities is the best since records began and 600 times better than it was in 1900.

UK emissions dropped 5.7% in 2023 as global emissions inched up by 1%. And let's not forget that the country is over halfway to achieving net zero by 2050 despite the economy growing by over 60% in the last 30 years.

And no, this hasn't been done at the expense of global inequality, which is the lowest for the past 150 years. How come I missed all the celebrations taking place about this good news? They must have been drowned out by the celebrations that COP28 agreed to 'transition from fossil fuels'. Apologies if this sounds a tad cynical; it's because it is.

Of course, I could present a list of things that have got worse, many of them resulting from the self-inflicted global shutdown in response to Covid.

My instincts tell me that the doom plague is not a rational response to the state of the planet. It seems that many people – my guess more young than old – have a default world view that is biased towards catastrophe rather than optimism. Perhaps the condition is a natural outcome of inflating the language, something I have already discussed. Extreme words like 'nightmare', 'crisis', 'emergency' and 'breakdown' are commonplace. The NHS is always on the edge of a precipice and we live in a perpetual state of being 'one minute to midnight' before some awful event occurs.

Those trying to remould society, the army of activists, have brilliantly exploited catastrophising by ensuring their messaging is always laced with the most extreme outcomes. They know that policymakers are terrified of being blamed for catastrophes and the media adores using the word in its headlines. In the past, sage advice was 'prepare for the worst but hope for the best'. Today, it is 'prepare for the worst and then some'.

We are inundated with news and content masquerading as news on TikTok, Google, Facebook, X and the digital version of the legacy media. If only the sentiment of news was neutral rather than inherently negative or as Tracy Jamal Morgan, the American stand-up comedian, expresses it: 'Bad news travels at the speed of light; good news travels like molasses.'

As one of life's natural pessimists, I find myself in a strange place, gazing at my compass for confirmation that things aren't that bad. I refuse to believe we are living through some sort of polycrisis or, worse still, a permacrisis.

Telling a depressed person to 'pull themselves together; things are better than they think' has never worked. Using the same technique when the malaise grips much of society will be equally futile. Hopefully, somebody brighter than me knows the solution.

Roughly 780,000 years ago the magnetic poles flipped. What was north became south. This happened in a geological blink of an eye (less than 10,000 years). Had you been around and using a compass, you would have seen it behaving erratically and then rendered useless. Something similar has happened with the belief system that I thought was reassuringly permanent. As I have described, my familiar moral waymarks have shifted position or disappeared.

My first thought was 'it must be me', but I kept encountering others who were equally, if not more, confused. Most of them were younger and had previously inhabited the left-leaning part of the old political spectrum. I was just lost. They were lost and angry that the beliefs they held dear were being abandoned. Throughout the writing of these essays this group of lost souls has swelled in size and has even got a name – heterodox thinkers.

Most of them are American and watch in disbelief as bastions of the old school of progressive thinking now hold views and behave in ways they despise. As I have discovered, much of academia, the media, government, tech companies and big business have distorted liberal thinking into a nasty, controlling ideology.

I am indebted to my fellow travellers who have been wrestling to understand why their world has been turned upside-down. In the final essay, I will build on their thinking and attempt to make sense of it all. Before that I have summarised the conclusions of each essay, just in case you need reminding.

ESSAYS IN BRIEF – KEY POINTS

The best business training I ever received was from IBM, the company that once dominated the computing industry. Before presenting to clients we were taught to prepare an 'elevator version' of our pitch. We had to visualise being in the elevator with the client and answering their question, 'So what's it all about?' You had to summarise your presentation into a version you could recite before getting to the tenth floor.

The only way of doing this is to leave out most of the facts, references and context, focusing on the main points that express the important conclusions.

Before we go into my final analysis of what's going on, let's review the elevator points for each essay – although, looking at their length, I would need the elevator to be moving very slowly and going to the 35th floor.

For the sake of brevity, I have avoided repeating my caveats and niggling doubts about judging today's institutions. The following concerns apply to all of the essays.

- I am viewing the world through the eyes of a 74-year-old. I have tried to exclude the prejudices and the decades of confirmation bias accumulated with age.

- I have done my best to discard my 'rose-coloured' spectacles, which view the past as being better than the present.
- The labels of human behaviour and beliefs change, but they are cosmetic differences; the fundamentals are unaltered.
- It's impossible not to be overly influenced by the current dominant narratives as they undoubtedly colour our perceptions. Hopefully, I have successfully put them to one side.
- Most of the book was written during 2023 when the UK and US were enveloped in doom and gloom. I am instinctively optimistic, and it was a fight not to be overly influenced by this malaise, which I pray is short in duration.

Please remember that summarising complex arguments results in them sounding too extreme, too black and white. You need to read the essays to understand all the shades of grey.

ACADEMIA – THE TRASHING OF A PRICELESS BRAND

I began this essay harbouring an idealised vision of academia as a place free from day-to-day pressures where new ideas flourish. I ended with serious concerns about its integrity and value. Of all the institutions I studied, academia gives me the greatest concern.

There's much to criticise about its workings but also much that doesn't attract attention and delivers huge benefits. Currently, all the attention is focused on its failings, something that has accelerated since the 7 October 2023 attack on Israel. Never have attitudes about academia been so politically polarised.

Trust in universities is at rock bottom. Doubts about their value and objectivity are at record levels. Even the accuracy and honesty of their research is being questioned.

Grade inflation has destroyed the credibility of the awards

system, with the highest level of degrees the norm, not the exception.

The notion of universities being isolated from the commercial realities of the world is long over. They are commercial operations fighting to attract the highest-paying customers (overseas students) and minimise costs. For most students, their investment in a degree is still financially worthwhile, but for many, it's not.

Universities have become mono-political cultures where the dominant ideology is increasingly at odds with the public's. Progressive views about identity and social inequality have replaced the old left–right arguments concerning economics and class.

Striving for equality and making universities more diverse and inclusive have resulted in the universal adoption of DEI theory, which is influencing all parts of the university's workings, administrative and academic.

When implemented at a tactical level, what was done for noble ideals is distorting the very nature of academic freedom. This is more pronounced in the US than the UK. I think the reason is abandoning the goal of equality and replacing it with 'equity', which can only be achieved by positive and negative discrimination.

Intolerance to opposing views has increased to the point where the concept of free speech is threatened. The majority of students believe silencing speakers is not only acceptable but sometimes necessary.

The curtailing of diverse opinions has spread to every part of academia – the recruiting of faculty, application for grants and the submission of academic papers. These were once determined by merit and now have to satisfy DEI considerations. The goals of the University of California Berkeley perfectly explain the change: 'Excellence in advancing equity and inclusion must be considered on par with excellence in research and teaching.'

The noisiest, most aggressive people in academia have a disproportionate effect on its future. The majority are probably sympathetic to their ideals but dislike their tactics. But, it's easier and safer to stay silent and keep your head down than oppose.

Student behaviour has always engendered feelings of incomprehension, annoyance and envy. Today, they are portrayed as a mix of fragility – with poor mental health and the need for protection from harmful ideas – with intolerance and quick to anger.

Those outside academia look on in disbelief, which is turning to anger. The goals and priorities of the institution are dangerously close to being so different from those of the public that, when ruptured, the respect will be beyond repair.

MEDIA – WHERE DID ALL THE TRUST GO?

The web has undermined the old advertising-funded business model, destroying many of the regional papers. Access to free content has damaged the finances of national publications. Digital technology enables the 24/7 availability of news channels, replacing legacy media's fixed cycles of reporting.

Attracting eyeballs is today's metric of success, not the thoroughness and objectivity of the reporting. The same applies to TV and internet news channels.

These different commercial conditions have affected the values and strategies of the mainstream media (MSM) and not for the better. Staffing levels have been reduced and journalists come from a narrower base of experience, a degree being required to enter the profession.

Despite striving to become more inclusive and diverse, the reverse has occurred. Mostly supporting the prevailing identity-focused culture, reporting has become more partisan.

News coverage has become sensationalised, with the subtlety of language being discarded and replaced with extreme expressions of what's right and wrong. Complex subjects are reduced to simplistic arguments.

For all these reasons, it's not surprising that across the Anglosphere, trust in the media is declining. In the UK and US, it is plummeting. Much of the public no longer see their priorities and beliefs reflected by the media, which has its own activist agenda.

Explanations for this problem are as polarised as the media's reporting. One group blames right-wing conspiracy theories for clouding the public's views. The other thinks the media has been captured by groupthink, with a vocal minority dictating the culture and what gets reported.

As employment in the media declines, it has increased in the fact-checking industry, often using journalist staff. The fear that legacy media and social media are a conduit for fake news that endangers society has driven its growth. Fact-checkers are the new arbiters of what's right and wrong, what's true and false.

Immune from the media's commercial pressures, these organisations are funded by governments, large companies and wealthy benefactors who have their own ideas about what constitutes 'the truth'. Their power to limit freedom of expression was revealed during the pandemic when the MSM abandoned all critical reporting and dissenting voices on social media were silenced.

Who decides if a statement is misinformation, disinformation or malinformation or if it will be hurtful and cause distress? These are the new conditions determining what's reported. Even the notion of objective reporting is questioned as being something distorted by Western history. Reporting of the 7 October 2023 massacre cast an unflattering spotlight on the extent to which parts of the media have willingly abandoned objectivity.

My prognosis for the future is distinctly negative. The more the media polarises, the more incentives it has to curate the news to please its readership. The very idea of it being 'mainstream', as in mainstream media, is fast vanishing.

POLITICS – MORE SHOWBIZ THAN STATESMANSHIP

Most people become politicians with the intention of doing good, although 'good' will differ depending on their politics. No doubt the money (not great) and the power it bestows (more perceived than actual) are also considerations. In the absence of effectiveness measures, their success is a subjective judgement. Well, here's my judgement: 1/10 or D- on the old exam grading structures.

Like the other institutions studied, measures of public trust are heading south. Only one in five people trust the government to put the needs of the nations first. That was in 2021, so I dread to think of today's figure. In the US, just 4% think their political system is working extremely well; two-thirds say they feel exhausted thinking about the subject.

The term 'political theatre' is often used to describe the process of government. This is done for good reason, as the similarities between politicians and actors and citizens and theatre audiences are uncannily similar. Most politicians aspire to a starring role, but few even get a speaking part. Audiences pay little attention to the actors until some faux pas in their private lives is revealed.

Our engagement with democracy is voting every four to five years, requiring little thought and taking a few minutes. Doing the weekly shop is more demanding. I have the uneasy feeling that this is a ritual because whoever wins, little is likely to change.

As amusing as it is to uncover the comical side of politics, it leads to a horribly serious conclusion: our system of government is unfit for purpose.

Politicians, be they lowly MPs, ministers or the prime minister, have far fewer degrees of freedom to govern than the electorate believes – certainly less than it understands. Their levers of control are surprisingly few and getting fewer.

Theoretically, politicians decide policy and civil servants make it a reality. This assumes the 'servants' appreciate their role and don't act as the masters. It also assumes they have the requisite skills and experience. Time after time, these assumptions are shown to be wrong.

There's a retinue of international organisations ever eager to control politicians' freedoms. The judiciary, national and international, is forever confining their scope of control. Then there are fiscal regulators that set the rules and dictate the scope of their policies. Politicians soon discover their power is a sham, yet they must act as if it's real because that's what the voters believe. In the absence of achievements, they provide a stream of rhetoric, keeping the audience happy with reasons to vote for them again.

We the audience, the citizens with the votes, are part of this nonsense. Despite perpetually being disappointed, we keep believing the system works, ever hopeful that the next group of players will be better than the last.

BUSINESS – CHARTING NEW PATHS OR LOSING DIRECTION?

Nearly half a century ago, I studied for a master's in business administration. Today's graduates learn much the same curriculum other than some additional modules about social responsibility. The body of knowledge of business has remained reassuringly constant.

Public trust has fallen in all of the institutions, with the exception of business, something that mystifies me. The most likely explanation is the constant pressure of the market ensures companies continually adapt. Those reacting to competitive pressure and changing cultural priorities prosper – Darwin's natural evolution theory applied to business.

Top among the social issues demanding new ways of thinking are the heightened concerns about the environment, racial equality and sexual diversity.

Sometimes, this sensitivity has turned to naïvety, and companies have made horrible blunders, much to the delight of the MSM, which has developed the narrative 'go woke, go broke'. These mistakes have all been made in companies' haste to appeal to minority groups with insufficient concern about antagonising their mainstream customers.

There's a more Machiavellian explanation for their motives. Promoting their concern about social issues is not only in harmony with the current zeitgeist; it deflects attention from the economic travails of their customers, some of which are their fault. This is especially true with the financial industry.

Companies face the challenge of managing a generational transition in their customers. The mainstay of most consumer businesses has been the Boomer generation. This is declining in numbers and spending power. Theoretically, they are being replaced by their children and grandchildren.

The economic travails of the past two decades have been especially painful for younger people. Many have been excluded from the prospect of home ownership by soaring housing costs. This, combined with the debts incurred in higher education, results in understandable resentment. Against this backdrop, companies are navigating the change to this new generation of customers and employees.

The financial rewards for senior managers in companies and employees in the digital industries have increased far faster than those of the average employee. Many business leaders have forged their personal reputations as social reformers as the size of their bank balances exploded.

With so much attention focused on the environment, fairness and inclusion, the management class has worked a wonderful trick of engendering trust while accumulating significant levels of wealth.

Expressing this point in more graphic terms, corporates have been extremely lucky that the anger of the perpetually angry has been diverted away from class and inequality to the muddy waters of identity politics, climate change and achieving equity.

Until now, companies have been able to demonstrate their adherence to the new social values through cosmetic actions that have avoided additional costs and radical change. Often, they have been able to profit from their newfound social consciences. This time is fast disappearing.

Displaying their environmental, social and governance (ESG) credentials along with their commitment to diversity, equity and inclusion (DEI) was relatively easy. Translating these ideals into tangible policies is far more difficult and dangerous.

ESG was an off-the-shelf 'feel-good' model that was easily adopted and profitable for the finance and consultancy industry. As so often, 'the devil is in the details' and has become unworkable when exposed to the complexities and uncertainties of business. When DEI just involved changing mission statements and running training courses, it resulted in some criticism. The further it expands into altering corporate processes, the more resentment it generates.

A beneficiary of the rush to DEI and ESG accreditation has been the 'trust mark' providers. These are supposedly independent companies that evaluate organisations, including companies, for their adherence to their benchmarks. The best-known of these is Stonewall.

When trust marks are evidence of a quantifiable and widely valued virtue, like improving quality, they can work. The further they venture into contentious areas, as has Stonewall, the more divisive they become and with that comes the risk of failure.

The unique position of trust that business holds is (in my view) under threat. The values of those insulated from the economic pressures facing the general population – senior managers and the ultra-wealthy – are being rejected. There's little overlap between the priorities of the elite and those of the masses. The further this rift expands the more vehement the response.

Already the measures of racial and sexual tolerance and willingness to adapt to environmental demands are declining. The more people are compelled, the greater their reaction.

National and supranational involvement in the workings of companies is another factor that damages trust. Increasingly, companies act upon government diktats rather than consumer pressure. The more governments interfere, the greater the alienation of customers.

Two megatrends that affect all businesses are the decline in Western values and their economies along with population ageing and mass migration. Neither of these is receiving adequate attention. All in all, the next decade of business looks much more challenging than the last.

LANGUAGE - FROM BEAUTIFUL TO BRUTAL

Much of this essay is about the natural evolution of words, how they come into and go out of fashion, how their meaning changes and how they are used to impress, insult and confuse.

The story then moves to the role of language in exercising power, control and influence. How language can manipulate public opinion, control narratives and exert social and political influence.

When money suffers from inflation, its value declines. Words are experiencing the same fate. In a noisy restaurant, everybody talks louder to be heard and soon everybody is shouting. The same is happening to our language.

Words that once had a precise meaning have become insults to silence debate. The full-volume nature of social media encourages short, sharp, put-down sentences devoid of meaning.

During the past decade, a more malevolent development has begun to limit our freedom of expression. No doubt done for the best of reasons, activist groups supporting social justice issues have attempted to dictate what can and cannot be said. Most often, this is done to protect minorities from harm and hurt; two words that have taken on a whole new meaning.

The most vocal and aggressive of these groups promotes transgender rights, demanding the banning of language that refers to the biological sexes, something that affects thousands of words and expressions.

The most concerning development (to me) is the outright suppression of expressing lawful beliefs – curtailing the freedom of speech. This began for the best of reasons (as many things do), responding to hostile forces (Russia and ISIS) who used social media for vengeful purposes.

Legitimate concerns about citizens' safety then extended to

the malicious use of social media influencing domestic events, especially those resulting in outcomes the establishment detested, namely Brexit and the election of Donald Trump. The pandemic and the controversy over vaccines and lockdown measures further fuelled this fear that 'fake news' was a dangerous, destabilising force.

As more has been discovered about the extension of the state's apparatus to limit personal freedoms of expression, the response has divided along political lines. Democrats believe it is necessary and to be welcomed. Republicans perceive it as a weapon used against them to undermine the democratic process.

What is not disputed is that governments in the US and throughout Europe have the mechanisms to influence (I would say control) social media companies and what they publish. This has created a panoply of new terms defining the rules of permitted commentary along with new companies empowered to determine what is true, false or dangerous.

These developments have led to much speculation about the parallels to the world George Orwell predicted in *1984*. Hopefully, we are not heading to his dystopian future, but it will be one where limits are increasingly applied to our freedom of expression. Some will call this censorship; others, providing safe spaces. And so the meaning of language will keep changing.

JUSTICE – TEETERING ON A SLIPPERY SLOPE

Understanding the effectiveness of the police and trends in the UK's crime levels was my initial objective for writing this essay. I soon discovered this would be impossible. The official statistics recording crimes keep changing, as does the public's willingness to report incidents.

My focus changed to investigating the role the law plays in our lives, how it relates to the other parts of the state (especially elected politicians) and how it is enforced.

Supporting the whole edifice of the system of law and order is an implicit agreement between the public and the government. In exchange for an efficient and fairly administered justice system, we obey the rules. Well, the vast majority obey them.

Mostly, the police work out of sight of the law-abiding majority. Drug and alcohol abuse, domestic violence and petty crime take up much police time. Two areas consuming increasing police resources are apprehending the small group of hard-core criminals who commit a significant amount of crimes. The other is their unwanted role as social workers in uniforms. The police are expected to intervene when other parts of the justice and social care system fail.

There are two parts of the justice system: the courts and the prison service. Both of these are working at full capacity. Both are failing by their own benchmarks to provide an adequate service, placing further pressure on the police.

The MSM contains regular accounts of the failures and misuse of the justice system. A common theme is the police ignoring crimes that concern the public and instead pursuing those seen as trivial. At the core of these stories is society's expectation of fairness – why is person X arrested but not person Y?

Politicians, not the police, set the rules. Too often, these are ill-conceived and impractical and done for short-term expediency or political point scoring.

The words 'hate' and 'harmful' have recently taken on a different significance. Both terms have legal implications that force the police to intervene in incidents that often bemuse the public. Crimes of 'hate' are sentenced more harshly despite the burden of proof being highly subjective.

How the police reacted to specific crimes involving black people has significantly affected their organisation and culture, in both the US and UK. After a prolonged investigation of the death of a black teenager, London's police were accused of being 'institutionally racist'. In the US, the videoed death of a black person being detained ignited an immediate and, at times, violent reaction resulting in the movement to 'defund the police'.

Among many in society, the police's operations are perceived as being fatally flawed. Whenever a case of police malpractice is discovered, it is held up as evidence of their institutional failure. This contrasts with failings in the healthcare system, which are dismissed as 'one-offs' and rationalised as resulting from the lack of adequate funding.

The constant criticism of the police in the US and demands for funding cuts have had unintended consequences. Police numbers have declined due to officers taking early retirement and difficulties in recruiting new staff. It's unknown whether this has resulted in the increase in crime reported in the major cities.

Public perceptions of the police are not helped by the numerous voices supposedly talking on their behalf. In both countries the structure of policing is complex and based on geography. In the UK, it is even more fragmented, with numerous staff groups representing officers of different races.

For most people, seeking justice in the courts is too expensive. A few have their lawyers' fees paid by the state, but most are faced with potentially horrendous costs. The notion that everybody is equal in the eyes of the law might be right in theory but only the wealthy can afford to enter the court's doors.

Policing is at the threshold where the actions of the vocal and visible minorities threaten the tolerance of the majority. Like an iceberg, most of what the police do is out of sight, engaged in the unpleasant part of society that most of us do our best to avoid. Those parts of the police's activities that are visible and reported too often convey the message their priorities are not those of the majority.

I fear that the first principle of policing, 'The police are the public and the public are the police' is no longer true, something that increasing numbers of people believe.

FINANCIAL AUTHORITIES – INCOMPETENT REGULATORS DON'T PROTECT US FROM GREED

There are three rules that will significantly reduce the risk of being a victim of fraud. Most people instinctively know them but repeatedly ignore them.

- Rule 1: If something sounds too good to be true, it probably is. When an investment claims 'guaranteed returns', 'market-beating performance', 'limited availability' or 'loss protected', you are in trouble.
- Rule 2: The Philosopher's Stone doesn't exist. Claims that the rules of investment are changed by some radical innovation often herald a crash in values. You can make money, lots of it, from these opportunities, but it's gambling, not investing.
- Rule 3: Our decision-making is more governed by behavioural instincts than rational thinking. Understanding these weaknesses by reading a book about behaviour science would be the best investment you will ever make.

Fraud and its causes are eternal. Wanting to get rich at the expense of others is a human frailty that transcends time and geography. The techniques used are timeless, yet they keep on working. There is nearly always a plausible explanation for why the investment opportunity is 'special'. By flaunting their personal wealth, the fraudster creates confidence and seems to demonstrate the investment's success. The urgency to complete the deal is the final component – this is a once-in-a-lifetime opportunity.

The thing that distinguishes the very best fraudsters is their instinctive ability to appear to uphold the latest cultural values. Most recently, the superstars of fraud projected a persona rejecting the accumulation of personal wealth; they were making money to help mankind.

Although not strictly defined as fraud, the failure of government institutions that manage the economy results in the same, if not worse, financial losses for the public. A miscalculation by the Treasury or the Federal Reserve can cause havoc with the value of investments.

Theoretically, there is an army of bureaucrats employed to police the finance industry to protect the unwary from being duped. They have one thing in common. They don't work. I can't think of any instance where so many people have been employed and been so ineffective.

BELIEFS – MY MORAL COMPASS IS BUSTED

If only I could buy a moral compass on Amazon because mine is busted. Most of my certainties are less certain; many have gone. I can no longer trust the heuristics, the mental shortcuts, that guided my behaviour. My system of beliefs is no longer fit for purpose.

Life was simple when political beliefs were on a spectrum ranging from the left to right. At the extremes were Marxists and Fascists. That was something of a mystery, since they seemed remarkably similar. Anarchists were always an anomaly that I never fathomed.

Those believing the state could solve all our problems were on the left. The right thought the state was the problem and that market forces were the answer. It was a simple model and easy to understand.

All the terms that defined the positions on the spectrum have lost their meaning. Depending on your viewpoint, being on the left or right has become a term of abuse. Appending 'ultra', 'far' and 'extreme' to 'right-wing' is tossed into sentences describing anybody not sharing the same opinions. You will be lucky to find two people who can agree on the difference between a liberal, progressive, social democrat and democratic socialist.

For most of my life, society strived to achieve equality by abandoning stereotypes and treating everybody the same, irrespective of their race and sex. This idea has not just become obsolete; it has become wrong. Supposedly treating people equally allows you to ignore their differences and needs.

Equity of outcomes is today's goal, a far more complicated concept because it requires understanding where in the hierarchy of social deprivation everybody belongs and then treating them unequally.

The earliest version of the statement 'You are with us or against us' is in the bible: 'Whoever is not with me is against me, and whoever does not gather with me scatters.' I had always thought it a polarising idea, since situations are rarely that simple. However, these sentiments are becoming popular as shared beliefs become the litmus test for social acceptance. Neutrality, or unwillingness to take sides, is seen as an acceptance of the unfair status quo.

This need always to have an opinion also applies to organisations, which appear impelled to reject neutrality and take positions about global events. Once started, this is difficult to stop and it's difficult to remain consistent.

Social media has enabled new ideologies about social justice to spread rapidly. The death of a black man in Minneapolis causes riots in Rome. The disclosure about the sexual misconduct of an influential man in New York leads to similar incidents being reported in London. Impassioned support for Palestine spreads rapidly throughout academia in the US and Europe and then into the wider population.

Opinion about why this happens is divided. Some claim it is the rightness and importance of the injustices that propel their popularity. Some believe it's because these events reduce complex issues to symbolic battles between good and bad that resonate with all the popular values.

Today's social activist is a strange mix of being caring and sympathetic to racial and sexual differences, intent on safeguarding the vulnerable from harm and hurt, and at the same time being cruelly unforgiving about those who offend their beliefs. The circumstances of the misdeed are immaterial. Once done, the perpetrator is marked for life.

This same absoluteness applies to people holding contrary beliefs. Notions about 'live and let live' have been abandoned. Holding certain opinions pigeonholes people not just as right or wrong but as good or bad.

Until recently, I instinctively used the heuristic that educated people make smarter decisions. It seemed obvious that education bestowed knowledge and reasoning ability. The more you had, the better. Perhaps this notion has always been nonsense, but it definitely is today. No longer should you automatically value what somebody says based on their educational credentials.

Throughout writing these essays, two themes have emerged: trust in our institutions is in freefall, and many of us are unhappy and anxious. If judged by its ability to guide us and improve our state of mind, then this new-fangled digital moral compass doesn't work very well. For the time being, I will stick with my old analogue version.

SO WHAT'S GOING ON? MAKING SENSE OF IT ALL

> The surest way to work up a crusade in favour of some good cause is to promise people they will have a chance of maltreating someone. To be able to destroy with good conscience, to be able to behave badly and call your bad behaviour 'righteous indignation' – this is the height of psychological luxury, the most delicious of moral treats.

Aldous Huxley, *Crome Yellow*, 1921

> Many institutions have been taken over by activists who behave as if they are theirs to dispose of. Trustees wink at the pursuit of ideological goals without popular consent. They have power without responsibility, while politicians have accountability without authority.

Prof Robert Tombs, 2024

Our institutions are facing 'troubles,' and I've had the luxury of time to explore why. I have tried to make each essay free-standing, spending time probing each institution's entrails and then diagnosing what afflicts it.

Albert Einstein supposedly said, 'If you can't explain it simply, you don't understand it well enough.' The conclusion that our institutions' troubles are the fault of them going woke is beautifully simple but meaningless. Now I must provide an alternative.

Is there a common verdict, or is each institution facing its own set of unique problems? Elon Musk has concluded the institutions and their leaders had caught the 'woke mind virus'. As much as I admire the man, I don't think that takes us much further forward.

You don't have to wait until this essay's end to discover my answer. The institutions are grappling with the same problems as they try and align with their perception of society's new moral values. Their effort to translate these beliefs into practical measures is at the heart of what's commonly referred to as 'woke' controversies. However, there are even more potent dynamics at play related to technology, economics and demographics that have cruelly revealed their structural weaknesses. Moreover, the pandemic has not only amplified their failings – it has made them all the more visible.

Before moving on to my diagnosis, I want to introduce two companions who have been looking over my shoulder as I wrote these essays. They are not real people but concocted characters with very different opinions and beliefs. One is aghast at what's happening to society, and the other believes change is essential and needs to be more radical and happen faster.

I can guarantee that you will sympathise with one and detest the other. Their clash of values explains many of the difficulties I will discuss.

EXTREME OPPOSITES – DIFFERENT VIEWS, SHARED ANGER

I know these are caricatures and that I have continually warned about the dangers of stereotypes. And yes, perhaps I have over-stated their positions. But it's important we understand the views of those battling to control how society evolves, those wanting the reins of power. This is my attempt to do that.

Ms 'Tomorrow-Belongs-To-Us'

This person is more likely to be young than old and non-binary, known as Jane, preferring the pronouns ey/em/eir. Using these was a step too far for my writing skills, so I stuck with they/them/theirs.

Jane, who typically would have aligned with Labour/Democrat ideologies, is disillusioned with party politics and has lost all interest in its meaningless, petty battles. The so-called progres-sives promised the earth and failed to deliver. Jane's disillusion-ment extends to nearly everything; it doesn't make them depressed, just very frustrated, angry and 'pissed off'.

Getting a job that has a purpose and isn't boring has been diffi-cult, especially in the gig economy. Jane's parents have been supportive yet remain baffled by their beliefs, opting to stay clear of contentious subjects, a list that is getting longer. The 'bank of mum and dad' could help them buy a house but Jane resists, not wanting to succumb to the corrupt capitalist system. Instead, they pay ridiculous amounts of rent or sofa surf.

Jane perceives the world descending into madness and nobody cares, certainly not those 'in power', the people who are elected and paid to sort things out. Everywhere they look are widespread injustices affecting the marginalised, a planet in peril and a popu-lace too complacent to enact even minor changes. Initially, Jane thought this resulted from a lack of understanding. Now they believe it's much worse; they are thick, ill-educated morons and would be happy to see the planet burn.

Jane's radical side had always been there but it's now integral to who they are. The hours alone during the lockdowns, thinking about what's happening in the world, shook them out of their passive state. The whole system is corrupt and busted. Jane realised that it wasn't just them; most of their friends felt the same way. If this was being an activist, then they had become one.

Jane's social media feeds were suddenly full of equally frustrated people. Everywhere they looked were people screaming with the same frustrations. Friends who wanted to sit on the fence and not take sides stopped calling.

Now they see that the country and its institutions are run by a clique of the white, male and old. Their mindset is stuck in a bygone era that's rigged for their benefit. Jane's generation is not like this; they have very different beliefs and priorities. They care about people and making society fair, not screwing it for profit. It makes them sick to think how many people have been deprived of their voice and their heritage. It's blatantly obvious that biological sex doesn't define who you are – and the whole bloody system is rigged to stop people of colour from succeeding. The term intersectionality is always used when talking about these issues, a word they think is ugly and pretentious. All they know is it is wrong and must be changed.

From now on, the needs of the marginalised take precedence. Change, rapid change, must happen if a climate catastrophe is to be averted.

OK, it's going to mess up the privileged lives of the powerful, but who cares; they had their chance and failed. The more annoyed they are, the more they complain, the better; it shows progress is being made. They are tired of their bleating the same arguments and excuses and will do whatever is required to silence their whining. Whenever the elite's power is challenged, all they can do is talk about 'how much has been achieved' and how freedom of speech is being threatened and their favourite criticism about everything 'going woke'. What pathetic excuses for aeons of failure.

Jane now realises their education was based on a horribly warped view of the world. History was written, and the rules have been set, by those who have prospered from the West's white colonial past. The bias is ingrained so deep in the way the system runs that it needs to be ripped out. People need to confront the sins of the past that have provided their comfortable, privileged lives.

The same thing is happening today, with the downtrodden being kept in place by the rich and powerful countries. Look at how America and Israel stole the Palestinians' lands and expect them to be nice and forget. All the media does is defend the oppressors' actions.

Much of their free time is taken up by direct activism. Getting into the face of the stupid idiots defending their broken world gives them a thrill. The excitement and camaraderie is fantastic, seeing the fear on their faces as they realise their pampered existence is being replaced by a kinder, inclusive, diverse and sustainable world.

Mr 'The-World-Has-Gone-Mad'

John is more likely to be older than young and is unapologetically, indeed emphatically, heterosexual. Even mentioning the term 'personal pronouns' generates a stream of spluttering about 'haven't people got more important things in their life than messing up the English language?'

John says, although it's not totally true, that he has given up watching and listening to the news because it annoys him so much. His wife keeps telling him there's nothing he can do about 'it' (just about everything) and that he should 'chill out', something that makes him even angrier.

He has worked hard all his life, followed the rules, paid his taxes and tried to be a good member of society. Now, his comfortable lifestyle is distinctly less comfortable. His mortgage repayments have increased along with the prices of everything in the shops. He doesn't really understand his pension statement, but it keeps saying he needs to invest more, money he doesn't have, and work for longer.

Covid and Brexit get blamed for this financial mess but he's not so sure. His American equivalent (Johnnie) has never forgiven the bankers for screwing up his finances and blames all the ills of society on them.

Among John's biggest bugbears is the nonsense about transgender rights. Both words trigger a stream of muttering. What rights, who gave them these 'rights' and where are all these transgender people the press keeps on about? John's brother is gay, and it's one of the few subjects they agree about. As for all the crap, a word that has crept back into his vocabulary, about inclusive language and rules about not calling women, women… His wife shrugs and tries to change the subject.

His daughter, a few years out of university, does her best to explain this new language and admits that it's mostly ignored: 'Dad, just go along with it; the press is obsessed with the subject and knows it winds people like you up, so stop reading about it.' She gives him the same advice concerning his other bugbear about 'net zero', a concept he refuses to understand. Discussions normally end with him swearing never to change his diesel car. What he would do with heat pumps is best glossed over.

As much as these subjects make him angry, they also have a strange fascination for him. Like a magnet, they draw his attention and condemnation, followed by head shaking and a stream of moaning. (Note: the author has a book, *The Joy of Moaning*, that would help John's condition (and that of his long-suffering wife). End of the advert.)

John has always felt he was an optimistic sort of bloke with lots to be thankful for: good health, a happy family and the prospect of a comfortable old age. Now, he is not so sure. More and more things annoy him, which is bad enough, but those parts of his life he took for granted are falling to pieces. Meetings with his mates are filled with complaints about the latest faux pas and indiscretions of politicians, how the NHS is getting even worse and their latest tale of abysmal customer services, especially from anything run by the government.

In the past, their chats ended in laughter. Now it's more likely to be with comments about thanking God they are not growing up in today's world.

If pushed to explain what bugs him the most, it's that everybody wants to change things for the sake of change. He doesn't see what's gained from obsessing about racism. How his parents behaved towards black people was wrong, but that was then; now, the pendulum has swung too far the other way. All this talk about minorities; what about the 'majorities'? Nobody cares about them; in fact, they are reviled. Why should he eat less meat, obey ridiculous speed limits and do whatever some local jobsworth dictates? He would never use the word 'powerlessness' but that is what he is feeling.

John hoped that the latter part of his life would mirror his parents', who seemed so contented. He now looks to his final years with dread. Maybe a change of government will make a difference. At least this idea makes him laugh, but not for long.

Unlikely bedfellows

I think it's safe to say that John and Jane aren't likely to be sending each other Xmas cards.

Their differences are immense and obvious. Jane brings purpose into their life by passionately and aggressively righting the wrongs they perceive John and his generation have created. John is retreating into his shrinking world of gloom.

If you were able to get them together (a skilled and muscular mediator would be a good addition) to focus on their similarities, they would be amazed at how much they have in common:

- Disgruntlement with the state of the world.
- Fear about the future.
- Squeezed financially.
- Lacking trust in the institutions – especially politicians.
- Anger – lots of it.

I also suspect that Jane would find John not that different from their father, whom they are fond of, despite his views. The same goes for John, who would recognise much of his daughter in Jane. Stereotypes are easy to attack; face-to-face contact with real people makes things much more complicated.

The institutions behave as if there are as many Janes as Johns, if not more. That's because Jane is determined that their values and priorities dictate society's trajectory by being noisy and uncompromising. They have jettisoned the old-fashioned niceties of persuasion and mutual respect.

Some of John's friends focus their anger outward, but most sink deeper into the safe world they know and understand. They don't have the energy or weapons to fight back. They surround themselves with like-minded people and hold on for dear life to those parts of their lives they value and bugger the rest. John doesn't know about 'hunkering down' but that is what he and millions of others are doing.

In the tradition of British fairness, I expect most people have some sympathy with both perspectives. Life's daily challenges give little time to dwell on Jane and John's obsessions. Perhaps they glance at the news quickly and then retreat to their favourite entertainment channels. Only when their family is affected do they pay attention. Let's call them the 'Too Busy'.

My contention is there are a lot more Johns than Janes and that these two represent the extremes of the spectrum of beliefs. Their numbers are swamped by those who are too busy to care.

Jane is the one seeking social change and shouting the loudest, and is emblematic of the new progressive mindset, so I will look at their beliefs in more detail before considering how they appear to be affecting society.

JANE'S PERSPECTIVE – TRYING TO MAKE SOCIETY FAIR

I have no idea what label Jane associates with their beliefs; however, I would take a bet it includes the words fair, just, safe, equitable, diverse and sustainable.

I am equally certain the media that's critical and furious about what results from them uses the terms 'social justice warrior', 'cultural Marxist' and most definitely 'woke'. The words identity, minority politics and intersectionality are bound to make an appearance.

I have tried to remove the emotions that invariably accompany a discussion of identity politics, the term I prefer, and attempt to understand its founding principles.

A full and frank disclosure: I don't know many people with Jane's views. My understanding of them is a composite formed after reading and listening to numerous Jane-like people espouse their beliefs in a variety of media. Apologies if I am misrepresenting them.

Identity politics

This is my understanding of the beliefs that encapsulate identity politics. Jane would undoubtedly use more colourful language. An academic would undoubtedly use more complicated and unfathomable language.

Society's institutions are controlled by and used to benefit its most powerful members. These privileged people have historically been predominantly white and male. The chief diversity officer at Johns Hopkins Medicine expanded the list to include Christians, heterosexuals, cisgender, able-bodied, English-speaking, middle-aged and property-owning people. She later withdrew the definition, saying it was poorly worded.

If the underprivileged are to succeed, the system that is rigged against them must be dismantled and replaced with one that is fair and inclusive of all people, not just the powerful.

Institutions are inherently biased because they are constructed on a Western cultural history that ignores the richness of contributions from other societies. This must be rectified by ensuring the educational system incorporates diverse perspectives and histories that challenge the narratives that perpetuate false stereotypes.

A person's identity is inextricably linked to their race, gender, sexual orientation, religion and disability. The combination of these characteristics determines the form of discrimination they suffer, often referred to as 'intersectionality'.

Just espousing the belief in equality, regardless of identity, is not enough – in fact, it reinforces the status quo. The goal is to achieve equity – equal outcomes – and that requires removing society's systemic inequalities and rectifying the resulting imbalances.

Institutions should reflect society's rich diversity by removing discrimination and exclusion based on people's identity. Many of these obstacles are obvious. Others are deeply ingrained in the system. The processes that govern the institutions must work for everybody while ensuring they reflect and respect minority cultures but don't appropriate them.

Privileged groups resisting the evolution to a diverse society are the same ones delaying the actions needed to stop the global threat of environmental disaster. Environmental and social justice movements are separate but often have shared beliefs, especially about the urgency of action.

The power exerted by the privileged affects all parts of the international economic and political systems. Nations whose wealth results from colonisation and exploitation have a duty to help the countries they exploited.

Only by engagement in all forms of activism will a fairer and environmentally sustainable society be created. The forces opposing an equitable world must be countered and silenced.

It appears to me that this vision of the world is based on a few underlying assumptions. These heuristics are the mental shortcuts people like Jane use to make sense of how society operates.

- The combination of a person's race, gender, sexual orientation, religion and disability determines their experiences within society and their relative power.
- Society's history and norms of behaviour are defined and maintained by those who exercise power. Absolute truth is a myth; the lived experiences of the powerful define the accepted truths.

- The distribution of power, influence and wealth is a zero-sum game. There is always a winner and a loser, an oppressed and an oppressor.
- Life chances are determined by our identity rather than any innate mental capacity or predisposition – more generally known as 'blank sheet' theory.
- The privileged in society maintain their dominance and subjugation of minorities by overt and covert means ranging from blatant discrimination to the subtle control of the language and culture.
- Only by continual activism will the power imbalances in society be redressed and environmental disaster averted.

Although many of these beliefs have a ring of truth, there is much about them that disturbs me. The concept of inequality, based on wealth and income, is measurable, albeit not that accurately. Unfairness resulting from a person's identity is complicated and subjective, involving multiple factors and impossible to quantify. Knowing if policies to improve diversity are working is even more difficult, a subject we will get onto a little later.

My amateur exploits as a historian convinced me about the wisdom of the saying, 'The victors write the history.' Identity politics appears to assume the victors were all the same: white and male. This seems like an inverted racist Western-centric view of the world, especially when research shows countries in Africa and the Middle East are the least tolerant.

The central tenet of these beliefs assumes that 'privilege' is a fixed commodity that must be reallocated, not grown. This is a zero-sum game ideology that is inherently confrontational. Winners must lose and be seen to lose. As we will see later, this attitude is especially strong among men who perceive women's gain in status as their loss.

The value of collective knowledge might be suspect and influenced by ingrained prejudice, but it is inherently more valuable than reliance on collective 'lived experiences' that are arbitrarily selected and subjective.

Much of the attractiveness of this ideology is its simplicity. There are clearly defined winners and losers, exploiters and the exploited, oppressors and the oppressed. I don't believe life is that simple and it seems to me this thinking results in policies based on crude stereotypes. Another name for seeing the world through the prism of blackness and whiteness, where each is attributed its own characteristics, is neo-racism.

Mao Zedong believed that transforming society to his vision required perpetual conflict and transformation. That idea didn't end well for the Chinese. I detect parallels between his Cultural Revolution and the continual activism of identity politics and environmentalists.

Of all the issues we face, the move from carbon-based economics is the most complex and difficult to achieve. There are marked similarities between activists concerned about the environment and those like Jane. The 'bad guys' are obvious and must be challenged. Complex decisions are treated as trivial.

Irrespective of my thoughts about these ideas, the most important question is whether they are working. There is some reliable data about how attitudes towards gender, race, sexuality and the environment have changed over time. Of course, many factors affect public attitudes, making it impossible to establish any causal links. All that said, these results cannot be ignored.

How attitudes have changed

These are brief accounts of attitudes in the UK and the US and how they have changed over time. I will make some comments about what the data means but, for now, let's focus on the facts; perhaps I should say 'my facts'.

Racial tolerance: Gallup has been measuring Americans' attitudes towards racial tolerance since 2001. For much of that time, the responses of black and white people were constant. However, during the past decade, both groups perceived a deterioration in race relations.

> *For the second consecutive year, U.S. adults' positive ratings of relations between Black and White Americans are at their lowest point in more than two decades of measurement.*

As recently as 2013, those believing relations were 'very or somewhat bad' were a third of the population yet by 2022 this figure had doubled.

The situation in the UK is very different. In 1990, one in ten people said they would not like to live next to people of a different race – today, that figure is 1% (World Values Survey). Ipsos MORI found much the same result, reporting that the country is more racially tolerant than ten years ago in all aspects.

The UK ranks in the top ten most racially tolerant countries; America is 69th (World Population Review).

Immigration: Both countries have similar beliefs about the importance of immigration. During the 1960s, the UK recorded over 90% of people opposing immigration. Research companies differ on the extent of the change, recording levels of opposition today as somewhere between 20% and 40%. From 2000 onwards, the US showed a steady increase in its desire for immigrant numbers to increase. This ended in 2020, when the trend reversed. At about the same time, concerns about immigration started rising in the UK.

You don't have to look far to explain this turnaround. Both countries have experienced a very visible rise in illegal immigrants entering the country. In the UK, the media is forever reporting the small boats crossing the English Channel and in the US, the numbers crossing its southern border.

Sexuality: The US and UK are less divided over their tolerance to different types of sexuality. In 1990, nearly a third of Britons said they would not like to have homosexuals as neighbours. Two decades later, this had fallen to 4%.

Since 1996, Americans have been more comfortable with same-sex couples having the same rights as traditional marriages. In

1996, less than 30% agreed with the idea; today, the figure is 71% (Gallup).

Attitudes to transgenderism are complicated by the fact that most people have ignored the issue. Two-thirds of Britons say they pay little or no attention to the media's coverage of the subject – only 8% say it's very important. However, when questioned about the potential implications, the response is significant. For example, the idea that transgender women should take part in women's sports and use women-only spaces is rejected by four to one. Overall, there has been an erosion in support for transgender rights since 2018 (YouGov).

Americans have equally mixed ideas about the subject; however, an increasing number of people support the idea that gender is the same as sex given at birth. Republicans and Democrats share this view, more so the former (Pew Research).

The view that gender and sex are indivisible is more pronounced among older people and those with a high school education or less. When broken down by race, black respondents are the most vociferous in holding this view.

The environment: The percentage of Americans who believe climate change is a global threat to the country has been declining since 2017. This change in attitude is most marked among Republicans, but Democrats are also losing interest (Pew Research). These findings were confirmed by Monmouth University, which also recorded young people losing a sense of urgency about the issue. Strengthening the economy is a much more important priority than tackling global warming.

British views are very similar, with concern peaking in 2019 and falling ever since. Worries about the increasing cost of living and the failing NHS are more important (Ipsos). Research by the Office for National Statistics gives slightly different figures, showing concern about the environment flatlining and ranking behind worries about economic conditions.

Presented with these findings, Jane and John would probably give the same response: 'They prove my point.' All the measures show improvements in tolerance, except for America's attitude to race. However, in the past decade, the improvements have stalled or declined.

John would say (very loudly) that he is vindicated. Society is inherently tolerant of social change but doesn't take well to the preaching and demonstrating of the likes of Jane. He would also add that importing 'American race politics' into the UK is stupid – just look at the difference in our histories and attitudes.

Jane would see the reversal in tolerance about transgender rights and the environment demonstrating the need to do more to squash the reactionary voices. Rather than seeing society's evolution as being towards their goals, they would criticise the paltry level of diversity that's been achieved and why this proves more intervention is required. And look at how racist America is and why it must become more inclusive and fast.

How can two people with such different ideas about society look at the same data and conclude it confirms their beliefs? I think the experiments conducted by psychologist Leon Festinger and his colleagues provide the answer. He studied what happens to cults when their predictions fail to materialise and how it's used to strengthen their resolve. Although written in 1956 his book *When Prophecy Fails* has a chilling message for us today.

I have used my fictitious characters to illustrate this human frailty that appears in each essay: facts have little part in determining peoples' beliefs and emotions. Forming a reasoned, fact-based view about race, sexuality and the environment requires a level of intellect and open-mindedness that most people don't have. Confronted with information, the instinct is to select those parts that support the already-held opinion. Worse still, to ignore it entirely or to discount its value with the comment, 'Well, they would say that wouldn't they?'

The numbers tell me that something has happened during the past decade to halt the long-term trends of increasing racial and sexual tolerance and willingness to tackle environmental threats. What that 'something' is will emerge in the next section.

HOW DID WE GET HERE?

All institutions are engaged in a struggle between Janes and Johns for their souls. If you don't believe institutions have souls, then think of it as a power battle to define their culture. Academia is dominated by Jane-type thinking, business less so; the others are somewhere between the two. This conflict generates the noise the media turns into clickbait with the hashtags of woke, culture wars, cancel culture and identity politics.

The public space is a noisy place as emotions run high, with little listening and much screaming. If you block this out and listen carefully, you can hear a rumbling noise that's getting louder as the foundations of the institutions come apart. Before revisiting the conflict between Jane and John, I intend to explore what's behind this foreboding sound.

Disillusioned gloom

The clearest symptom of things going wrong is the extent of people's negative attitudes. There's a daily torrent of research showing that mental health problems are worse than ever. Nearly a quarter of US adults have a mental illness, and nearly 10% also suffer from substance abuse. The British aren't much happier. Mental illness is the main reason for people being economically inactive. Just over 20% of UK adults are not looking for work despite job vacancies being at record highs. The worst hit are young people and children. Over 15% of US children, aged two to eight years old, have a diagnosed mental, behavioural or developmental disorder. More than 10% of American kids have an ADHD diagnosis; the same percentage have a diagnosed anxiety disorder.

It's easy to explain these shocking levels of unhappiness as resulting from the disruption to normal life caused by Covid. John would dismiss the figures, saying that just suffering from life's usual ups and downs is now labelled as a mental illness. No doubt there is some truth in both explanations.

I don't think these events are a complete explanation because the rise in unhappiness started before Covid. If you believe the results of Gallup's *Global Emotions Report,* it seems we have been getting more miserable since 2012. The latest report (2022) found worry, stress and sadness at record levels during the pandemic, and I bet things have got worse since then. This research measures the symptoms but doesn't explain why it's happening, however.

The first two explanations for this gloom pandemic seem blindingly obvious. All my essays concluded with comments along the lines of 'the public doesn't trust you' and that there's a 'mismatch between your priorities and those you serve'. I think it's a reasonable conclusion that if you don't trust and believe institutions are working in your interests, it makes you feel uncertain, vulnerable and generally a tad unhappy.

I have already provided lots of evidence about these two issues. Here is some more that drives home the magnitude of the problem.

Mismatch in priorities: When the 1,500 experts from academia, business and government met at Davos in 2024, their top concerns about the future were 'extreme weather, AI-generated misinformation and disinformation and societal and political polarisation'. None of these are mentioned when Americans and the British are asked about the things keeping them awake at night.

Economic problems top the list of things worrying the public in both countries. How will their families cope with the high cost of living and inflation, the things that most affect their immediate wellbeing? Both publics are also worried (and annoyed) about illegal immigration. The British also fret about the state of their health service, Americans about their dysfunctional government.

The environment, racism and LGBTQ+ rights are way down the list of priorities.

Ironically, the theme of Davos 2024 was 'rebuilding trust'. Perhaps a good starting point would have been to align their priorities with those of the people who fund the event.

Lack of trust: If the folks at Davos realised they have a problem with trust, then so should those governing our institutions when every measure of this vital commodity is heading south. Just reading the titles from the market research gives the game away:

> *Confidence in U.S. Institutions Down; Average at New Low. Gallup*
>
> *UK has internationally low confidence in political institutions, police and press. World Values Survey*
>
> *Social fabric weakens amid deepening divisions. Edelman Trust Barometer*
>
> *Trust in national institutions has declined across the EU. Eurofound*
>
> *Young adults are more sceptical of government and pessimistic about the future than any living generation before them. WSJ/Pew*

Having worked on global surveys I am suspicious of their accuracy but it's impossible to ignore these monotonously consistent findings. Trust in our national institutions is evaporating. It is as simple and awful as that. Another, and not surprising, factor is that this loss of trust is contagious. Institutions and nations are losing trust in each other. Since 2012, McKinsey has been measuring the degree of global cooperation, which went steadily upward until 2020, when it stalled and then fell.

So far, I have covered many different subjects and quoted lots of research statistics. This is a good place to stand still and summarise what it all means and what questions remain to be answered.

We are witnessing a radically new political belief system trying to displace the existing one and causing – what shall we say – friction. Meanwhile, the public is questioning the very things that are core to these new beliefs: tolerance of different races and sexualities and concern about the environment.

At the same time, our trust in the institutions that support our wellbeing is evaporating, with a widening gap between what is important to them and to us. Perhaps the two reactions are linked? These symptoms of institutional failure explain much of the rumbling noise I can hear.

The word that is conspicuously missing from my explanation is 'why'. Jane and John have long ago answered the question to their satisfaction. Jane believes the evidence vindicates their position that the system is systemically busted and needs a reboot with their ideology at its core. Those facts that question this belief are dismissed as disinformation. John blames Jane and her – he refuses to use the preferred pronouns – like for all the problems. He thinks the institutions' priorities are imposed by their 'woke' managers (who all think alike), so it is no wonder normal people don't trust them.

It's about time I told you what I believe.

Distracted and ineffectual government

The least trusted institution is the government, and the least trusted people are politicians. In a couple of research reports, journalists take the top spot; everywhere else, it's members of Parliament and Congress. We shouldn't be surprised since it was the same in 2020, 2015 and 2010 (Edelman Trust Barometer).

For at least the past two decades, we, the public, believed in a fairytale that somewhere there were competent politicians who would make the right decisions and take care of us. This never worked out, yet we cherished the belief that the next bunch would be better. Covid shattered this fantasy.

I think the post-Covid lack of trust is different from the historical distrust we have had for government. How it responded to the pandemic destroyed forever the myth of competence. For a couple of years, the machinery of government was exposed to 24/7 news coverage, inspecting every word and decision about just one subject. Covid. Subsequently, the aftermath has revealed not just a litany of mistakes but also crass amateurship. Rightly or wrongly, everything that's now going wrong with the economy and in society is being tagged as the fault of the government and its Covid policies.

The emperor's new clothes are lying in a pile on the floor, revealing a flabby, unfit institution that can't deliver on its promises. Many of my friends would disagree, believing Covid was such a rare event and of such magnitude that mistakes were bound to be made. They would probably chuck in the comment, 'Do you think you would have done any better?'

My answer would be 'absolutely not', but that's the point; politicians are just ordinary people we expect to behave in ways we can't. We anoint them with our votes and believe it confers special abilities and knowledge we mere mortals don't possess. Then we compound the myth by convincing ourselves that the machinery of government is efficient and trustworthy even though all the evidence says it's not.

It's not a pretty picture. The closer you look, the louder the rumbling sound as bits of the institution collapse. Covid revealed a failing of government we couldn't ignore, but it is by no means the worst. The full sordid story is explained in 'Politics – more showbiz than statesmanship'. These are the five failures of government that most concern me.

Responsibility without power: Many of the factors affecting people's lives are not controlled by elected politicians, although they get the blame when things go wrong. Lots of decisions about economic matters are made by independent organisations (e.g. the Bank of England and the Office for Budget Responsibility). The markets are always ready to pounce if they deem policies to be unacceptable.

Large swathes of decisions have been delegated to the 1,000 quasi-autonomous non-governmental organisations; others are made by executive non-departmental public bodies like the NHS. Then there is the judiciary, which is increasingly willing to intervene if it thinks politicians have exceeded their powers. Oh, and the raft of international organisations that can influence national policies (e.g. UN, WHO, World Bank and IMF). Finally, there are the remnants of the controls the EU still exerts over the UK.

And you thought politicians had the power to do stuff. What little influence they have is asymmetric. They can easily make our lives harder by raising taxes and restricting our freedoms but are woefully constrained in making things better.

America has a whole different set of things that constrain politicians, including the written constitution and the tensions between state and federal legislatures.

The machinery of government has gone feral: Once upon a time, so the story goes, politicians made decisions and the machinery of government made them happen. I am not so sure this ever was the case. Fifteen years ago, the Labour Party was told by its favourite think tank:

> *Whitehall is poor at reflecting on its purpose, strategic thinking, dealing with inadequate performance, managing change effectively, learning from mistakes or working across departments.*
>
> *The anachronistic and severely inadequate constitutional conventions governing relations between the civil service, ministers, Parliament and the public have become a recipe for ambiguity, confusion, weak leadership and buck passing.*

There are a couple of things I would add to this damning

description. Since then, its efficiency and dependability have got worse and, in the past decade, it has developed a mind of its own and openly delays or ignores government policies.

Avoiding unpalatable decisions: A trillion in numbers is 1,000,000,000,000. The amount of debt that the US, UK and EU countries have to fund are all measured in trillions – $37, £2.6 and €13.8, respectively.

These numbers are so big that they are impossible to visualise. Think of it this way: in 2023, just under 10% of all spending by the UK government was on debt interest and repayments; in the US, it was 16%. The EU debt servicing payments would be somewhere in the same ballpark. In the first half 2024, the US spent more on interest payments than it did on either defence or Medicare.

If this were a short-term issue and there were credible plans to repay the debt, then it might be OK. Instead, two more bills of horrendous size are in the post and have to be paid – net zero and the ageing population.

Europe is ageing faster than the UK and the US, which means its base of young taxpayers is shrinking. Heaven knows how much the transition to a zero-carbon economy will cost – more about this in the next section.

The answer to this conundrum is that there isn't one because nobody dares to do the sums. I am not being flippant; I am being brutally honest. Decisions about what to do about each of these subjects are delayed or fudged.

Failure is coloured green: In 2019, a not very memorable UK prime minister left the UK a legacy of legislation that committed the country to achieving net zero by 2050. Nobody had a clue what this meant or how it could be achieved, but it sounded like a great idea. Parliament made the decision to go ahead in less than an hour based on the flimsiest of evidence.

Today, most countries have agreed to slash their CO_2 emissions with legislation and targets to achieve net zero everywhere. Even so, Google reports that the term is searched less than

'Donald Trump', one of those snippets of data that I am sure has a profound meaning, but I don't know what it is.

The fun began once the virtuous objective was handed down to national and international bureaucracies to fathom out how it could be achieved. A torrent of targets and rules erupted that are now being tested in the court of public opinion and found to be not just wanting but useless. Telling car purchasers what sort of car to buy, householders how to heat their homes, farmers how to reduce the disastrous results of their cows' flatulence, drivers where to drive and how existing electricity generation capacity must be closed in the hope that something better replaces it... Excuse the rant!

Shutting down planet Earth to cope with Covid had immense repercussions that are dwarfed by what's involved in moving to a zero-carbon economy. Then there are the inconvenient results of Russia cutting off its energy supplies to Europe and declaring war on Ukraine.

And let's not ignore the feat of international diplomacy that enables China to dominate the world's markets for EVs, batteries and wind generators while increasing its production of CO_2.

Setting aside whether the idea of net zero is right or wrong, I fear that governments will keep retreating from or diluting their arbitrarily set targets in the face of public pressure. Every step back weakens their authority and ability to enforce the remaining rules.

Employing lots of people like Jane: The next section discusses how Jane and their fellow travellers have been affecting institutions, so I will leave the details until then. The key point here is that all parts of the UK government have adopted identity-related policies and language in some way. However, it's been done in the same fragmented, bureaucratic way the government does everything. I must confess to finding it all rather comical.

One moment, politicians are telling the public that they are determined to stop the spread of woke ideology, and the next, the media is reporting that another government department is launching an inclusion campaign. These make terrific clickbait articles that follow the same formula. Examples are given of the new language (e.g. expectant mothers are now called expectant people) and details of the costs incurred. For example: 'Woke new NHS guidance stating that "not everyone who experiences menopause is a woman" sparks outrage' (March 2024). The result is fuming readers and further proof of politicians' powerlessness.

As I write this (July 2024), the American presidential election is in turmoil, as the reality of Biden's cognitive collapse has been painfully revealed. UK politics has lurched to the left just as the rest of Europe heads in the opposite direction. All sense of political authority is draining from the Western World.

With this litany of failures, is it any wonder that things are so bad? Is it any wonder that trust in government has evaporated?

Who shouts the loudest wins

My character Jane is one of the noisy, virtuous and vulnerable people getting so much attention. I've discussed their beliefs and why I am concerned about them. Now, I'll focus on the reasons behind their success.

The author Margaret Mead wrote: 'Never doubt that a small group of thoughtful, committed citizens can change the world. Indeed, it is the only thing that ever has.'

So perhaps no explanation is required; Jane is continuing the heritage of thoughtful and committed citizens. Being part of the best-educated generation ever could be another explanation. Maybe anger is driving their success. Sky-high property prices and rents force more of Jane's generation to live at home with their parents than any other generation since the Great Depression.

Of course, social media's global reach massively enhances their ability to amplify their voice and influence people. The illusion of consensus has never been easier to generate when none exists.

All these factors play their part, no doubt. However, I believe some other, less understood behaviours are behind Jane's success. Before beginning, I must admit to having no proof that Jane and their friends are a minority. I am making a huge assumption that the 'Too Busy' and Johns are the majority. Some recent events have reassured me I am right, as we will soon discover.

'Activism is my rent for living on the planet': These words of Alice Walker, the American novelist, would be Jane's rallying cry. Institutions appear influenced by the message and are impelled to declare their opinions about social issues and demonstrate how they are seeking to change the world. This is most pronounced in the media, where objective writing has been replaced by blatantly partisan reporting. I exaggerate a little but not much, as I explain in the essay 'Media – where did all the trust go?'

Those with Jane's beliefs working in business provide a steady flow of instances of companies broadcasting their support and allegiance to one cause or another. Sometimes these activities result in controversial advertising and products demonstrating their inclusive credentials. Most go unnoticed. Occasionally they go spectacularly wrong.

Continually trying to change society must be exhausting. The author Mark Fisher described this relentlessness, anger and campaigning as 'po-faced moralism, it's joylessness, it's resentment-fuelled feuding'. Once started, it's difficult to stop and to ensure consistency. If you are supporting XYZ cause, why not ABC or HIJ? Why is one deserving of your emotional energy and the other ignored?

However much it annoys other parts of society, its effectiveness is undisputed – up to a point. There is a world of difference between successful evangelism and making converts.

Simple messages with a binary response: Stripping complexity and nuance from the public arena gets attention. Banishing uncertainty enables your commitment to run at full throttle. There are no caveats, no acknowledging valid opposing views, just a world of defined winners and losers, exploiters and the exploited, oppressors and the oppressed.

But does ultra-simplification and a rush to emotional certainty lead to dangerous decisions, or is it the other way around? Perhaps the 'you are with us or against us' technique has always been the way to impose your views on the placid majority. If so, then supporters of the identity politics catechism of beliefs are a case study for the technique's success.

The media is fond of describing Jane and their like as a religion or cult, which is not meant as a kindly comment. But what's the difference between Christianity's Ten Commandments and Jane's Creed? Both demand belief without proof and a binary view of what's good and bad. The answer is that beliefs are just words; it's their implications that matter.

A time of poly- and permacrisis: I think we live in a time of passionate ignorance. What angers people and inspires their commitment are things they are unlikely to understand. How much do you know about the science of global warming, let alone the solutions being implemented to ameliorate its dangers? No doubt you have views about the conflicts in Ukraine and Gaza and how the government handled the pandemic. Is the political party in power doing the best it can to manage the economy or making a total mess of things? I bet you have an opinion. I bet you have really strong views about one or all of these subjects.

What we hold dear doesn't result from an in-depth analysis of the facts; it comes from a mix of existing prejudices topped up with supporting commentary from a reassuring news source. Don't be upset by this statement – I am just as guilty as anybody.

In his book *Dirk Gently's Holistic Detective Agency*, Douglas Adams describes the 'Electric Monk' that practices religion and believes in things, thus saving humans the trouble of doing so.

It seems our Electronic Monks have malfunctioned, adopting an ultra-pessimistic view of the future, plunging us all into the deepest gloom. Perhaps this is an outlandish explanation, and what's really happening is that language, especially that used by the media and those manipulating it, presents events in their bleakest form. Everything is, or is about to be, a crisis or worse.

The 101 primer for activists explains the value of inflating language to always portray the darkest outcome, to get coverage, to make an impact and to further the cause. What this does for our mental health, existing in a state of permanent polycrises, is another matter.

Aggressively vulnerable and unforgiving: Today's social activism is a complex mix of compassion and sensitivity towards racial and sexual diversity, forever protecting minority groups. They are vulnerable, ever fearful of being harmed, hurt or worse. Those daring to question them are pursued with a vengeful and unforgiving vehemence. Perhaps I am overstating the case. However, I can give you a long list of academics, entertainers, writers and journalists who would agree 100%. They will show you the evidence, the X pile-ons and worse.

This uncaring kindness, wrapped in a cocoon of vulnerability, is often called 'cancel culture' and is the most unpleasant characteristic of Jane's ideology. What can't be denied is its effectiveness in silencing opponents.

My armchair psychologist's explanation of what's happening is very simple. Professing caring values is perceived as an excuse for committing hurtful actions. The enemy is demonised, allowing the normal rules of decency to be abandoned. Then, the baser emotions of bullying take hold and it's all about the thrill of exercising power.

Lots of things have surprised me as I have journeyed through the institutions, but the symbiotic relationship between the noisy, virtuous and vulnerable and the elites is the weirdest of them all. Even now, I am not sure if I understand how it works, but I will try and explain in the next section.

Elites adapt, thrive and control

The 'elite' is a broad term that includes those in the 'top 1%' – the obscenely wealthy, the extremely wealthy, executives of large companies and the higher levels of the public sector. High income is not the only criterion for membership of this club. My definition extends to the upper echelons of academia, charities, entertainment and the media. The common characteristic is the power bestowed by their position and wealth to influence our lives.

Despite all the economic and social upheaval of the past couple of decades, the elite have thrived. They have enhanced their own prosperity and authority by wrapping themselves in virtue. I am still unsure whether they managed this by luck or cunning manipulation, though I have a suspicion.

Although well-credentialled, they aren't necessarily the brightest of people, so my guess is that it was luck. They benefited from the bluebird of all bluebirds when identity politics displaced social divisions based on class and wealth.

What follows is my explanation of their good fortune and its consequences.

They learnt the language and espoused the beliefs: Tara Henley is a Canadian journalist who writes about elites and the new left. This is her explanation about the inversion of the old political spectrum:

> *Many of the new left's decision-makers are highly educated, wealthy, well-meaning, and entirely cut off from the working class, save for a few quick Uber Eats handoffs. And while this version of the left takes increasingly radical positions on cultural and social issues, it is largely uninterested in pursuing leftist economic policies.*

Her comments are about the 'new left', but they also apply to the elite. Not long ago, rich capitalists and the left had little in common. Now they do. The former adapted, the latter radically changed.

This is most apparent in US academia, especially in the elitist of the elite, Ivy League universities. Renowned for their deeply embedded left bias, they were the early adopters of the diversity, equity and inclusion (DEI) agenda that now pervades their organisations. The media, large corporations and government departments weren't far behind.

Advocating support for DEI became the mark of an enlightened leader. The 2020 Fortune/Deloitte survey of CEOs found that an astonishing 96% claimed that DEI is a personal strategic priority for them and that they will prioritise investing in DEI initiatives in nearly every area of business.

In the space of a few years, the highest-paid people in the country claimed to be leading the fight against racial, sexual and all other forms of injustice. Soon, they were joined by the uber-wealthy. Was this Lazarus moment genuine or a calculated embracing of a low-cost, high-virtue ideology? I have no idea; all I know is that it worked.

With the new left's attention now focused on fairness and inclusion, the elite worked a wonderful trick of engendering trust while accumulating astronomical levels of wealth. The essay 'Business – charting new paths or losing direction?' details this amazing conjuring trick.

Diverging beliefs of the elites and the masses

Occasionally, something happens that the elite didn't expect or want. The masses are asked a question and reply with the wrong answer. The UK's decision to leave the EU and America's to elect Donald Trump as president were two of the biggest 'wrong' answers. Another shock occurred when the elite's diagnosis and rules for countering the pandemic were ignored and questioned.

More recently, two referendums were held that came to the 'wrong' answer. Australians were asked if they wanted their constitution changed to recognise the First Peoples of Australia by establishing an 'Aboriginal Voice'. Surely, few could object to making Australia a more inclusive country – 60% of the population thought it a bad idea.

The Irish were asked to make a couple of tweaks to their constitution. Rather than defining a family solely based on marriage, the proposal was to add the term 'or on another durable relationship'. The other idea was to delete references to the role of women in the home and their role as the primary providers of care. Both of these were rejected with a thumping 70% majority.

Watching the response to these 'wrong' decisions is as amusing as it is consistent. The notion that the masses got it right is never considered; rather, 'they' failed to understand what was involved and were influenced by disinformation. The horror at the decisions reinforces the need to communicate better and silence those spreading false information. This rationalisation adds a few more notches to the gap between the educated establishment and the rest.

Perhaps you are thinking, 'the "rest" got it wrong, so does that make me a member of the elite?' The answer is not necessarily; it means your views are in the minority. That raises the next question – do you have a right to impose them on the majority? If you answer yes and believe in the long term it's in their best interests, then welcome to Club Elite.

When the *FT* was rationalising the Irish vote it concluded: 'The more evidence we see of hardening attitudes, the more work we need to do to understand why.' Rarely do I agree with *FT*, but on this statement, we are one.

The final example concerns the elite's unwillingness to question the orthodoxy of the transgender movement until they don't have a choice. In April 2024 Dr Hilary Cass published her final report about the UK's gender identity services for children and young people. This is the first paragraph of the 400-page document:

 This Review is not about defining what it means to be trans, nor is it about undermining the validity of trans identities, challenging the right of people to express themselves, or rolling back on people's rights to healthcare. It is about what the healthcare approach should be, and how best to help the growing number of children and young people who are looking for support from the NHS in relation to their gender identity.

The report's 32 recommendations came as no surprise since concerns about the 'treatment' of young people identifying as the opposite sex have been widely expressed for years. But Cass's report was unequivocal about the lack of evidence that the hormone drug therapies administered to children actually worked and their potential side effects. She described the culture of the centres treating children as 'toxic', suppressing dissent from those doctors questioning the ethics of the treatments.

I expected Cass's report to have the same fate as Sewell's investigation into race and ethnic disparities in the UK. He questioned the dominant narrative that the disparities resulted from systemic racism and concluded the problems were complex, with numerous factors contributing to the differences. This ignited the wrath of the race activists, aided by their media supporters. How dare a black man question the central tenet of identity politics! More details of this incident can be found in the essay 'Justice – teetering on a slippery slope'.

The reaction to Cass's report was very different, probably because it was about children and experimenting with untested drugs – something even the disinterested public balk at. Within days it became a national issue. There was nothing new in her report. All the horrors Cass documented had been identified and publicised by whistleblowers, but here was the former president of the Royal College of Paediatrics and Child Health forensically detailing the atrocious mess.

The momentum to have Cass's recommendation accepted soon became unstoppable despite the efforts to attack her credibility by the advocates of the drug treatment. Suddenly those who had stayed silent, despite knowing about the problem, found a voice, declaring their concerns and supporting her recommendations.

In the US the authorities are still looking the other way, unwilling to confront the transgender activists. Like so many conflicts it will likely conclude in a court action.

Money buys you influence: It seems Dale Vince, the multi-millionaire, realised the irony, or was it hypocrisy, of funding the climate protesters Just Stop Oil, which regularly disrupted London's traffic. His wealth ensured he wasn't inconvenienced. By transferring his funding to the Labour Party, it can be argued he will cause even more chaos, but that's another story.

It's unlikely you will see Michael Bloomberg on a scheduled air flight – he prefers to use private planes – yet he pledged $500 million to lobby US states to close their coal power stations to help save the planet.

There are hundreds, probably thousands, of very wealthy people using their money to advance environmental and social causes. And why shouldn't they spend their money how they want? A century ago, Rockefeller, Frick and Carnegie were doing good deeds; today it's the titans of technology and finance (Bill and Melinda Gates, Mark Zuckerberg and Priscilla Chan, and Warren Buffett).

So much of what they do is to be applauded. However, it starts to rankle when their beliefs have negative consequences for the majority; their wealth ensures they are not affected. The American Rob Henderson labelled holding principles that bestow virtue on someone but cost the person nothing as 'luxury beliefs'.

There's a fine line between the wealthy using their money 'for good' and for imposing their beliefs. I think we could do with more of the former and less of the latter.

On a lighter note, it is amusing watching people brandishing placards and making demands that were created by activists funded and directed by the rich and powerful. I am reminded of the scene in *The Devil Wears Prada* when the young, cynical and idealistic Andy giggles as her boss Miranda – based on the editor of *Vogue* – argues about the stylistic difference between two identical-looking belts.

Andy works in the world of fashion but wears an inexpensive baggy jumper as a symbol of her independence and independent thinking. Miranda turns to her and begins a monologue:

> *You... go to your closet, and you select... I don't know, that lumpy blue sweater, for instance, because you're trying to tell the world that you take yourself too seriously to care about*

what you put on your back, but what you don't know is that that sweater is not just blue, it's not turquoise, it's not lapis, it's actually cerulean.

She then explains how it originated in the haute couture houses of Yves Saint Laurent and Oscar de la Renta and was popularised by designers and retailers:

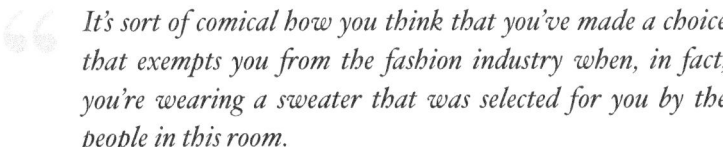

> *It's sort of comical how you think that you've made a choice that exempts you from the fashion industry when, in fact, you're wearing a sweater that was selected for you by the people in this room.*

The next time you share your startling insights about the environment, sexuality or whatever, spend a moment thinking about where they originated.

Caring intolerance: I have already discussed the strange mix of aggression, vulnerability and callousness that accompanies so many discussions about identity politics. These attitudes are not just the province of individuals; in recent years, governments and corporations have exhibited the same reactions, something that's not surprising since their policies are executed by people with the same mindset.

Who would have thought that Canadians, the gentlest and most understanding of people, would impose the most extreme hate law legislation? The Canadian author of *The Handmaid's Tale* (Margaret Atwood) was among many criticising the new Online Harms Bill, which extends the punishment for hate crimes to life imprisonment. During the pandemic, the Canadian government ended the truckers' demonstrations by invoking the Emergencies Act, giving itself unlimited powers. The federal courts later found these actions were not justified.

Legislation being passed in Scotland (Hate Crime and Public Order Act) and Ireland (Incitement to Violence or Hatred and Hate Offences Bill) gives the state unparalleled powers to suppress public discourse it deems hurtful. During the pandemic, departments of the US state worked with (some say coerced) social media companies to suspend the accounts of those it accused of spreading disinformation. At the time of writing, the US Supreme Court is determining whether they acted illegally.

The essays about business and academia include numerous accounts of how these institutions used their power to silence those with views deemed incompatible with their beliefs.

Michael Gove is a politician with whom I agree and disagree in equal measures. These paraphrased words perfectly explain the sentiment I have been trying to express.

> *We face a challenge of the coalition between the privileged and the resentment industry. Major figures and institutions were aware that the decisions they took enriched them. They have done incredibly well out of the division of spoils in our country and needed to insulate themselves from the envy, resentment, and indeed sense of injustice that is out there, so they have co-opted individuals from the resentment industry to be their collaborators.*

Collateral damage – the unintended consequences

My characters, Jane and John, have very different attitudes about the need to change society. The former believes more is needed; the faster, the better. The latter cannot understand why it's happening and detests its consequences. Perhaps it's an 'age thing' that the young thrive on change while the old find it frightening. Perhaps I am making a huge generalisation!

The drivers of change are numerous and impossible to quantify. Some are obvious, like the emergence of identity politics; others result from the echoes of past economic and technological upheavals. Of course, the reverberations of the pandemic and the conflicts in Ukraine and Gaza are all too evident.

Wandering through the institutions, I encountered the collateral damage of change, those outcomes of events that weren't planned or predicted yet have had significant consequences on our lives. These are the ones I think are most important.

The language minefield: Has there ever been a time when choosing the wrong word could be so dangerous? Maybe it was worse during the Inquisition, witch trials and in totalitarian regimes. Uttering a phrase that sets the 'hate' and 'harm' bells ringing is enough to get cancelled and a visit from the police. If you think I am exaggerating, then look at the legislation about to become law in Scotland and Ireland.

All of the institutions seem to have spent the past couple of years churning out language guides listing words they don't like and alternative phrases. Some of this has been concerned with race, disability and appearance but most have wrestled with words describing a person's gender and biological sex. The premise is that certain words and phrases have the power to trigger, annoy, harm, hurt or some other negative emotion.

It is all too easy to descend down the rabbit hole of arguments about the rights and wrongs of this hypersensitivity and the results of making the language bland and ugly, all in the cause of not offending the numerous offendable groups. ChatGPT had no difficulty listing 50 types of people where care in the choice of words is required.

My conclusion is that this surfeit of language rules results from the clumsy and bureaucratic application of DEI ideology – more on this a little later. In addition, it is a negative externality in which the few enjoy the benefits while the majority bear the costs. Perhaps the benefit is the genuine appeasing of hurt feelings but I suspect it is more about the bestowing of power.

Language is being repurposed not to improve communications but to signal the relative power of different groups. My fear is that every newspaper article about 'woke language guides' widens the divisions in society, just a little.

The sprawling DEI bureaucracy: It's impossible to know what triggered the institutions to unquestioningly embrace the nostrums of DEI. Anybody would think the concept of diversity and inclusion has just been invented. McKinsey was publishing reports about the financial benefits of diversifying the workforce back in 2015.

From the 1960s onward, America has been attempting to redress the huge racial inequalities that existed in its society. The widespread adoption of equal opportunities and affirmative action has resulted in significant advances.

In the UK the Race Relations Act was passed in 1968 and the Commission for Racial Equality began in 1976. In 1999 the UK's policing was first accused of being institutionally racist, forcing it to make major changes that are detailed in the essay 'Justice – teetering on a slippery slope'.

Tolerance of sexual diversity has a similar story. The attitudinal research I looked at earlier in this essay all pointed to society becoming more tolerant. During the past few years, however, this positive momentum has stalled and, in some cases, reversed.

As we have seen, the events associated with #MeToo and #BlackLivesMatter totally changed the narrative. After a short period of introspection, institutions decided a radical change was needed. Advocating support for DEI became the mark of an enlightened leader. Budgets were allocated, senior management engaged and the stellar rise in DEI began.

There are lots of interpretations of what happened next; this is mine. After a short time, senior management's attention became focused on a much larger issue: coping with the pandemic. The budgets had been approved and lots of people were employed with diversity, equity and inclusion in their job titles, plans were made, initiatives were begun and the show was on the road. A new stratum of people working in the middle to lower parts of the organisation had the assumed authority to do just about whatever they wanted.

After the initial rush of enthusiasm, the high ideals of DEI became just another part of the organisation vying for power. The initiatives were embedded in the bureaucracy with diversity training courses to attend, forms to fill out and no doubt numerous meetings to attend. Because of the unbounded remit of DEI, it extended into all of the institution's processes, causing conflict, lots of it. The achievements of DEI, however they were defined, didn't materialise, and the voices of criticism from within and outside the organisation intensified.

The *Harvard Business Review* published an article in 2022 that pretty much reflected these views: 'The Failure of the DEI-Industrial Complex'. The author, who works in DEI, is even more damning than me:

> There's a big, poorly kept secret in the Diversity, Equity, and Inclusion (DEI) industry: the actual efficacy of an uncomfortably large proportion of our 'flagship' services, talking points, and interventions is lower than many practitioners make it out to be.

This bureaucratic phase of DEI will undoubtedly evolve. However, hundreds of thousands of people are now dependent on it to pay their mortgages and further their careers. It has a life of its own and will no doubt continue to provide the media with stories about banned words and 'privilege' for some time to come.

The widening gap in beliefs: For a couple of days in March 2024, the UK press was obsessed with changes made to the England football team's strip. In a rare show of unity, the prime minister and the leader of the opposition criticised the new design, a view echoed by the mainstream media. The BBC thought it was all a storm in a teacup.

What could have caused such a reaction? Nike and the Football Association (FA) had decided to change the St George's cross (coloured red) to a mix of navy, light blue and purple.

Nike called this a 'playful update'. Others interpreted it as an insult to the English. Many believed it was intended to please the LGBTQQIP2SAA community. Whatever the rationale, it was soon branded as a symptom of the woke virus.

My interest in football is measured in minus numbers, so I had no idea about the history of the England team strip. Apparently back in 2011, devotees of the sport pointed out, it had included a St George's cross in red, blue, green and purple. That design was justified because it represented the country's diverse cultural makeup. At that time, nobody seemed concerned about the colourful cross.

I recount this story to illustrate the change in the public's sensitivity to decisions perceived as being forced upon them to satisfy the elite's agenda. Both the FA and Nike have 'form' for clumsily promoting their vision of a diverse world. Here we go again with changes made to make 'them' feel good while others pay the bill. Whether this is true doesn't matter; it is a narrative that many believe.

The quantitative research shows that the elite's priorities are not shared by the public. My qualitative studies come to the same conclusion. In the section 'Diverging beliefs of the elites and the masses', we saw the gap between the opinions of governments and those of their citizens. I believe institutions are alienating large numbers of people in their hurry and desire to achieve their identity politics ideals. Most of the time, these token changes have been received with a resigned shrug of the shoulders. When changes impinge on people's lives, however, the response is more hostile. The more the elite push for their vision of the world to be accepted, the greater the pushback.

You would expect that the displays of rejection would temper the desire for change, but this safety mechanism has stopped working. It seems the wants of the customer no longer count. The defence would be that given time and careful explanation, the wisdom of their actions will be embraced. I would call this arrogance wrapped up in caring words.

I cannot see a happy or even a benign outcome for the polarisation that's occurring. A booming economy would be the natural release valve, but nobody is counting on that happening. When people believe they are being ignored, that their standard of living is declining and nobody cares, then heaven knows what the outcome will be.

The new left has abandoned tolerance: In July 2020, *Harper's Magazine* published a letter with 153 signatories criticising the spread of illiberalism in the US. This is an extract:

> *The forces of illiberalism are gaining strength throughout the world and have a powerful ally in Donald Trump, who represents a real threat to democracy. But resistance must not be allowed to harden into its own brand of dogma or coercion – which right-wing demagogues are already exploiting. The democratic inclusion we want can be achieved only if we speak out against the intolerant climate that has set in on all sides.*

The magazine openly espouses a left-of-centre perspective, hence the references to Donald Trump, illiberalism and right-wing demagogues. Despite this bias, the signatories were worried that the left's reaction to this perceived danger was destroying the very thing it claimed it wanted to protect.

They were right to have these fears. My explanation of what's happening is perhaps too extreme, but here goes. I distinguish the new from the old left as those, like Jane, who view the world through the prism of identity. Most of the elite fall into this category, although I am not sure if that is for reasons of convenience, fashion or genuinely held beliefs.

The left, both new and old, is paternalistic, believing it knows how others should live. Up until recently, this was well-meaning; now it's not. Those opposing their views are no longer people to be convinced by superior arguments; they are enemies to be defeated. When their opposition is Donald Trump and his supporters, it increases the vehemence by an order of magnitude.

In the name of 'saving democracy' the US justice system is blatantly being used by the state to attack him and his supporters.

Similar shouts of 'democracy is being threatened' are heard throughout Europe. Germany is aping the US in its techniques to neuter the AfD political party. France is not far behind with the state's attack on Marine le Pen. Once upon a time, the media would critically interrogate what was happening, but now it acts as an echo chamber shouting its condemnation of the ultra-right-wing populists.

Much of the old left (and me) look on in horror, watching the new left become as intolerant as it accuses its enemies of being. If the new left wins, the price will be the alienation of a large section of the population. If it loses, it will have established the precedent for its opponents to do the very things it once fought to oppose.

Academia, what have you done? Academia was the first and most enthusiastic convert to the beliefs and consequences of DEI ideology. Has it become a beacon of success or a grim predictor of the damage it can cause? My essay, 'Academia – the trashing of a priceless brand', firmly concluded the latter.

The universities show what happens when an institution's founding principles are barged out of the way by new ideals. Rewarding excellence and freedom of thought and expression has been replaced by achieving equity and diversity targets. Proponents of this change would deny that one has replaced the other. Rather, merging the two has led to better outcomes.

Perhaps this happens in a perfect world with perfect people. What I encountered was not a harmonious union but one side enforcing its will over the other. Diversity trumps excellence. Inclusion trumps freedom of expression. Equity results in a box-ticking mentality that distorts student selection, recruitment of academics, awarding of grants and publishing of research.

To make matters worse, if that's possible, universities' business models are unstable due to their reliance on high-fee-paying overseas students. The UK's top universities (the Russell Group) get 57% of their fee income from non-UK students. As universities look more like credential factories, where their products are only distinguished by their reputation, so trust in their brand becomes paramount. Pandering to the perceived values of their domestic students may alienate their international customers.

Finally, there's the ongoing scandal over journal papers' research findings being impossible to replicate and the long-term effect of degree grade inflation.

Any doubts I had about the severity of academia's problems were confirmed by the reaction of America's leading universities to the 7 October slaughter of Jews by Hamas. The institutions most vocal in their support of inclusion and protecting their students were revealed as tolerating levels of antisemitism that shocked America.

Academia is now centre stage in America's polarised political battles. What an awful mess.

Narratives that can't be questioned: I want to conduct a thought experiment. We are in a laboratory studying climate change using AI technology that's hundreds of times more powerful than today's. Instead of confirming the heating effect of CO_2, it finds a new cause for sea temperature warming. Only the AI's massive pattern recognition power could identify how the Earth's magnetic field changes were aligning with a long-term phase of solar flare activity. Within a hundred years, temperatures are expected to rapidly decline, with a mini-ice age the most likely outcome.

Remember, this is a thought experiment, not a crackpot rebuttal of the current science.

This experiment tests the question: Despite this model repeatedly coming to the same conclusion, what's the likelihood this explanation would replace the current theory of CO_2-induced change? My fear is that the answer is zero. There is so much financial and personal investment in the current theory being right that nothing will displace it. Some science has moved to creating incontrovertible truths that are defended at all costs. Some scientists have become more activists than academics.

Research grants to study the new theory wouldn't be forthcoming. Publishing research findings would be difficult. Any academic supporting this theory would face career-death. I fear the mechanisms of investigative science would be used to stifle contradictory theories rather than encourage them.

We know something similar happened during the pandemic when scientists questioning the dominant narrative were attacked and silenced. Subsequently, most of their claims have been vindicated but, at the time, the scientific 'community' convinced itself that the righteous approach was to stamp out debate. The media and governments played their part in stifling dissenting voices.

Perhaps what I am describing is the inevitable result of the rising intolerance within the institutions. When this unwillingness to countenance disagreement stifles the scientific process, it scares me rigid.

Reversing past gains: This final comment shouldn't be described as collateral damage but rather as self-inflicted injuries. Whatever you think about my analysis, the evidence shows society is becoming less tolerant. In what world can these new ideologies be successful when the very things they are supposed to be improving are going into reverse? The section 'How attitudes have changed' contained the research findings supporting this view.

Dissecting society into groups by identity and then ranking them might please the winners, but it angers the losers, and there are lots of losers. The relentless haranguing of those disagreeing with your views doesn't convince; it annoys. Punishing people in the name of the environment doesn't make converts; it stiffens opposition.

As I write this section, new research from Ipsos finds a backlash against immigrants and increased resentment toward elites. Three-quarters of Brits believe 'The political and economic elite don't care about hard-working people.'

Half of Brits believe promoting women's equality is now discriminating against men. This figure has more than doubled in the past five years. The same response was found in the US, Germany, Italy and Spain.

In a separate study, the BBC found that 70% of sportswomen

oppose competing with trans women. Most of them said they felt uncomfortable or very uncomfortable about speaking out on the issue.

Not for a moment do I think those pressing for radical change will be affected by adverse research findings. They will rationalise the research as proving the inherent racism and sexism in society and use it to justify more extreme actions.

Back in the real world, some of the old demons of intolerance that I thought were long buried are re-emerging.

WHAT NEXT?

The TV adaptation of Liu Cixin's science fiction novel *The Three-Body Problem* starts in 1966 with China's young Red Guards brutally murdering a university professor because of his belief in Western physics. For the following decade, millions of people are killed as these young people try to rid Chinese society of the 'Four Olds' (old ideas, old culture, old customs and old habits).

I cannot help but see echoes of these impassioned young Chinese political devotees in today's diversity warriors and eco-activists. The certainty in their eye that they are right and right is on their side. However, that's not my reason for relating this story; it's to illustrate how much can change in a few years. After the Cultural Revolution collapsed the country was transformed into the world's manufacturing centre and now vies with America for the top position economically and militarily. A phenomenal change in less than half a century.

Western countries have a long list of troubles, some of which I have described in my essays, but overall, I am optimistic about the future. All the problems we face are solvable, and I am sure they will be solved. It is so easy to forget the wonders of human ingenuity.

In just four years, nearly 70 million Chinese escaped from poverty. India's achievements are nearly as impressive. The infant mortality rate worldwide is less than half what it was in 1990. If this is possible, just think about what affluent and relatively rich Western countries can achieve. China was able to transform its culture and economy in a single generation. During the pandemic, we suspended the planet's commercial activity. Despite some horrendous (and unnecessary) mistakes, most people survived unscathed. The advances being made to tackle climate change are far better than the media reports. The models that much of the forecasting is based on still use a set of assumptions (RCP8.5) that are no longer relevant. This assumes emissions consistent with a five-fold increase in the use of coal and virtually no policies to limit CO_2. Reality is much better than this.

Of course, we have an astonishing ability for screwing things up and inflicting unnecessary chaos and harm. But, the net effect of our endeavours, in the long run, is usually positive.

Concluding that 'it will be all right' and that in a couple of decades, we will wonder what all the fuss was about seems a cop-out. I could end with a list of Dick Stroud's predictions. Unfortunately, my crystal ball is malfunctioning and, in any case, forecasting the future is bound to be wrong. What I can say for certain is the 'woke' explanation for what's happening doesn't begin to address the complexity of the situation. If only Elon Musk was right and conquering the 'woke mind virus' would end our travails. The same with Dominic Cummings' theory that modernity suffers from a madness that has gripped the intelligentsia. As we have seen, it is much more complicated.

I am certain that a handful of issues will determine how the next few years unfold.

The most immediate and by far the most dangerous is the gap between the elite, both real and imagined, and everybody else. You are probably bored with me talking about this, but their sense of entitlement and rightness oozes from the pores of the institutions.

In March 2024, Ipsos surveyed 21,000 adults in 28 countries. People in all but one nation (Singapore) believed their country's society is broken. South Africa topped the list of most disgruntled countries and Sweden was number two!

They all identified the main divide in their society being between ordinary citizens and the political and economic elite. Most countries believe the solution is a strong leader 'to take the country back from the rich and the powerful'. This is an ominous conclusion since this year (2024), roughly 4 billion people vote in elections.

I have given numerous examples of what's generating this anger. For the final time, let me summarise the causes in a few sentences. Those controlling the institutions are failing in their primary role. Economic and social issues demanding fixing are ignored. Instead, the elites attempt to impose a culture that satisfies them. They have abandoned listening and treat opposing views as stupid and wrong. When they don't get their own way, they bully their opponents in the name of being caring.

The gulf between 'us and them' is reaching dangerous levels as the consequences of the elite's policies evolve from annoying to damaging. How this conflict resolves depends on their remoteness from the anger and disgruntlement.

Those running companies will desperately cling to their ideals but, eventually, the discipline of the market always wins. As much as governments elevate their demands over those of the consumer, they will only delay, not change, the outcome.

Academia's remoteness means it will be the slowest to respond. While the credentials it sells are in demand, it will remain cloistered from reality, isolated from democratic control. Its monopolitical culture and lack of diversity prevent it from adapting. It has the highest density of clever people making daft decisions, most of them brimming with the ability to delude themselves into thinking they are right. Perhaps the pain caused by its unstable financial model provides the discipline for it to evolve. I do hope so.

The great unknown is how politics and the machinery of government will evolve. I think my earlier comment describes how many people feel: 'The emperor's new clothes are lying in a pile on the floor, revealing a flabby, unfit institution that can't deliver on its promises.' Would a strong man or woman who dispensed with the niceties of democracy do any better? Somehow, I doubt it, but the threat of one taking control might just make the ruling elite wake up and smell the coffee.

Whether they do or don't will not stop reality from intervening. Their make-believe energy policies are unravelling. DEI's nostrums sound ever more fanciful as the public experiences their consequences. The head-in-the-sand approach to dealing with the economic and demographic mega problems ratchets up the pressure demanding radical decisions.

I doubt that the government machine, whoever is in charge, will anticipate and adapt. What will occur will be a succession of failed policies that are hurriedly ditched for new ones. I foresee a long period of hyper-reactive rather than proactive government. The more negative the public mood, the greater the pressure for the political machine to align with public sentiment.

I expect Ernest Hemingway's words about going bankrupt apply to the machinations of government. A character in *The Sun Also Rises* asks 'How did you go bankrupt?' and is answered 'Two ways. Gradually, then suddenly.' Somehow, the government will muddle through, but I don't think it will be pretty.

And what of our polarised society? Let's pray that we don't experience the historic way that a looming external threat unifies societies. That cure could be worse than the problem. What are the chances of Jane and John finding a shared understanding? Are MAGA Republicans likely to be sharing Thanksgiving with progressive *New York Times* readers?

Part of me is pessimistic since ingrained prejudices are hard to dislodge. Perhaps the disdain between opposing parts of society needs to get even worse, manifesting itself in such disturbing ways that both sides are shocked and soften their views. Maybe Jane and their friends will suffer from catastrophe exhaustion. There's only so long you can maintain white-hot crusading anger. Generation Alpha – born 2010 until 2025 – might mimic past generations and have diametrically opposite beliefs to their parents.

Let's not forget that large group of people, the 'Too Busy', who just want to get on with their lives – eventually, their wishes will prevail. I sense they are getting tired of Jane and their shouting and the relentless gloom of John and his friends. This large slice of the population acts as the dampener, stopping extreme lurches in direction. Well, at least, I hope it does.

Wouldn't it be wonderful if the partisan media could rediscover the love of objective reporting? Occasionally there is a sign that some still cherish objective reporting. When Obama's adviser for strategy and communications chastised the *NYT* for not 'saving democracy or stopping an authoritarian from taking power' – I think he was referring to Donald Trump – the paper's executive editor acidly replied that the paper was not the White House's propaganda office.

However, as long as customers are hooked on simplified stories to top up their confirmation bias needs, that's not going to happen. The alternative media, the Substacks and podcasts, will keep growing to satisfy those wanting more than panic porn and clickbait articles. Commercial considerations will be the final arbiter of the media's future shape and direction. Its trajectory will closely follow how society either further divides or reconnects.

Finally, there are the known unknowns. Those things that we know are occurring but can only guess about their outcomes. I am not going to muse about the ongoing wars and conflicts. I don't have any special knowledge and find the subject too depressing.

Will AI decimate the middle and lower reaches of the credentialled class? We have experienced the agrarian, industrial and digital revolutions. Are we about to live through one that changes the value and nature of intelligence? Perhaps it will break down the barriers the elite have erected and make them as vulnerable as those they disdain. I suspect that's wishful thinking.

I remember the days of marvelling at the wonders of my Intel 286 computer. Today, I use an M3-powered MacBook Pro. With AI technology at about the same level as my old personal computer, it is inconceivable what it will achieve when it evolves to the equivalent of my Apple. Yes, I think it could upend the relative value of intelligence, knowledge and physical skills. Let's not forget AI consumes enormous amounts of energy, so that might limit its development.

When Western countries realise that the centre of economic gravity has lurched to the East, how will they respond? Currently, we are in the denial phase and a long way from accepting the reality. If we follow the classic grief model, we still have anger, bargaining and depression to go. It would be nice to think the challenge will have an invigorating effect, but I suspect a long sulk is more likely. For all the talk of unconscious bias, the West still struts around as if the rest of the world is following its lead. Not only should the West 'check its privilege', it must come to terms with its decline.

Will we 'fix' the problems caused by population ageing and the shortage of babies? So far, the attempts have been amateurish and uncommitted. I can't see why the future will be any different. No doubt there will be friction as Millennials and Gen Z take over from the Baby Boomers. However, I think too much attention has been focused on intergenerational issues and not enough on the divisions between men and women.

I have already explained that men believe that favouring women has gone too far. It seems that in much of the world, the attitudes of young men and women are polarising. *The Economist* found that two decades ago, young men and women (aged 18–29) had much the same beliefs. That's no longer the case. In the 20 rich countries surveyed, women are becoming more liberal and men more conservative, at an astonishing rate. American women are more likely to be Democrats; men tend to vote Republican. Another global trend is females are more prone to negative emotions than men. It's unknown if that's a side effect of being liberal. Throughout all stages of education, girls outperform boys. The premise that *Men are from Mars, Women are from Venus* is truer now than ever.

It once seemed that the evolution of DEI was an intergenerational issue – the idealist young versus the set in their way oldies. Now I am not so sure. Currently, the agenda is set by women. About three-quarters of those working in HR and DEI are women. Female business leaders value DEI much more than their male counterparts (McKinsey). The battles of the sexes takes on a whole new meaning.

There are many more 'this or that might happen' issues, but I think these are the most important.

My understanding of our institutions is orders of magnitude greater than when I began. Hopefully, yours is as well. Their failings are serious and mostly self-inflicted. Incompetence and conceit, not the distraction of wokeness, are to blame. That word is well and truly banished from my vocabulary.

Something else has happened during my journey, giving me an unexpected gift. This is best explained by two quotations, separated by a few centuries.

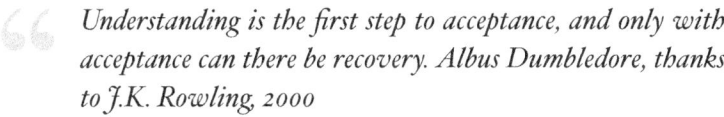

Understanding is the first step to acceptance, and only with acceptance can there be recovery. Albus Dumbledore, thanks to J.K. Rowling, 2000

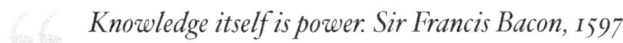

Knowledge itself is power. Sir Francis Bacon, 1597

Long ago, I realised the benefits of power. Perhaps the greatest is that once you understand what's happening and realise you can't change it, you can move on to more rewarding things.

WORDS THAT MAKE YOU THINK

Each of the essays begins with a couple of quotes. These were chosen to stimulate thought, to set the scene for what you were about to read. Deciding which to use was difficult. So many wise words and a few not so wise! Rather than discarding those that didn't make the cut, I decided to include them in a final chapter. I expect they will make you think, laugh, wince and everything in between. Enjoy.

Academia – the trashing of a priceless brand

 University administrators, who are under a fiduciary obligation to conserve and protect the independence of their universities, ought to use care and prudence in pursuing goals extraneous to education and research.

Robert Post, professor of law, Yale Law School

 The largest cultural menace in America is the conformity of the intellectual cliques which, in education as well as the arts, are out to impose upon the nation their modish fads and fallacies and have nearly succeeded in doing so.

William Buckley Junior

Many intellectuals with high accomplishments seem to assume that those accomplishments confer validity to their notions about a broad swath of issues ranging far beyond the scope of their accomplishments.

Thomas Sowell, economist and social philosopher

There is one thing a professor can be absolutely certain of: almost every student entering the university believes, or says he believes, that truth is relative.

Allan Bloom, *Closing of the American Mind*, 2008

The strongest brand in the world is not Apple or Mercedes-Benz or Coca-Cola. The strongest brands are MIT, Oxford, and Stanford. Academics and administrators at the top universities have decided over the last 30 years that we're no longer public servants; we're luxury goods.

Prof Scott Galloway, New York University, 2020

The public is paying the price for a broken system of publishing research – the sooner they realise it, the better.

Carl Heneghan, professor of evidence-based medicine, University of Oxford

> If ignorance is a disease, Harvard Yard is the Wuhan wet market.

Bill Maher, TV commentator

> The old scientific institutions for peer review and publication (hijacked during Covid to spread misinformation about misinformation) – they're all disintegrating in a self-reinforcing cycle of collapsing performance, collapsing trust and moral authority, spreading chaos, growing accusations of 'madness', and a widespread feeling that our system has been stretched to or beyond some invisible-but-critical threshold.

Dominic Cummings, Substack, May 2024

Media – where did all the trust go?

> Journalism's allegiance is to the truth, not to a specific political agenda. And the truth, more often than not, is profoundly messy. The task of the journalist, as with the artist, is to learn to cope with that complexity.

Tara Henley, Substack journalist

> Without facts, you can't have truth. Without truth, you can't have trust. Without trust, we have no shared reality, no democracy, and it becomes impossible to deal with our world's existential problems.

Maria Ressa, Nobel Peace Prize lecture (2021)

In a sense, journalism is going through the same fate
as the serious novel. The fewer people are interested
in it, the more insular and masturbatory it becomes.
Which in turn causes fewer people to be interested
in it.

FT journalist Janan Ganesh, June 2023

Is our real problem 'a loss of trust in mainstream
media like the New York Times which play a vital
role in democracy' (the mainstream Insider view) or
is this mainstream media itself the biggest source of
lies and fake news and thereby undermining public
confidence in democracy?

Dominic Cummings, blog June 2023

What the public is telling us boils down to this: Stop
taking money from the government. Stop indulging
in moral panics. Stop ignoring dissenting views. Stop
letting your personal politics blind you to the facts,
making you vulnerable to mistakes. Stop refusing to
acknowledge mistakes when you do make them. Stop
inserting your views into the news.

Tara Henley, *The Massey Essay: The Trust Spiral: Restoring faith in the
media*, 2024

Trump's manipulation and every one of his political
lies became more powerful because journalists had
forfeited what had always been most valuable about
their work: their credibility as arbiters of truth and
brokers of ideas, which for more than a century,
despite all of journalism's flaws and failures, had been
a bulwark of how Americans govern themselves.

James Bennett, Former *New York Times* opinion editor

> In the span of a decade or so, essentially all professional media not explicitly branded as conservative has been taken over by a school of politics that emerged from humanities departments at elite universities and began colonizing the college educated through social media.

Freddie deBoer, Substack journalist

> Our reverence for the truth might be a distraction getting in the way of finding common ground and getting things done.

Katherine Maher, CEO and president of National Public Radio

Politics – more showbiz than statesmanship

> Central government is too metropolitan, too short-term, too siloed, too rivalrous and too focused on the preoccupations of Westminster and Whitehall.

Lord Mark Sedwill, cabinet secretary, valedictory speech, 2020

> The British civil service is not nearly as good as it thinks it is, and it is nominally directed by ministers who are often mediocre, if not stupid, and downright ignorant of the fields they are expected to manage.

The Times leader article, March 2024

> One should esteem men because they are generous, not because they have the power to be generous; and in like manner, should admire those who know how

to govern a kingdom, not those who, without knowing how, actually govern one.

Machiavelli, *Discourses*, 1517

Is the only future for British party politics ever more regulation and tax, supported by No 10 as media and entertainment service with elections pretending to be about significant differences between elites which are trivial?

Dominic Cummings, blog post, June 2023

The left now holds power in almost all the important cultural and moral citadels of the country.

Peter Hitchens, *The Abolition of Liberty*, 2004

It's not government's maliciousness that I fear but its incompetence.

Dick Stroud

Any organisation that is not explicitly rightwing sooner or later becomes leftwing.

Robert Conquest's Second Law of Politics

We have statutory bodies controlled by statuary regulators – Parliament might just as well not exist.

David Starkey, *Parliamentary Sovereignty*, 2023

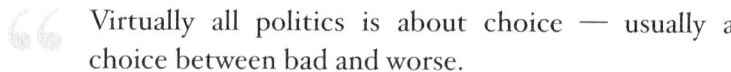

Virtually all politics is about choice — usually a choice between bad and worse.

Trevor Phillips, *The Times*, 2024

Our public servants want to save the world but don't want to clear up the litter. We feel we are living in some kind of dictatorship of virtue, but the virtue is virtual virtue.

Theodore Dalrymple, 2023

Business – charting new paths or losing direction?

It is the highest impertinence and presumption... in kings and ministers, to pretend to watch over the economy of private people, and to restrain their expense... They are themselves always, and without any exception, the greatest spendthrifts in the society. Let them look well after their own expense, and they may safely trust private people with theirs.

Adam Smith, *The Wealth Of Nations*

It's all about bucks, kid. The rest is conversation.

Gordon Gekko, *Wall Street*

Unless the woke mind virus, which is fundamentally anti-science, anti-merit, and anti-human in general, is stopped, civilization will never become multi-planetary.

Elon Musk

Does the evidence really show that diversity is the key to business success, or is this a case of confirmation bias – accepting a claim uncritically just because we want it to be true? When you take off your blinkers and look at the evidence with a clear head, you can see the glaring errors in these widely touted diversity studies.

Alex Edmans, professor of finance at London Business School (2024)

Change before you have to.

Jack Welch, former CEO of GE

The first principle is that you must not fool yourself – and you are the easiest person to fool.

Prof Richard P. Feynman, commencement address at Caltech, 1974

Language – from beautiful to brutal

Clarity of writing usually follows clarity of thought.

The Economist Style Guide

Thanks to words, we have been able to rise above the brutes; and thanks to words, we have often sunk to the level of the demons.

Aldous Huxley, *Adonis and the Alphabet*

The difference between the right word and the almost-right word is the difference between lightning and the lightning bug.

Mark Twain, *The Wit and Wisdom of Mark Twain*

To achieve activists' ambitions of deconstructing systems, terms must have dual meanings – a common, ordinary and reasonable meaning, and a specific, activist meaning.

Prof Peter Boghossian

'Emergencies' have always been the pretext on which the safeguards of individual liberty have been eroded – and once they are suspended it is not difficult for anyone who has assumed such emergency powers to see to it that the emergency persists.

Friedrich Hayek, *Law, Legislation and Liberty*

Complete liberty of contradicting and disproving our opinion, is the very condition which justifies us in assuming its truth for purposes of action; and on no other terms can a being with human faculties have any rational assurance of being right.

John Stuart Mill, *On Freedom of Thought*

The real misinformation almost always comes from our rotten regimes and the old media. And remember, this same rotten system is responsible for advice today on multiple wars and biosecurity, AI etc...

Dominic Cummings, Substack, 19 January 2024

> It used to be the case that very conservative voices were the places from which you would hear that such and such a book should be banned or is obscene. But the thing that's different now is that it's also coming from progressive voices. There are progressives saying that certain kinds of speech should not be permitted because it offends against this or that vulnerable group.

Salman Rushdie, CBS's *60 Minutes*, 2024

Justice – teetering on a slippery slope

> We call for a national defunding of police. We demand investment in our communities and the resources to ensure Black people not only survive, but thrive.

#DefundThePolice petition on BLM website

> Free speech does not mean free speech: it means speech hedged in by all the laws against defamation, blasphemy, sedition, and so forth. It means freedom governed by law.

James versus Commonwealth of Australia legal case

> Equal justice under law.

Above the entrance to the US Supreme Court

> Defend the children of the poor and punish the wrongdoer.

Above the entrance to the Old Bailey court in the UK

There are more instances of the abridgment of the freedom of the people by gradual and silent encroachments of those in power than by violent and sudden usurpation.

James Madison, Speech in Virginia Convention, 1788

Let there be little doubt that Republican zealots will seize upon any precedent established by Democratic zealots when the circumstances allow it. History proves that neither party can be trusted to apply the law neutrally and in a nonpartisan matter.

Alan Dershowitz, *Get Trump: The Threat to Civil Liberties*, 2023

Financial authorities – incompetent regulators don't protect us from greed

It is no exaggeration to say that since the 1980s, much of the global financial sector has become criminalised, creating an industry culture that tolerates or even encourages systematic fraud.

Charles Ferguson, *Inside Job*

The most difficult subjects can be explained to the most slow-witted man if he has not formed any idea of them already; but the simplest thing cannot be made clear to the most intelligent man if he is firmly persuaded that he knows already, without a shadow of doubt, what is laid before him.

Leo Tolstoy, 1897

> You've got your average person's mortgage. Fixed rate, 30 years... Boring, safe, small pay off... Right? But when you have thousands of them all bundled together... Suddenly the yield goes up and the risk is still low cause it's a mortgage and who the hell doesn't pay their mortgage?

Lewis Ranieri, inventor of the mortgage-backed security, *The Big Short*

> The financial crisis was not an act of nature. It was man-made, and it was preventable. Regulators had the power to stop it, but they chose not to act.

Elizabeth Warren, US senator and former special advisor for the Consumer Financial Protection Bureau

> The financial crisis showed that financial regulation was out of date, out of step, and out of control.

Andrew Lo, professor of finance at MIT

Beliefs – my moral compass is busted

> Support for democracy is in freefall among young people now... My sense is that young people want to engage with politics around specific struggles they believe in... When you are a warrior for a specific cause you don't have to compromise. The bread and butter of formal politics is the art of compromising. You have to be aware of trade-offs. That smacks to young people of losing your purity.

Kevin Casas-Zamora, secretary general, International IDEA

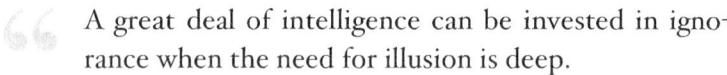

A great deal of intelligence can be invested in ignorance when the need for illusion is deep.

Saul Bellow, *To Jerusalem and Back*

I would rather have questions that can't be answered than answers that can't be questioned.

Professor Richard P. Feynman's notebook

I think the more experience that you have of life — and history is essentially a source of vicarious experience — the more sceptical you are likely to be about any magic bullet solution.

Lord Jonathan Sumption, UnHerd interview, 2023

Take away the 'high-fallutin' talk about 'countering hate' and 'reducing harm' and 'anti-disinformation' is just a bluntly elitist gatekeeping exercise. If you prefer to think in progressive terms, it's class war. The math is simple. If one small demographic over here has broad control over the speech landscape, and a great big one over there does not, it follows that one group will end up with more political power than the other. Which one is the winner?

Matt Taibbi, testifying before the House Judiciary Committee, November 2023

The point of all this nonstop messaging is to take a stand, but also to be seen taking a stand, to position yourself on the appropriate side, and to head off criticism for not taking a stand. Once you join this game, it leads you straight into a tangle of hypocrisy and double standards.

George Packer, staff writer at *The Atlantic*, 2023

Of all tyrannies, a tyranny sincerely exercised for the good of its victims may be the most oppressive. It would be better to live under robber barons than under omnipotent moral busybodies.

C.S. Lewis, *God in the Dock: Essays on Theology*, 1972

At any given moment there is an orthodoxy, a body of ideas of which it is assumed that all right-thinking people will accept without question. It is not exactly forbidden to say this, that or the other, but it is 'not done' to say it... Anyone who challenges the prevailing orthodoxy finds himself silenced with surprising effectiveness. A genuinely unfashionable opinion is almost never given a fair hearing, either in the popular press or in the high-brow periodicals.

George Orwell, *The Freedom of the Press*, unused preface to *Animal Farm*

So what's going on? Making sense of it all

We've arranged a society based on science and technology, in which nobody understands anything about science and technology. And this combustible mixture of ignorance and power, sooner or later, is going to blow up in our faces.

Carl Sagan, 1996

Many institutions have been taken over by activists who behave as if they are theirs to dispose of. Trustees wink at the pursuit of ideological goals without popular consent. They have power without responsibility, while politicians have accountability without authority.

Prof Robert Tombs, 2024

Things fall apart; the centre cannot hold;

Mere anarchy is loosed upon the world,

The blood-dimmed tide is loosed, and everywhere

The ceremony of innocence is drowned;

The best lack all conviction, while the worst

Are full of passionate intensity.

W.B. Yeats, *The Second Coming*

The language of postgraduate seminars at Harvard turned into the language of Democrat presidential candidates and some of the social customs which started on Ivy League campuses became the social customs of broad swaths of the American and British elite.

Yascha Mounk, interview with the *Times Education Supplement*, 2023

Is 'distrust in our institutions' a big problem, maybe the biggest (SW1 conventional wisdom) or is our real problem that there's too much trust in our institutions by political-academic-media Insiders.

Dominic Cummings, blog, June 2023

Without facts you can't have truth.

Without truth you can't have trust.

Without these three things, we have no shared reality, can't solve problems, and have no democracy.

Maria Ressa, Nobel Peace Prize winner

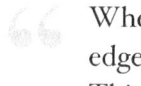 When people believe that they have absolute knowledge, with no test in reality, this is how they behave. This is what men do when they aspire to the knowledge of gods.

Jacob Bronowski, *The Ascent of Man*, final episode at Auschwitz-Birkenau where a million Jews were murdered

 Everybody knows that the dice are loaded

Everybody rolls with their fingers crossed

Everybody knows the war is over

Everybody knows the good guys lost

Everybody knows the fight was fixed

The poor stay poor, the rich get rich.

Leonard Cohen, *Everybody Knows*, 1988

Young's Law says the more progressive a country is when it comes to sex and gender, the more authoritarian it is when it comes to speech and language.

Toby Young, founder of the Free Speech Union

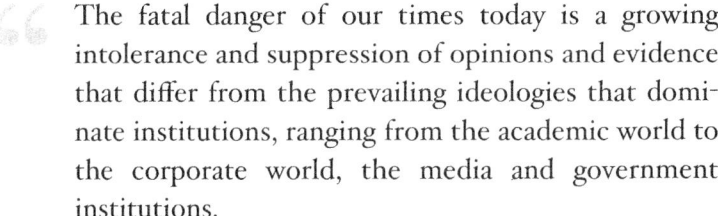
The fatal danger of our times today is a growing intolerance and suppression of opinions and evidence that differ from the prevailing ideologies that dominate institutions, ranging from the academic world to the corporate world, the media and government institutions.

Thomas Sowell, American economist, social philosopher

Falsehood flies and truth comes limping after it.

Jonathan Swift, *Political Lying*, 1710

ACKNOWLEDGEMENTS

I have dedicated *Goodbye Trust* to the Reverend Alfred Barwick.

He was an author, artist, plumber, sportsman and businessman and somebody who tried to do good with his life. He was a teacher and trustee at the Ragged School in Hoxton, East London. His life was dedicated to helping the poor. He made me very proud to be his great-great grandson.

The Godfather is my favourite film, by a long, long way, a movie that Mario Puzo and Francis Ford Coppola packed with memorable quotes. Who hasn't heard of 'I'm going to make him an offer he can't refuse'?

My favourite is: 'I refused to be a fool dancing on the strings held by all of those big shots.' I think this sentiment helps explain why I wrote this book. It's my instinctive reaction to question the conceited and powerful. My guess is it's something I share with the writers who have provided so many of the ideas for *Goodbye Trust*:

Michael Shellenberger, Matt Taibbi, Tara Henley, Prof Jay Bhattacharya, Professor Carl Heneghan, Dr Roger Pielke, Peter Hitchens, Coleman Hughes, Greg Lukianoff, Yascha Mounk, Lee Fang, Brendan O'Neill, Lionel Shriver, Bari Weiss, Nellie Bowles, Freddie Sayers and many more.

I would also like to thank OpenAI for creating ChatGPT. It didn't write any of the book but was a constant companion generating ideas and a loyal research assistant.

Thanks to Suzanne Arnold, who, as always, takes my words and turns them into readable text.

Finally, my darling wife Stella, thanks for your patience living with somebody who spends too much time locked away with his laptop.

Who is Dick Stroud?

My website **dickstroud.com** contains all you might want to know about me and the books I have written. Yet more stuff is available on **goodbyetrust.com**. But if all you want are the top-line facts:

- Edging closer to 75 than 70.
- All the usual academic credentials.
- Once knew a lot about marketing and the internet.
- Still knows something about marketing and demographics.
- Writes for fun and to keep active.

GLOSSARY

'BLAH' WORDS... Words used to signal the writer's progressive credentials rather than to have a precise meaning.

BOOMERS... The generation born between 1946 and 1964.

CANCEL CULTURE... The practice of publicly rejecting, boycotting or ending support for people or groups because of their views or actions.

CLERISY... Originally the word was used to describe a secular group of learned individuals. More recently it has been associated with elitism and detachment from the general public.

CONSPIRATORIAL CONSERVATISM... A critical term used by the new left to denigrate those not accepting of their worldview.

COP... Convention of the Parties: the United Nations climate change conferences that review progress made by member countries to limit climate change.

CSR... Corporate social responsibility: the management concept of combining social and environmental concerns with business operations.

CULTURE WARS... A conflict or struggle for dominance between groups within a society or between societies, arising from their differing beliefs and practices.

DEI... Diversity, equity and inclusion: three values that organisations profess are important to their culture. Sometimes equality is substituted for equity.

DISINFORMATION... False information deliberately spread to deceive or manipulate people.

DOMINANT NARRATIVE... The prevailing or widely accepted storyline, perspective or interpretation of events within a particular society, culture or discourse.

DOMINIC CUMMINGS... A UK political strategist who managed the official leave campaign in the EU referendum and worked for Boris Johnson when he was prime minister.

ELITE – negative definition... Those with a disproportionate influence over others that is achieved because of their wealth, position or education.

ELITE – positive definition... A select group that is superior in terms of ability or qualities to others in society.

FIRE... The Foundation for Individual Rights and Expression. A non-profit civil liberties group with the mission of protecting freedom of speech on college campuses in the United States.

GASLIGHTING... Persuading somebody, so as to exert power, to question their perception of reality.

GEN-X... Born between the mid-1960s and the late 1970s.

GEN-Z... The cohort born between the mid-1990s and the early 2010s.

GEN-ALPHA... Born between the early 2010s and mid-2020s.

IDENTITY POLITICS... A political ideology that emphasises the importance of social identity, such as race, gender, sexual orientation, ethnicity, religion.

IPCC... The Intergovernmental Panel on Climate Change. The United Nations body for assessing the science related to climate change.

KATHLEEN STOCK... An academic and writer who staunchly defends the rights of women.

LEGACY LEFT... The views of the left before they were superseded by the canon of beliefs associated with identity politics.

LEGACY MEDIA... The mass-media institutions that dominated before the digital age: including print media, radio and television broadcasting.

LGBT+... Lesbian, gay, bisexual and transgender.

LGBTQQIP2SAA... Lesbian, gay, bisexual, transgender, queer, questioning, intersex, pansexual, two-spirit, asexual and ally.

MALINFORMATION... True information that is shared with the intent to harm someone or a group.

MBA... Master of Business Administration. Usually, a postgraduate degree providing the tools and knowledge required in business.

MDM... Misinformation, disinformation and malinformation.

MILLENNIAL, also known as Gen Y... Born between the early 1980s and the mid-1990s to early 2000s.

MISINFORMATION... Incorrect or misleading information that is inadvertently spread, often without intent to deceive.

MONO-CULTURE... When a group or organisation is dominated by a single set of cultural values.

MSM... Mainstream media. Large mass news media that influences many people and both reflects and shapes prevailing currents of thought.

NCHI... A non-crime hate incident: involves an act motivated by hostility or prejudice towards a person with a particular characteristic.

NEW LEFT... Those with a political view that extends beyond economic inequality, focusing on gender equality, environmentalism and anti-imperialism.

NGO... A non-governmental organisation: a not-for-profit entity working independent of government. They are often active in encouraging social change.

NOSTRUM... A proposed solution for social or political problems, often considered ineffective or overly simplistic.

NYT... *The New York Times:* the prestigious American newspaper known for its left of centre coverage of national and international news, politics, culture, arts and investigative journalism.

QUANGO... Quasi non-governmental organisation: a body with a role in the processes of national government but that is not a government department and accordingly operates outside ministerial control.

TDS... Trump derangement syndrome: the extreme reaction to the mention of Donald Trump. This might include a cascade of invective and irrational rambling.

TED talks... Short, powerful presentations delivered by experts and thought leaders aimed at sharing ideas, sparking conversation and inspiring change.

TRIBAL GROUPTHINK... The phenomenon where individuals within a group or community conform to prevailing opinions, beliefs or behaviours without critically evaluating them.

UN... The United Nations, the international organisation established to promote peace, security, cooperation and development among member states.

WFH... Work from home rather than in the office. Often this is called hybrid working when people work from both locations.

WHO... The World Health Organization: the UN agency responsible for international public health. It coordinates global health initiatives.

WSJ... *The Wall Street Journal:* the American business-focused daily newspaper that is widely respected for its coverage of financial news, business trends, economics and global markets.

Printed in Great Britain
by Amazon